MORALITY'S CALLING

IN GLOBALIZATION

The importance of separating it from religions

and giving it worldwide validity

Jose Vargas

2009

e-mail: josevargasg@lexium.com.mx

English version edited by Victoria Treviño

CONTENTS

Foreword

The structure of this work is somewhat unusual; for this reason, in addition to the six-page Introduction that follows, I am venturing here to tell the prospective reader - in plain English- why he or she should read it.

I hope that my want of eloquence will be partially offset by my keen desire to share with the reader my concern for the present and the future world, based on its past, and to find practical ways to address its issues.

The most noticeable characteristic of today's world is that it is the result of breakneck progress in which the impelling forces had been, for more than a century, advances in scientific knowledge, technologies, sanitary measures, medicine, and the "massification" of communications. These drivers propelled the world into the age of motor transportation, electricity, telephone, television, and computers, and have permitted it to multiply its population four fold and put all its peoples into commercial, informative, and tourist contact.

But the problem is that those advances had combined with conflicts between different ideologies and national and religious loyalties, which bear on the normative aspect of conduct. These confrontations have caused fighting two world wars that have affected all of humanity as far as upsetting their standards of moral values. The first war was so tragic that it left the world stunned and then fostered the birth of two terrible totalitarian ideologies, which dragged humanity to the second war that reached levels of cruelty, hate, and bitterness that still have us in a trauma.

Suffering is but another name for the teaching of experience, the saying goes, and, indeed, humanity learned the lesson, at least, of not fighting "total" wars again. However, it has kept advancing at an increasingly accelerated pace while divided into two radically different ideologies, both believing to possess the key to future happiness. Both ideologies also clashed with traditional religious views, in such a way that humanity's joint "material" progress was not matched by similar headway regarding the fairness of "the rules of the game" of each ideology or their averred goals. Furthermore, traditional religions took exception to many other spiritual aspects.

After a lengthy confrontation, one of the ideologies, soviet communism, collapsed and the other, liberal capitalism, seemed destined to prevail. But it then transpired that all the flaws, crassness, and injustices of the winning ideology came into sharper view, as it stood alone as responsible for all the problems in that world. The most notorious: the huge differences in standards of living between the four "worlds" into which humanity can be divided.

But it so happens that this economic and social justice problem, serious as it is, is only part of the overall problem, which also includes the following issues: 1) Control of weapons of mass destruction, for even if an ideology collapses, its component powers do not disappear. The use of conventional armed forces -when should they be deployed- must also be addressed. 2) Control of fossil fuels and their greenhouse effect-causing carbon dioxide emissions, plus many other related problems that are damaging the Earth's environment or eco-system. 3) Lastly, global commerce, the flow of venture capital and large-scale loans, and their counterpart, worker migration, must be regulated.

How is humanity, working as an organized group, going to solve these problems? All are two-dimensional, and should be broken down: One could be known as the "material" dimension, which includes its scientific, technical, structural, and economic solutions. The other is the "spiritual" dimension, encompassing the public morality we call "justice". If we reexamine the aforementioned "global" issues, we could ask ourselves: Who is the enemy of humanity? And the answer has to be: Humanity itself. In other words: Humanity is such a colossus that its huge destructive power and its tendency for internal strife when defending "interests" have to be offset by its equally huge constructive power and its capacity for consensus when group leaders realize it's in everyone's best interest. In our era, what must be understood is that development has to unfold in harmony with the Earth's environment and has to be shared by all peoples and nations.

If we take for granted that we have the knowledge, technology, organization, and money needed to solve the "material" aspect of these issues, and that there are no foreseeable obstacles to achieving what will be needed in the future, then the only thing pending for solution is the problem of consonance, a dimension in which general agreements are lacking, both regarding "the rules of the game" and the goals to be achieved. Why are we in this situation? I think it's because the ethical basis of our morality is limited and controversial.

Why does our morality possess these "flaws"? For two main reasons: First, because the morality which slowly took shape in our genetic makeup during our hominid evolution, was "designed" for operating in small groups. Of course, the instinctive aspect of our morality is just a help and a guide to form our own operative morality, which also factors in education and experience. Second, because once our ancestors arrived to high self-consciousness, they had to understand their relationship with other humans and with the outside world by means of a magical-religious outlook, which became so important so as to include morality, even if it had only normative functions for the survival and development of the group until then.

Thus, the genetic component of our morality is highly "concentric" or limited in its range, and the whole of morality became embedded into religious beliefs and practices. How can we correct these traits, which became "flaws" in light of our present needs? It seems to me that by two different means: 1) Extending its range until it encompasses the whole of humanity, by means of suitable education, and 2) Separating morality from religion through the knowledge that their coupling was a historical event which may not longer be justified. This will also require projecting where we want to arrive at and how, and conceiving the appropriate social discipline to do so successfully. Doing so will also provide the answer to the existential question about the meaning of life.

I see no difficulties in convincing ourselves that morality should span the whole of humanity, as religions themselves have preached in this sense, albeit at odds with their practices at times and whilst fighting one another. What I do see more difficult is extricating morality from the various religions, and possible only if we convince ourselves that they are social disciplines of very different origins and functions: Starting with our hominid ancestors, morality has walked with us for millions of years and is as necessary today as it was then, even if its range must now be expanded. Religion, in contrast, appeared only some 50,000 years ago, as a consequence of having arrived to high self-consciousness and as a means of coming to grips with the awe of our situation. I think that we can now do so without resorting to pure speculation.

Those who see the problem of separation from another point of view, may ask: We agree that morality and religion are different in origins and functions, but why bisect them if they seem to work well together? The answer to this is that they have not worked well together for some time: If we take the Catholic Church as an example, from at least the 14th century there were serious problems regarding its handling of political authority, which had to be wrested from the Papacy and the clergy at the price of numerous wars and conflicts over the next six centuries until, by the mid-20th century, it had been stripped almost entirely. Even then, they abused what little moral authority remained in their hands by ruling the private lives of their faithful. An example is their stubborn opposition to contraceptive birth control, for the absurd reason that the methods are "artificial", as if all medical procedures which diminish mortality were not.

Besides, they attack contraception by hiding this nonsensical policy behind the smoke screen of their opposition to abortion, an issue where they are on more solid footing. However, it is precisely their absurd opposition to contraception that has led many women to resort to abortion.

In short, we are in a difficult era which allows few errors and failures in general attitudes. If we entrust –led by tradition or custom- such an important decision-taking moral authority to a group of people without any democratic responsibility to an electorate, based only on their arbitrary interpretation of some writings held as divinely inspired, then we would not be abiding the most important "commandment" I believe humanity now has: to control its own numbers. In addition, we would deny ourselves a reality-wide search for the ethical basis of a morality that will ensure the survival and development of our descendants.

Another example of religion obsolescence would be Islam, for if its faithful interpreted the dictates of the Koran and the Sharia literally, they would have to live in intolerant theocracies, complete with the death penalty by stoning for adulteresses and the hand amputation of robbers.

Don't people have, then, freedom of belief? Sure they do, but not to impose it on others, not even to members of their own family, although they possess the right to educate their children in their own religious faith.

We can neither discard religions as something worthless or devoid of importance, nor take for granted that they will soon disappear. They have accompanied our species during some 50,000 years and still, for many, offer answers to their questions regarding the meaning of the world and of life, which secular society has failed to furnish.

Morality's dwelling within religion is far from having produced solely bad results, however. Among its positive yields, the following are worthy or mention:
1) The strengthening of morality's compulsory status by making its norms sacred; 2) The mushrooming effect of morality's applicability by way of the religious belief in the brotherhood of man under the fatherhood or motherhood of the divinity; 3) The setting of limits to human rulers' arbitrary decisions. One has only to remember the atheistic totalitarian ideologies of Communism and Nazism to miss and yearn for said protection by religions' heteronomy.

Morality's dwelling within religion also had its negative aspects, such as: 1) Making moral norms excessively rigid and slow to respond to the changing circumstances which normally occur as generations succeed one another in human groups; 2) Gradually making morality's precepts different from those of other groups, mirroring how religious beliefs and practices diverged among those same groups, until they became mutually unacceptable and even repellent.

Each of my assertions must have historical backing to be acceptable. That is the rationale for my embarking on a painstaking verification of morality and religion's ways at each stage of history. In order to make this analysis as accurate and meaningful as possible, I describe my "working hypothesis" at the end of Chapter III. Point 5 states:

"As we proceed with our overview of human history, we will see that: a) in both friendly and hostile interactions among different human groups, the core morality proves very stable, so much so that time and again it serves as the bedrock to establish relations; and b) on the other hand, the religious aspect –or "theological"- in particular, will tend to be divisive and to flare into conflict. But we will also see that it can be stopped short and undergo radical modification, which will never occur with morality."

This hypothesis is confronted with events narrated in each one of the following chapters, resulting in the leading thread of the whole work. The only thing left to answer is this question: What can all this tell us about the present historical juncture or about the future?

We provide the answer in the final Chapter XI: The Historical Present and the Projected Future. There we say that the code of conduct for countries at the global level should rest on those socio-political disciplines that better ensure the arrival of humanity to the projected scenario in a stipulated time frame.

How to make this project compulsory? By means of an effective government of global affairs which would be in charge of (in short): a) Controlling weapons of mass destruction and overseeing police use of conventionally armed forces; b) Controlling the production, transport, and massive use of fossil fuels, and preserving the planetary ecosystem or world environment; and c) Controlling global commerce, massive capital flows and worker migration; d) Communications using satellites and space exploration.

What voting mechanism could we propose that would be considered fair for all nations? I think that the only type of mechanism that has any chance of being accepted by all countries, large or small, rich or poor, socialist or capitalist, Eastern or Western, would be one that is proportional to the ability of each country or geo-cultural group of countries, to be a player on the global scene. The only practical way there is to ponder that ability is by measuring the capacity of each nation to produce riches, which means using its Gross Domestic Product or a similar but adjusted indicator, as its Purchasing Power in Parity or PPP index. This voting power would be used mainly in directing and supporting a "global affairs government".

For those who may think that linking a voting mechanism to production is crass materialism, two things to take into account: 1) All modern democracies began their political life permitting only those citizens who were owners of real estate -the ones supposed to have the wherewithal- to vote; 2) It is urgent, given the issues it would have to control, that a "global affairs government" be able to take mandatory action. So, if that can be achieved with a voting mechanism deemed unfair in some aspects, but which proves to be effective, it can be tweaked to address other needs as confidence grows.

These would be the reasons I would advance for reading this book, making clear that my only intention is to call attention to the issue and prompt others more capable than I to feel intrigued and involve themselves in this affair of giving morality -and the ethics that studies it- a firm foundation, so that the precepts built on it yield a benefit for humanity.

****

I warmly acknowledge the invaluable help, motivation, and considerations I received from my wife Blanca Rosa, my sons José, Tomás and Pablo and daughters Cecilia, Inés and (-in law) Laura and from all the rest of my family, through all the years it took me to complete this book.

INTRODUCTION

If we are interested in knowing what other people think about the most basic existential problems at the turn of this millennium, the first thought that strikes us is the diversity of civilizations and standards of living there are in the world. The problems we are referring to are the relationships of an individual with him/herself and with others, in concentric degrees of nearness; with the biological and physical worlds -ultimately, cosmology; and even with a parallel spiritual or supernatural world, if part of his/her religious beliefs.

So, if we intend to fathom this issue, we have to circumscribe to a manageable proportion, first by limiting ourselves to those societies built within the confines of Western Civilization and then referring only to those persons who have attained a certain educational level. We may be justified in doing so by the probable fact that it is this limited group, probably numbering about one sixth of humanity, which will chart the heading that the rest will eventually follow.

If we limit ourselves to Westerners' beliefs, the first salient feature is that the existential conceptions of many people are still rife with religious characteristics -both in beliefs and in practices- that many philosophers and writers predicted would soon disappear. If we peruse the history of Western Christian churches, we will see that in the last century and a half they have held on to the waning and declining role that had befell them for the previous six centuries. But we would also see that some aspects of religion have not only been preserved but have in fact flourished in some parts of the West, in a manner that seems to contradict, or at least assuage, those predictions.

We can rapidly trace Christianity's declining fortunes in the West in both its Catholic and Protestant branches: After achieving official religion of the Lower Roman Empire status, it inspired and organized the conversion of the barbarian peoples invading the western part of Europe, and then reached its medieval pinnacle in the 13th century as one of the two political powers of Western Christianity. Over the following two centuries, it lost much of this political power, which was seized by the emerging "national monarchies" of France, England, and Spain, or by the "provincial monarchies" of Germany and Italy. During the 16th century, the Roman Catholic Church even lost its theological monopoly as a result of the Lutheran and Calvinist revolts; and then, after 120 years of "wars of religion", all church officials were expelled and excluded from international treaty and law negotiations.

During the 17th and 18th centuries, writers like Hobbes, Locke, Montesquieu, and Voltaire succeeded in their drive to convince the governing bodies of those nations which were adopting a liberal juridical structure, to consider unacceptable any attempt by a politician to bolster his position by claiming a divine mandate or sanction to govern. In exchange, the churches were left free of any political interference in their theological affairs, resulting in a climate of complete tolerance.

On the heels of this "Great Separation"(1) between politics and theology, the new scientific method came into its revolutionary own, driven by the observations, experiments, and writings of Galileo and others, and acquired a philosophical structure by virtue of the fact that most scientists accepted the proposed method for practicing and communicating science advanced by Descartes. This new science began to replace religious dictum in physics and chemistry with no major fallout, but upon reaching geology it not only displaced but contradicted cosmological Biblical history, as astronomy had done before.

By then, the French Revolution had broken out, and wreaked havoc on organized religion to such a degree that for some time it seemed possible that the end had come not only for the Catholic Church, but for some Lutheran churches as well. But once the Napoleonic Wars had ended in 1815 and the attempts to "return to the Old Regime" had failed by 1830, an unexpected thing happened: A kind of religious renewal took root in the Western World that lasted for the duration of the 19th century and through 1914.

What were the causes behind this? That is the gist of Chapter VIII, but we can briefly state them here:

1.- The main cause was that political rights were extended to a broader swath of the population, where many of the people benefited had preserved their religiosity.

2.- Another cause was the reappraisal of religious feelings by writers of the "romantic movement", inspired largely by Rousseau.

3.- The third cause was that philosophers began to notice that even if science was making great strides in explaining the material world, it had next to nothing to say about the "ought to be" in human behavior. Kant, for example, demonstrated that it was impossible to prove the existence of God, but recommended it -as well as the existence of the human soul- be assumed, in order to avoid falling into despair.

Worth noting is that the religious revival was not the only or even the most important trend of thought in Western Europe and North America in that period: The Industrial Revolution was in high gear and science kept its rapid pace, with Darwin finding the explanation for biological evolution, including man's. Meanwhile, Marx and others pointed to the problem of "man's exploitation of man" in society and tried to find a way of forestalling it, while yet others were unleashing Western dynamism on the rest of the world. Nevertheless, it is important for us to study the characteristics of this new religiosity, mainly insofar as the role it played in shaping the mindset which lent itself to making humanity descend into the World Wars. For this we will take Mark Lilla (2) as a guide.

The last half century -and this applies to the whole world- has witnessed more discrepancies in making or accepting a consensus on how we ought to behave and why, notwithstanding our knowledge of how the world is. Our intent here is, precisely, to try to understand the reasons for those discrepancies and to attempt to find a solution, even if far fetched. First, let us try to stake out both areas and their contrasting features.

As far as scientific knowledge is concerned, i.e. meaning based mainly on applied math and known facts about matter and energy –like physics and chemistry- or about life -like biology- there is perfect worldwide agreement. Scientists of every nationality cooperate in building on this kind of knowledge, and constructors use very similar techniques to erect a skyscraper in Kuala Lumpur and in Manhattan, trains speed over magnetic suspension systems in China as well as in Germany, and spacecraft are launched in similar ways in Baikonur and in Cape Canaveral.

However, it would seem that as soon as we venture into disciplines related to what public or private behavior ought to be and why it qualifies as correct, good, law-abiding or ethical, we leave firm ground and step into a real quagmire. While it is true that one can certainly trust that between human groups or individuals there will always be large areas of agreement about what kind of behavior is considered morally correct -so much so as to make us suspect that we all share the same innate feelings- nevertheless the indubitable fact remains that in many concrete cases discrepancies immediately emerge, particularly in the face of new activities. The most sobering aspect of these situations, however, is not that discrepancies arise, but that there may not even be an agreement on what evidence will convince both parties in conflict to accept a concrete solution in good faith.

The "ought to be" area for behavior is sizeable, because it not only includes social customs and mores, but also the moral codes making them systematic, the ethics that studies their philosophical structure, and the religions that make some of them sacred. Also deriving from them are the laws regulating the private and public lives of people in political units, their dealings with other political units, and the studies regarding politics, equity, and justice which ensure that judicial systems are acceptable to our reason.

Why is there such a marked difference between the general consensus in the scientific arena and the many and sometimes intractable disagreements in the "ought to be" area of behavior? I will briefly mention here the main reason being advanced by modern scientists, philosophers, and other thinkers.

The certainty of science, from its humble beginnings of early man's technologies up to its grandiose present state, has always stood the test when confronted with the reality of the world. Although sometimes different "realities" might appear to exist in different places -in the plains vs. the mountains or in cold vs. hot climates, for example- eventually it has always held true that the physical, chemical, and biological basic principles stand the test everywhere.

In contrast, social customs and mores and their moral codes were only confronted with the test of being relevant, adequate, and favorable for the survival and reproduction of the individuals integrating the groups that embraced them.

Today's world has a very important and impressive socio-political structure, and humanity arrived at it by means of its morality, sense of justice, politics, religions, and laws. But when compared with the "exact" and biological sciences, the "humanistic" disciplines addressing what human behavior should be seem to us to have an unsteady basis, like great buildings whose foundations rest on sandy soil instead of on solid rock.

I venture here to say that the solution to this huge, worrisome problem -the contrast between the steadfastness of the exact and biological sciences and the lack of it in the behavioral disciplines- will lie in attempting to firmly anchor the latter in the whole of reality, even if we can only arrive at a hazy and indistinct picture of how to achieve it.

This book's intent is as follows:

1.- To review the biological evolution of life up to our own species, in order to familiarize ourselves with the facts of space, time, and circumstances in which they occurred, with an emphasis on the brain's growth rate.

2.- To probe what today's leading thinkers can tell us about the origins of morality and sense of justice. Then, to dwell on gaining a grasp of the momentousness of the onset of high consciousness, articulated language, and a magic-religious view of the world.

3.- To examine the triad of quantum leaps represented by the arrival to the Superior Paleolithic, the Neolithic, and the "first generation" civilizations. We will focus on the ecological impact that man began to have on his environment, both as a result of his growing numbers and of his more efficient technologies. Then, we will examine the birth and early development of religion, both as a teleological explanation for (the purpose of) the world, and as a vehicle for making moral codes and socio-political institutions sacred.

4.- To survey the arrival of several peoples to the "second generation" civilization tier, with an emphasis on their religions' axial or "moral value" transformations toward a more strict and encompassing moral code. We will also review the birth of democracy and the beginnings of philosophical thought.

5.- To review the political and cultural components of Hellenism, and the philosophical and religious currents that it spawned. That will provide us a cultural reference for understanding the origins of Christianity, from its roots in Jewish monotheism, its adoption by many Middle Easterners, its intellectual structure in

Greek philosophy, and its triumph in the Lower Roman Empire, to its success in converting the barbarians, the birth of Islam, and its adoption by Middle Easterners.

6.- To trace the development of the "third generation" Western Civilization in its "infancy and youth", through its arrival to humanistic Renaissance, overseas expansion, and religious Reformation.

7.- To examine the Modern Age from 1560 to 1830, beginning with the wars of religion and the birth of the modern scientific method, through the arrival of several peoples to a limited and balanced government, the Enlightenment, and to the industrial and political revolutions.

8.- To analyze the genesis of the clash between science and religion, in the context of the unfolding of the industrial revolution, the democratization of Western societies, and its impact on the rest of the world.

9.- To understand the unexpected and traumatic experience of the two World Wars, stopping to examine the circumstances which turned WWI into an enormous tragedy. Then, we will delve into the two terrible totalitarian ideologies which raged in the two decades between the wars. We will then see the strange but fortunate way in which WWII was won, a way which allowed today's world to base its coexistence on two principles accepted and upheld by the human genre. Regardless of the fact that those principles are not new, their modern application is, indeed, a novelty.

10.- We end our historical journey reviewing the Cold War and the Information Revolution in three stages. First: The period of maximum ideological confrontation up to 1968. Second: The period of political detente and socio-economic change. Third: The collapse of the Communist system.

11.- We finish by pointing out what "ought to be", in the present Globalization, the basis for defining the new aspects of morality that would permit this troubled behemoth of humanity to survive and develop in harmony with its environment. To have a chance of achieving that, an effective "Government for Global Affairs" has to be put in charge of only those functions we identify as being global. Finally, a voting mechanism is advanced that hopefully all nations will find acceptable and fair.

*   *   *   *   *

Before plunging into the substance of the book, I would like to clarify my outlook and perspective on this issue: since we will engross ourselves in trying to understand the origins, development, and current state of the intellectual disciplines of what human behavior "ought to be", much of our study involves analyzing both religious feelings and their institutions. Hence, I consider it only fair to state my position in this regard.

I will take a stance that includes a view of the world in which only the natural forces operate, following laws which we can deduce through our experience and reasoning. This is contrary to the acceptance of the existence of a parallel "spiritual" world, in an incorporeal sense, which would include God and the soul of every human being.

Therefore I will refuse to acknowledge the existence of individuals or institutions in a position to decree what a deity ordains in regard to human behavior, based on their interpretation of scriptures held as divinely inspired or following traditions related to them.

The rationale behind this is that I see no evidence supporting those self-attributed powers and, on the contrary, clearly see their historical origins. In other words, I do not acknowledge that there has ever been a phenomenon of "divine" revelation. I am, however, well aware that the scriptures considered sacred by many people may be a trove of human wisdom and include profound truths.

On the other hand, I think that the concept of the monotheistic God, or of the oriental Nirvana or Tien, are noble creations of humanity, in two main aspects: in declaring the existence of a universal order and deriving from that notion a set of behavioral obligations for us, and in recognizing the brotherhood of humanity. For these reasons I view those concepts, in their most abstract and non-institutionalized form, as a veritable patrimony for all of humanity.

Finally, I think that we can say that for some religions, whose faithful are part of societies that have adopted the scientific view of the physical and biological world and the liberal democratic system, their churches are little more than empty ceremonial shells. This is true of many areas and social classes of Western Christianity, both in its Catholic and Protestant branches, and it is my belief that this situation is protracted by two major intellectual omissions by both scientists and philosophers, who have failed to achieve widespread agreement on the following two areas:

1.- Answering existential questions regarding human life and the universe.

2.- Identifying the ethical basis for morality and the sense of justice.

These are precisely the omissions that we will try to redress, albeit even partly, in the following pages.

Chapter I.- Biological Evolution up to the Human Species

1.1.- Early Life

Although we are still in the dark regarding precisely how the transition from inert matter into initial life took place on this planet, as soon as we arrive at the double helix of ribonucleic acid (RNA) and desoxyribonucleic acid (DNA) there is a general agreement on biological evolution. In reviewing its first stage, I will follow Andrew Knoll's [1] lead.

If our planet Earth was formed some 4.5 billion years ago (bya), during its first 500 million years even its surface was in a fluid paste state. Some 4 bya its surface became solid, forming an irregular sphere, its hollows filling with sulfurous water. Covering its oceans and those emerged parts of rock and sand was a nitrogen atmosphere.

Sometime after this geological shakeup, molecules of carbon, hydrogen, and nitrogen must have formed, in some cases with such complexity that they were able to nurture and then replicate their structures' scaffolding. Traces of such "bacteria" have been found in rocks formed 3.5 bya. These and other similar but oxygen refractory organisms, called "archaea", must have filled the primitive oceans with life, and started to react chemically with the water and the rocks at the bottom. The most important impact of this early life was the slow oxygenation of the atmosphere.

Some 1.2 bya, life on this Planet made one of its most important strides, the eukaryote cell, complete with a nucleus, protoplasm, and a bounding membrane, having also symbiotically assimilated some bacteria, called mitochondria, as organs functioning for it. As long as these organisms maintained its unicellular structure, it conserved its spherical symmetry.

Some 100 million years after that, "kingdoms" of life started to differentiate: The plant kingdom acquired another specialized organ, called a chloroplast, which make plants able to process its own nutrients, out of matter diluted in water, with the help of solar light, by means of a complicated chemical reaction called photosynthesis.

Another branch of life, the one unable to manufacture its own food but must obtain it from outside sources, is divided into two kingdoms, one of them of fungi, which obtain its nutrients from rotting organic matter. The third kingdom, the animal kingdom, began to produce fixed "colonies", like the sponges, with specialized cells, i.e. ones for maintaining water flow, others for digesting the living matter floating in it, and still others for forming the structure for the whole.

1.2.- The Emergence of Individuals and the Explosion of Life (2)

Specialization continued in the animal kingdom until the first individuals floated freely in the ocean waters, some 600 mya, in the shape of jellyfish, formed by two concentric bags of cells, with only radial symmetry, plus sensory tentacles and cilia.

Some of the jellyfish specialized in crawling on the sea bottom, losing in the process part of their symmetry, keeping only the bilateral one, thus forming flat worms, with just one opening for both ingestion and excretion.

The next and very critical step that yielded the model for all "superior" animals on this planet consisted simply of a tubular worm, with three concentric bags of cells, with an opening for ingestion at the front and another for excretion at the rear, complete with means to feel the environment and to displace itself in it.

Having produced this model, the animal kingdom was ready to have its "Cambric Explosion" around 545 mya, when a great Ice Age was over and the oxygen level in the atmosphere was high enough to provide the energy needed for large animals. It is called an "explosion" because it is then that all of today's "phyla" of animals were formed. We will focus only on the two most important of them: the "primitive mouthed" one, which produced the arthropods and the mollusks, and the "correct mouthed" one, which produced the chordates.

The two branches differ in the following: Both have a digestive system along the center of a tubular body, but arthropods have their circulatory system in the upper or back portion and the nervous system in the lower portion of their bodies, whereas the reverse is true for chordates: the nervous system is in the back or upper part and the circulatory system is in the front or lower part (evident in us if we position ourselves "on all fours"). In addition, arthropods have the skeleton in the outside of their bodies, while chordates do so in the inside. Mollusks lack a skeleton, but their bodies are folded over themselves, as if forming an "U".

In sync with this "explosion" in the animal kingdom, the plant and fungi kingdoms were performing a comparable feat: They were "conquering" the continents, which during the last 3 billion years had been only barren expansions of rock and sand, albeit being moved by volcanism as tectonic plates, and molded and eroded by rainwater. This conquest was led by the modest symbiosis of plant algae and fungus known as "lichens", which grew on rocks that receive some humidity and proceeded to form the soil in a slow process. Vegetation which developed roots and hard stems or trunks with many little tubes as slender as hairs: the surface tension of water lifts the column to ascend through those tubes as high as this molecular force is greater than the weight of the water column; thus, nutrients dissolved in the water can reach the leaves, where photosynthesis take place. Vegetation took advantage of any humid soil and advanced inland wherever there was enough water.

In the oceans, meanwhile, the chordates were evolving from worms to eels, complete with a cranium as the command center of its nervous system, but still with a round mouth, capable only of nibbling small pieces of food. From them evolved sinewy animals with jaws, like rays and sharks, and then fishes with solid skeletons, which thrived and occupied all available niches in the oceans.

Arthropods divided into crustaceans, arachnids, and insects, with the latter making the jump to participate in conquering the continents, some 450 mya, and finding the land already covered by cryptogam vegetation. The insects entered in symbiosis with some of them, with phanerogam (or flowers and seeds) plants, which insects aid in reproduction in exchange for sipping the flowers' nectar, evolving as a result.

Some 365 mya, in continents' coastal waters and waterways, fish with two pectoral and two pelvic fins evolved lungs, and later became four-legged amphibians. Then, 300 mya, a branch of the amphibians evolved water-resistant skin and their females laid shell-encased eggs, so these reptiles were able to advance inland in those continental areas with hot or temperate climates. This reptilian fauna almost disappeared some 250 mya, together with a large part of the marine fauna, in the wake of the worst catastrophe studied to date, probably the result of a meteorite impact.

Roughly 35 million years later, two branches of the surviving reptiles developed a high metabolic rate, i.e. a very efficient transformation of nutrients into biological energy. In order to achieve this, animals have to maintain their bodies at a constant high temperature, which they succeeded in doing by means of two different "strategies": Dinosaurs by growing tremendously in size, so corporal mass would grow much faster than its surface area; and primitive mammals, by developing a thermal insulating material on their skins, called hair.

During the following 150 million years, dinosaurs were the lords of the continents, some returning to the seas, others taking to the skies. The mammals, for their part, never went beyond being creatures of little size, nocturnal habits, and insect-based diets. Their only evolutionary progress was the positioning of their four legs under their bodies, instead of the sprawling posture inherited from the reptiles, allowing them faster movement.

This situation suddenly changed around 65 mya, when another meteorite struck the Earth, causing a comparable, yet less catastrophic, event than the one before. All dinosaurs became extinct, save one class which had specialized in small size and developed another thermal insulating material: feathers. The humble mammals also survived, so both classes of warm-blooded animals shared the main earth niches, birds taking the sky and mammals the land, with exceptions.

Mammals still had small sharp teeth, adequate for catching insects, but as their expansion exposed them to many other food sources, some evolved molars for eating herbs, others incisors for nibbling, and still others canines, for killing other animals. By choosing special niches, some had no need to specialize their teeth or the rest of their body much. We will focus on those which chose the arboreal niche: Primates.

Simply living in trees requires a somewhat intense use of brainpower, for three main reasons: There is great advantage in living in groups that can mount an organized defense against predators, which requires knowledge and an assessment of the other individuals in the group. The second is that an arboreal diet requires an intelligent search for food, compounded by the fact that color vision is highly useful, as it saves an animal valuable energy by refraining it from climbing trees with still-green fruit. The third reason is that any locomotion atop tall trees is dangerous if the animal does not grab the correct branch or liana. Doing so requires calculating precisely not only the lateral position but also the distance in depth. Defining that distance is better helped by a frontal placement of the eyes, as the brain can then fuse the input and translate it into a precise image.

Between 25 mya and 7 mya, the Earth's main landmass entered an era of very stable hot and humid climate, called the Miocene, so that an enormous rain forest covered it from Western Africa to Eastern Asia. The Primates order had evolved by then to the level of Old World monkeys, i.e. baboons and macaques, but then leaped another step in that vast jungle, to the level of anthropoids. The first family of this new suborder we call the gibbons, whose main evolving changes were that their two upper limbs developed a ball and socket shoulder joint and that their tail was reduced to an insignificant coccyx.

1.3.- The Hominid Evolution (3)

Between 7 mya and 2 mya, the climate of the main group of continents (the Old World) entered a drier geological era, known as the Pliocene, with the enormous rain forest disappearing from many areas and being substituted by either deserts, like the Sahara and Arabian, or savannas, like the Sahel, between the Sahara and the Guinean jungle, or in the highlands (2,000 feet above sea level) of Eastern Africa, at equatorial latitude (where Kenya and Tanzania lie today).

The gibbons living in the receding forests of that plateau had two options: to retreat with the jungle towards the Congo River basin, as the ancestors of the gorillas and chimpanzees did, or stay in the savanna. The ones who stayed quickly evolved into a new genre called australopithecines, whose fossilized remains, dating from between 4 mya and 2.5 mya, have been found.

The physical evolution of australopithecines performed a great leap in our direction, because they adopted an upright posture for their 4 feet 3 inches (1.30 mts.) height by modifying some important aspects of their anatomy: Their spine acquired an "S" shaped double bend for supporting the weight of the upper body, head, and arms. The arms became free of any locomotive function and could be used for handing sticks or stones.

Their pelvis also evolved, becoming narrower and stronger, in order to support the weight of the upper body in its center and transmit it to both of its hip joints and down to the lower extremities. This narrowing began to be problematic for female childbirth, although not so much at this stage, since an adult's brain had a volume of 450 cubic centimeters (c.c.) and weighed one pound, comparable to that of a chimpanzee.

The upright posture and freed arms, complemented by the loss of body hair, except on the top of the head, and its substitution with sweat glands, gave the australopithecines tremendous advantages for living in the savanna, as they could locate a carcass at great distances, by circling vultures, and trot or walk rapidly to it. If no lions or hyenas had beat them there, the australopithecine group, once having learned to operate as a team and to use sticks and stones, could keep vultures and jackals at bay while they grabbed part of the prey and took it with them. (4). We know little of the social life of australopithecines, but it seems that they lived in mutually binding groups for defensive and feeding activities, led by several polygamous males.

Some 2.5 million years ago, the Earth entered the present geological age, called Pleistocene or Ice Age, caused by the movements of the tectonic plates which, among other things, formed a "land bridge" between North and South America, barring the flow of water between the Atlantic and Pacific oceans at the torrid zone. At that same time, the Strait of Gibraltar was opening, filling the Mediterranean basin with seawater.

In the early Pleistocene, individuals of a new genre called *Hominid* appeared in the Eastern African plateau. One of them was *Homo habilis,* which was 4' 7" (1.40 mts.) tall and had a 675 c.c. brain (weighing 1.5 lbs.). This was 50% larger than the brain of their australopithecine ancestors, but since their corporal mass had also grown 25%, the ratio between brain and body weight only increased 20%.

This evolutionary fact is even more outstanding if we take into account that brain tissue is the most ravenous consumer of nutrients and oxygen, ten times more so than other tissues, so the share of circulating blood needed to sustain the brain increased to an extent that its use in another system had to be curtailed. That seems to have been the digestive system: from then on our ancestors, with their reduced amount of bowel mass, were unable to feed on foliage, as the anthropoids do.

This decrease in types of food that could be ingested forced our ancestors to obtain more nutritional foods, such as berries, nuts, eggs, and meat. To do so required developing two capabilities: They had to be able to cover large distances by foot and defend their turf against other groups; and they had to be able to obtain carcasses and hunt more efficiently. Indeed, the earliest stone tools, made with roughly 32 strikes, have been found among the remains of these *Hominids*. Also, the area where their remains were found expands out of the Eastern plateau to cover much of the rest of the African Continent. This ushers in the first step of human culture, called the Lower Paleolithic.

The hunting and gathering activities of *Homo habilis* and other related species were only possible in very close-knit groups. This need was aggravated as females needed the assistance of others during childbirth, and the help of her male partner in raising their offspring during their lengthy infancy. The latter was easier for the females because their ovulation periods were not apparent to the males, so the females had a better control of whom to assign the paternity of their children. The mother's line only recognition of children and the shared responsibility of all adult males of the group over all females and offspring, regardless of paternity, derived from these new facts.

Some 1.8 million years ago, a new species, *Homo erectus,* evolved from one of the earlier ones. It was 4' 11" (1.50 mts.) tall and had a 900 c.c. brain (weighing 2 pounds). So, even if its body had grown 23% and its brain 33%, the brain to body ratio only grew 8.4%.

The high new brain ratio was evident in two main aspects: They manufactured hand axes by striking stones roughly 64 times; fastened or attached to one end of an appropriate shaft, men could throw them at a distance by means of a "programmed rapid movement" (we will examine it again further ahead). Thus, they became the first animals that could strike and kill at a distance. The other headway was their territorial expansion, first to Southern Asia and from about 900,000 years ago to the southern portion of Europe as well. There they had to withstand the first modern ice age, 600,000 to 500,000 years ago.

It was during the second Ice Age, 400,000 to 350,000 years ago, that our own species made its appearance, albeit in its archaic form, with a height of 5' 3" (1.60 mts.) and 1,125 c.c. brain volume (weighing 2.5 lbs.). That translates into growths of 21% in body size and 25% in brain size, with a 3% higher ratio. There is evidence that they were eventually able to ignite fire at will, make tools by striking stones 128 times, kill large animals, and clothe and shod themselves with their furs. This enabled them to inhabit the temperate zones with cold winters of Europe and Asia, and cook their meat and other food, making it more easily digestible. Thus, they arrived to the cultural level of the Middle Paleolithic.

During the third Ice Age, 200,000 to 140,000 years ago, the archaic form of *Homo sapiens* gave way to two new subspecies: One in Europe, called *H.s. Neanderthal,* with the same height of 5' 3" (1.60 mts.) but more robust build -an adult male could weigh some 165 pounds (75 kgs.), and 1,500 c.c. brain volume (weighing 3.3 lbs.).

The other subspecies, ours, called *H. s. sapiens* or modern man, originated in Africa, with a height of 5' 7" (1.70 mts.), a mean weight of 150 pounds (68 kgs.), and 1,350 c.c. brain volume (weighing 3 lbs.). The anatomical differences of the heads of the two subspecies were that the Neanderthal cranium was larger in the back (occipital), but had smaller frontal lobes. They also lacked the protruding chin in the lower jaw.

1.4.- The Conditions for the Ascent to High Consciousness (5)

The first anatomically modern individuals of our own subspecies were not necessarily able to use their full brain capacity, because, at the onset, they were too few and isolated in Africa. The same holds true even when some of them reached the Middle East about 108,000 years ago, at the beginning of the fourth and last Ice Age, and then spread to India and Southeast Asia. Then, between 73,000 and 57,000 years ago, came the coldest spell of all, making living conditions very dire.

It wasn't until a little warmth tempered the climate, that members of our own subspecies were able to attain a modicum of both high consciousness and articulated language. That was evidenced by their all starting to display extraordinary dynamism in the following five traits:

First, they ascended to the Upper Paleolithic cultural level by manufacturing tools and weapons by striking stones up to 256 times and using techniques like indirect percussion, pressure scaling, and boring. They also employed other materials, such as bones, horns, antlers, ivory, teeth, claws, and shells, enabling them to make such fine tools as hooks and needles.

Second, they took hunting techniques to a level in which they could kill whole herds of large animals, using ploys such as chasing them with ignited torches in order to drive a whole herd over a precipice or into a morass.

Third, they began their great migrations toward the temperate zones of the Old World: One branch ventured into China, eventually resulting in the Mongoloid race. Another branch, the Cro-Magnon, made its way into Europe some 45,000 years ago, where it met the Neanderthal subspecies, which became extinct some 10,000 years later. The white or Caucasian race derived from this branch. From the "core group" of those remaining in Africa, represented by the Bushmen, three other races emerged: Pygmies, Nilotics, and Guinean-Bantus. Members of the "core group" which had migrated early to Southern and Southeastern Asia had now all but disappeared, but they still make up most of the population of New Guinea and the rest of Melanesia; the Australian aborigines also belong to this ancient race. Later on, the white race also occupied Northern Africa, the Middle East, and India, and the Mongoloid race extended to Southeast Asia and Japan.

The peopling of the Americas began some 20,000 years ago in eastern Siberia, where some tribes adapted to living year-round in exceedingly cold climates thanks to their learning how to fashion parkas by stitching several furs together with needles made of certain fish bones and animal sinew as thread. This allowed them to accomplish all the activities needed for survival. During the second and last stage of extreme cold climate during the fourth ice age, 27,000 to 16,000 years ago, a land bridge, called Beringia, emerged between Siberia and Alaska. In their everyday roaming, a number of human groups therefore wound up crossing into that part of America. When the great thaw began, they were cut off from Asia and also barred from going south until, roughly 12,000 years ago, a large passage opened in the ice sheet covering much of Canada and they eventually reached the Great North American Prairie. Some of them kept going south, all the way to Mexico and then South America, reaching the extreme southern tip of Patagonia some 10,500 years ago.

Fourth, when our ancestors attained high consciousness, they must have posed themselves the basic existential questions about the meaning of life, in their relationship with other humans and the world around them; but since there were so many things beyond their knowledge or control, all seem to have reached the following conclusion: That like themselves, natural forces possessed purpose-driven will, so they ascribed "soul" or *animus* to them, thus ushering in the "primitive animism" stage of magic-religious thought. This is evidenced by three types of traces found: 1) The burial of their dead, sometimes in fetal position, accompanied by ornaments and flowers. 2) Modeled clay figurines, many of females with exaggerated gender features, thought to represent fertility goddesses, as well as weapons decorated with an esoteric design 3) Rock art in hill faces or cave walls, seen as representing their symbolic vision of the world, using geometric figures and animal and human shapes, though they may also had served as territorial or ceremonial markers.[6]

Fifth, during the transition stage of the last great thaw, when the arctic biota in the temperate zone of Europe and Asia began to be replaced by forests of deciduous trees and by deer and boars, the hunter-gatherer groups living there domesticated the first animal species, the dog. This led to their invention of the bow and arrow, to kill game flushed by the dogs.

To conclude this chapter about biological evolution, we will try to roughly visualize the way of life of our ancestors who had reached high consciousness.

The basic human group was the hunter-gatherer clan or horde, comprising always at least 7 adult males, and more typically 12 to 15. Men were in charge of hunting, and women and children of gathering. The whole group may have numbered 50 or 60 people, so they had to claim a territory of some 4 sq. miles (10 sq. kms.) per person, which means a total area of some 240 sq. miles (600 sq. kms.) to roam.

Their organization displayed very strong solidarity, both for defense and food collection, aspects in which they were self-sufficient. For reproduction, however, they needed to be associated with a larger unit, called a tribe, because they heeded the incest taboo and had to practice exogamy. So the tribe was comprised of 6 to 12 clans, all related by blood and sharing the same language and culture, so the complete human group could include half a thousand individuals.

A very widespread tradition was to celebrate tribal reunions, once a year or even more frequently, for exchanging nubile age daughters and sisters, but also for celebrating rites, making deals, and just having plain fun.

Chapter II.- The Ascent to High Self-Consciousness

2.1.- The Evolutionary Pressure of Living in Groups

Thought is the organized functioning of the whole nervous system of an animal: It captures information about the world that excites its senses, processes it in its inherited brain structure, and builds when needed additional circuits based on its own experience. It can send signals to the body for action, and retain received information, for either short or long periods, in what we call memory. We will refer here to these processes in human beings.

The main neural circuits that integrate our brain were "designed" by natural evolution so that animals, and later hominids, were able to solve environment adaptation issues such as growing, surviving, and reproducing. These basic issues encompassed many others, like learning group customs, finding food, eluding predators, and securing access to a sexual partner. Each requires different attitudes and aptitudes, so the brain developed different modules, each specialized in addressing one type of problem.

We've seen how the brain grew in size through the evolution from anthropoids to australopithecines and the successive species of hominids. Also, how "costly" it was, in terms of blood flow, to properly feed the brain tissue. Now, we'll see in the following chart the phenomenon called "encephalization":

SPECIES	HEIGHT Mts.	BODY WEIGHT kilos	BRAIN WEIGHT grams	ENCEPH. INDEX *	% of Human Index
Gorilla		127	506	1.609	25
Orangutan		53	413	2.352	36
Chimpanzee		36	410	3.006	46
Australopithecines	1.30	28	450	3.902	60
Homo habilis	1.40	35	675	5.048	77
Homo erectus	1.50	43	900	5.860	90
Homo sapiens archaic	1.60	53	1125	6.363	97
H.s. Neanderthal	1.60	75	1500	6.770**	103
H.s. sapiens (modern)	1.70	68	1350	6.539	100

*The encephalization index was proposed by H. J. Jerison in 1973. It is calculated as: (the brain weight in grams divided by the product of 0.12 multiplied by the body weight in grams) elevated to the exponent 0.67. He deduced it from the real brain and body weights of all types of vertebrates, his index being the mean value of the tendency. Since that mean value equals one, the indexes of all primates, the gorilla included, are well above it. [1]

**The explanation usually offered for the fact that *H.s.sapiens* or modern prevailed in Europe over the slightly more encephalized *H.s. Neanderthal*, proposes a qualitative difference in favor of our African ancestors, who had a larger frontal sinus filled mainly with cortical tissue, even if *Neanderthals* had a larger occipital part, filled with a more ancient type of tissue. (2)

We've already seen the three reasons (the need to live in groups, good judgment in obtaining food, and specialized vision) which led primates to have more intelligence, generally speaking, than other mammals. We now have to explain the increase in brain to body weight ratio after australopithecines.

Neuroscientists have a way of pondering the relative importance of functions: by determining which portions of the brain are engaged in each. They have thus concluded that the most fundamental division of the brain involves two "domains" - one in charge of the ecological aspects, the other of the social ones. The ecological domain can be subdivided in physical and biological, the first in charge of representing objects and detecting movement, and the second with what we may call the faunal and floral aspect. The social domain, in turn, can be subdivided into individual and communitarian aspects. Individual aspects include language, gestures, body postures, and the development of a "theory of the mind" that would enable him or her to find out what others think, mainly by detecting if they cheat or lie. The communitarian aspects include the functions of identifying and learning how to deal with immediate family members, relatives, members of the group, tribal strangers, and outsiders, and acquiring and practicing the communitarian ideology.(3)

This distribution of the brain's processing power tells us that the fact that hominids lived in increasingly larger solidarian communities required more intense brain activity for the functions related to living in groups. Primatologists have discovered that one of the ways to maintain "civility" inside the group is by members delousing and grooming one another. Besides the function of friendship and companionship that these activities may have involved, they must also have been a means, for the performing individual, to learn the attitudes and possible reactions of his or her partner. But the problem was that the larger the group, the more time-consuming these activities would be, as they are carried out one-on-one. (4)

Starting in the days of australopithecines, which began losing body hair and having more solidarian groups, these civility customs became increasingly less adequate for getting to know enough of the community members, so it is possible that at this stage they began to be substituted by gestures and grunt modulation.

In the hominid stages, groups not only became larger and more solidarian in both defense and feeding, but members also relied more on each other, like the women who had to be assisted in childbirth, and the infants who had to be protected and taught. This situation surely placed heavy evolutionary pressure in favor of the survival of those individuals able to obtain more information from his/her relationships with others, and to correctly guess their probable behavior in multiple circumstances. In order to obtain the required information, their brains had to have the power to process, and then to express, what we may call "reputation management" or simply "gossip". This have been corroborated by the fact that according to estimates, between 60% and 70% of our conversations, even today, still concern these matters. (5)

2.2.- The Acquisition of Language

The "reputation management" or gossip theory may explain the evolutionary convenience of language acquisition, but not the development of the body mechanisms and cerebral processes that would make it possible. That is the following stop on our journey.

One anatomical fact lets us clearly see how evolution worked its way toward finely articulated language: Chimpanzees, the living species closest to us, have the entrance to the larynx immediately behind the root of the tongue, so it does not share a common passage with the esophagus. The same is true in human babies, allowing them to breastfeed and breathe at the same time; it is only during infancy and youth that the entrance of the larynx descends to its final position, allowing the vocal chords, located in the "Adam's apple", to vibrate by pulmonary air ascending through the larynx. Above the chords is a common passage called "pharynx", whose volume can be modulated by movements of the tongue, which forms its frontal wall. (6) The human ear, in turn, evolved toward the most adequate shape to decode oral sounds. (7)

This continuous evolution must have occurred throughout the entire sequence of hominids, which is to say from 2.5 million years ago to present times, but took a crucial step some 350,000 years ago, when the cranial base moved toward the back in an arched shape, thus making room for the vocal chords.(8) Notwithstanding this anatomical breakthrough, full articulation of language may have occurred only as recently as 50,000 years ago, because not only did it require a vibrating and modulating air instrument, but also that the brain's processing capability had advanced sufficiently for a human group to have assigned words to concrete objects and simple actions, complete with rules for ordering those words in a coherent manner.(9)

Which "processing capacity" took humans to articulated language and to high consciousness? Following Curtis G. Smith, we can say that most neurologists now agree that it has to be the only two modes of processing information in the brain which are uniquely human, and that no animal possesses: 1) The bilateral specialization of the brain in two hemispheres, and 2) Holographic thought uses the whole brain and therefore it is not possible to locate, because it superimposes over other types of neurological activity, and produces statistical results impossible to determine beforehand.(10)

How did the human brain attain this processing capability? Neurologists keep agreeing that the basic process in holographic thought is parallel processing, in which incoming information is divided into two or more components which are processed simultaneously in different circuits, and then compounded, thus yielding complex, high quality information. This process has been clearly and precisely explained for the sight sense by John E. Dowling. (11)

How and why did the first parallel process develop? Kathleen R. Gibson thinks it arose from the need to kill prey at a distance, which required throwing projectiles with precision. To accomplish this, the hunter had to coordinate the distance and speed of the animal being seen with sending adequate instructions to his muscles of a "programmed rapid movement", like those of a spear thrower or a pitcher or someone striking a nail in a wall.(12)

Turning now to the specialization of both hemispheres, we can now see that in keeping with the mind's increased "social domain" capacity, due to "reputation management", the "ecological domain" may also have benefited, mainly in regards to hunting, defending against predators, and protecting against the elements. These corporal activities require a high degree of coordination, and might also have led to parallel processing. Smith thinks that this capability might also have led to processing abstract symbols in the "social domain", and if so, language could have begun being articulated. He explains this possibility thus:

The signals that the five senses send to the brain, for detecting an animal, for example, are coded only by means of adjectives, such as: small, black and white, shrill, and stinky; then, each circuit process its information in parallel and another circuit compounds it and concludes: It is a skunk. With it the proper name is born. But that is not all: the brain also receives information from each muscle engaged in the action and from each segment of skin which stretched, plus other visual signals regarding distances and movements, wrapped in codes that refer to the space and movements in the world outside the body. When all those actions or states of matter are coded into words, the verb is born. (13)

2.3.- The Origins of Morality

Early reputation management, and that of the aptitudes and attitudes of "others", which probably had a feeble start in australopithecines, takes us to the beginnings of morality itself in hominid groups, for behavior assessment involves more than a simple description of facts: it also requires an approval or condemnation.

In its most essential aspect, acquiring morality means that those behavior assessments stir emotions in us. Since their initial evolutionary stage, hominids already possessed many emotions; i.e. they had circuits, wired in their brains, which sent signals for action to glandular or muscular mechanisms. The most typical were anger, fear, and sexual arousal, which permitted them to overcome or elude dangers, or take advantage of favorable situations. The new emotion that they were acquiring with the onset of morality is known as "guilt" or "remorse". It resembled the also recently developed emotion of "disgust", in the sense that both require a certain conceptual capacity which only humans have attained via their arrival to high consciousness and articulated language. 14)

Based on what standards did early humans judge the behavior of "others"? It seems that, in primitive man's groups, the following types of social relationships were included in the domain of the "ought to be":

1.- Loss of prestige or condemnation of anyone performing acts harmful to
   others.
2.- Established standards of equality and reciprocity.
3.- Attitudes and actions must be in keeping with each individual position
   within the group.
4.- Certain bodily functions, such as sexual acts, bathing or washing, eating,
   and excreting, were regulated by purity or contamination criteria.(15)

This new morality also wired its own brain circuits which triggered glandular or muscular mechanisms, thus aiding in an instinctive compliance of the most basic aspects of these obligations. However, many aspects had to be learned by each new generation. As a matter of course, a tendency appeared in human groups to let the inertia of custom prevail, to respect tradition, or to be content with the transmission of moral codes. For this reason, when groups divided and parties went their own way, even if the tendency within each group had been to avoid change, the differences among them could keep increasing, until new contacts, friendly or hostile, made their customs converge. On the other hand, the environment was so harsh that those mores which proved to be obstacles to a successful adaptation were soon eliminated.

Once the basics of the rules for peaceful and cooperative living within human groups had been "internalized" -when instinctive mechanisms led individuals to obey the rules and learn them in full- one could say, as per Kant, that the categorical imperative had been born, which barred, by means of a guilty feeling, that an "evil" action be considered acceptable, for all its appeal.

Where we are at odds with Kant is that the imperatives could have assumed universal status in those early times, because they were markedly concentric: very strong at the familial level and within the clan or horde, less so at tribal level, very weak outside it, and easily turned into hostility toward any strange or foreign group which threatened to attack the tribe or seize its territory.

It is important to clearly understand the survival advantages inherent in the appearance of moral feelings. From then on, the primitive human individual was in a position to judge his/her own actions, and to inflict self-punishment through feelings of guilt or remorse in the wake of a transgression. Humans had no alternative to living in the group to which they belonged either by birth, adoption or marriage, so this meant that the main requirement for their own survival, well-being, and development was one and the same as for the group. We humans, however, can be weak-willed when it comes to helping our community and that could induce us to cunningly ponder our course of action in way convenient to us. That's when our moral instinct makes it painful for us to follow such a course, heading off our intentions and having us act immediately for the common good.(16)

In this sense, even moral judgments that we make about ourselves have a public dimension, role, or purpose, and exercising it is also judged by others, turning the most oft-repeated judgments in a kind of benchmark, against which anyone's behavior can easily be appraised and categorized. Aided by these categories, an effective interpersonal commitment takes hold in human communities, for example, the regulation of cooperative strategies, which are always given in a conditional way by each of the members.(17)

In summarizing this capacity for making moral judgments, we can say that it was handed down to us by our ancestors in the form of "hard-wired" circuits in our brains, and the glandular and muscular reaction which they trigger. These innate structures help us, throughout our development, to acquire and learn the intricacies of a community's customs, mores, and moral system.

We can say that morality teams with the adaptation strategies of individuals living in large and solidary groups, causing all members to regulate their behavior in ways that lead them to inflict no harm to others, be fair in their dealings, acknowledge their position in the group, and abstain from polluting. These strategies have been reinforced by mechanisms that trigger emotional feelings of guilt or remorse, and have evolved at roughly the same pace as the brain toward high self-consciousness and articulated language.

These strategies proved to be adequate for regulating humans' social life, and succeeded in fostering the survival and reproduction of group members. Doing so also ensured the group's cultural continuity. But we must note that these strategies were and are not anchored in the reality of the physical and biological phenomena of the world, for they were not "designed" for that. Besides, let us not forget that these strategies were reinforced with feelings, which are not easy to change in a short time.

This caveat does not mean that the moral system is of little importance: It was a determining factor in mankind's arriving to its lofty present-day level, and helps sustain it there. But it does mean that moral systems have differed from one another, slowly and only in secondary aspects, though they can eventually converge. They can also lose a common reference insofar as to which behavior is "correct" or "true" in some particular instance or case. Nowadays, in fact, there are frequent disagreements not only between individuals or groups but also between social classes -even between entire societies. Disagreements are difficult to settle when the disputed matter involves basic aspects that ignite passions, because in those instances each part seeks to impose its own standards on the other, which often finds that unacceptable.

What should we do about those disagreements, now that we are supposed to know the real origins of our morality? First, we mustn't allow ourselves to panic or adopt a pessimistic attitude, but rather view as a plus that, despite those differences, the main core of our moral system is common to all humanity. The fact that millions of agreements among individuals and groups of very different cultural backgrounds take place all the time bears witness to that. Second, once pinpointed the problem, we should try to anchor our moral system in the aggregate reality of the world, daunting as that might seem. We will endeavor to figure out how we could go about it in the closing chapter of this book.

2.4.- The Meaning of High Self-Consciousness

We now proceed to consider the importance of the arrival to high self-consciousness by quoting a paragraph by John O'Manique:

"I see within the evolutionary process true novelty: the emergence of qualitative changes. Two of these stand out: the emergence of life and the emergence of self-consciousness. The emergence of life within the process of physical/chemical evolution from basic energy to complex organic compounds initiated a new kind of development: biological evolution. In a similar way, but with much more profound, extensive, and dramatic consequences for us, the birth of self-consciousness was the foundation of human development. These transformations marked new kinds of evolution with new capacities following a newest of laws for their further development."[18]

O'Manique says that he sees reflection as the cognitive dimension of the final development of the human mind: what makes it arrive to self-consciousness and to articulated language. From that point on, individuals begin to create culture, though still subject to many limitations, which he describes thus: "1.- Humans determine much of their own development within environments (culture) that they themselves construct. 2.-Human self-determination and culture, although constantly transcending their physical and biological foundations, do not completely escape the conditions of those foundations."[19]

He goes on to define self-consciousness as: "…consciousness of (or awareness of, or reflection on) the self-as-self and of all that the self is conscious of: things, symbols, ideas and concepts, feelings, beliefs, and other selves *as other*.) [20]

How was it that someone arrived to self-consciousness? He states that Daniel Dennett advances that: "...on some occasions when no other member of the community was present to respond, the communicator heard and then answered his or her own message.....The recognition of one's own meaningful utterances and of a response to that meaning could have been the first glimmer of self-consciousness — an awareness of the self that could in some way be articulated." He or she would then have transmitted this consciousness to the others, who would then have acquired it and, after a while, all would have been able to interact at a new level of cooperation and mutual awareness. Nascent language would have helped to open up new ways to communicate. (21)

Of course, together with generosity, altruism, and cooperation also came selfishness, rivalry, and aggressiveness, but there is no doubt that within the human groups that survived a climate in favor of positive attitudes must have unfolded. That can be inferred because we know that a fair amount of autonomy and self-determination in individuals, even if constrained by natural and cultural environments, is necessary for progress, and that individualism prevail only if the group's functioning is guided by systems of morality and justice.

We have now established: Human beings who had arrived to high self-consciousness, lived in communities where morality and justice prevailed, and communicated by means of an articulated language, began to create culture. How did they go about it? They structured efficient means for carrying out their activities, and then and there, for the first time in history - bar a universal teleology - purposes, objectives, and aims emerged.

The combination of the sense of morality and justice with the fulfillment of purpose yielded a new concept of moral values, which we may call "good and evil". One and the other were, simply, what was or was not convenient for the community in the long term. The concrete components of each concept, of what constituted good or evil, were agreed upon after lengthy, mature discussion and soul-searching regarding their own typical behaviors and their likely long term consequences. Usually, the main examples of good behavior took on the shape of models or paradigms of conduct. Those values, it also happened, could undergo modification over the course of generations, if the circumstances of the group or the environment changed. (22)

Thus, albeit vaguely at first, the concept of what "ought to be" took root in individuals as a conviction of what constituted good or bad actions, as a way of choosing what was convenient in the long term. The elevated self-consciousness gave those ancestors the capacity to overcome, with their newly enlightened will, some of their natural tendencies when they were convinced that those inclinations went against what the espoused norms dictated.

Science and art also emerge in all communities of high self-conscious human beings, probably along these lines:

In interpersonal communication, either by language or other means, an honest, sincere attitude came to be valued as events unfolded, given that life conditions were so dire that the environment allowed few errors or lies. Hunting, for example, has a better outcome if accurate and comprehensive data is available pertaining to the prey and dangers involved, and if everyone performs his role wisely and bravely. When all manner of knowledge regarding a certain type of activity becomes systematic, then it reaches the level of technology. When the principles that rule technology become conceptualized, then it becomes science.

Technology also gives birth to another type of activity: if someone, for example, making an object is struck by the idea that besides its purely functional features it would be fine to add other figural elements, emphasizing its purpose or its colorfulness, then that object becomes something special. When the rest of the community comes to appreciate those additions as symbolizing something, to a degree that it becomes a need, then the concept of beauty is born, and the activity of creating it becomes art.

The abovementioned purposes, objectives, and aims led the members of those primitive communities to feel the need to have some control concerning their own development. This feeling prompts each individual to claim said control for him or herself; its being acknowledged by all elevates this need to a "right". In the wake of said acknowledgment, everyone becomes "open" to helping others in his or her purposes, or at least abstain from interfering with them. (23)

Respect for the rights of others takes us to the overall concept of justice, which O'Manique defines as an equitable distribution of the available resources among all members of the community for the development of each. This hypothesis differs from the prevailing Western concept of justice, at least from Hobbes onwards. (24)

In primitive communities, this mutual recognition of rights and the equitable distribution of available resources are doubtless linked to the concepts of obligation and rights, but not with that of equality. Although it is undeniable that at that cultural stage there was total social equality among hunters and gatherers, it was forced upon them by the harsh conditions of life, which made the goals of survival and solidarity overwhelming. However, as soon as those conditions become modified in the Neolithic, equality gradually faded.

2.5.- The Origins of Religion (25)

We are going to conclude this chapter by expounding what was listed at the end of Chapter I as the fourth trait of the Upper Paleolithic, which is the emergence of three types of evidence for primitive man's belief in supernatural forces. We will now venture to see how those beliefs drove those men to try and understand, imagine, and get a fix on those forces, then try to relate to them and, if possible, to control or, at least, appease them.

We must remember that those ancestors, 65,000 to 45,000 years ago (no tombs, figurines, or paintings have been found before that time), probably had only recently attained high self-consciousness and developed articulated language, which is why they felt themselves possessors of a mysterious -for them- will, which allowed them to chart their own purpose.

In order to explain this wondrous ability they discovered in themselves, they imagined that their will emanated from a kind of soul or incorporeal spirit, although mortal and ephemeral. They simultaneously became aware of the cosmic, meteorological, and biological levels or dimensions of reality, and many of its phenomena surely struck them as terrible, menacing, and, above all, unpredictable. So, as an early step to make sense of them, they had to mentally picture them as similar to themselves, in the sense of possessing a soul or *animus* also capable of having purpose, albeit on a grander scale and with longer life. Thus began the "primitive animism" common to all humans.

Hans Blumenberg had this to say on how he thought our ancestors structured that "animism" into their communities:
"Human beings do not bear the absolute (which their own consciousness makes them sense). They have to try the most diverse means of interposing some distance. First, when primitive man overcame "the absolutism of reality", they dampened their dependency on that immense and menacing power by structuring myths: They transformed reality into a profusion of stories and its horrors into plays, by means of a "division of powers" (among Nature's forces). That is why we are obliged to the myth, we cannot renounce to it. (Our ancestors) sheltered in caves, as their descendants (do it) in institutions, and there (both groups) develop culture, interiority, and reflection, and with all that keep at a distance absolute reality, whose immediacy is dangerous."(26)

In order to relate to those *anima* which they had imagined, primitive men proceeded to structure the world of the sacred, i.e. the unusual, that which is not a part of "normal" activities of life, which became "the profane". How is it that the human mind could, indeed, imagine an entire incorporeal or spiritual world, with such an ascribed power that it came to rule many aspects of the life of individuals and their group?

The answer to this, that many researchers (27) are arriving at, is the following:
Having man attained high self-consciousness, comparable to ours, and in an almost total absence of any scientific knowledge about our mind and the world, there was practically no other option, for the following reasons:

1.- Every individual in his or her ordinary life comes to have "visions". Our consciousness is like a spectrum: on one end lies a complete state of awareness, which we use for relating with the environment and solving concrete problems. In the middle lie increasingly abstract and introspective thoughts ranging all the way to "daydreaming", where unreal images and situations can be meaningfully dealt with. That's followed by dreaming, at the other end of the spectrum. In primitive cultures, visions and dreams were accorded such significance, that their contents were usually told to the others.

2.- On special occasions, the entire group participated in celebrations or rites that included rhythmic dances accompanied by music and singing, that usually put people in an increasingly collective euphoric mood. Sometimes such an event culminated in the performance of a specially trained or sensitive person, proficient in inhaling or drinking stimulating or hallucinogenic substances, reaching such a degree of paroxysm that could be infectious to the others.

3.- From all these memories of visions, dreams, and euphoric or exciting experiences, the members of the group, led by the chief or shaman, slowly arrived at a consensus of their meanings, until they structured such myths that better "explained" the cosmic, meteorological, and biological phenomena and their relation to them.

Through the combination of individual <u>experiences</u> and communal <u>practices</u> , the group would reach a consensus regarding their <u>beliefs</u> in the world of the sacred (28). Then the members of the group tried to relate to the supernatural forces they had identified, displaying two different types of attitudes that is convenient for us to differentiate:

The first type of attitude displayed when relating to the sacred was a pragmatic one, which we may call "utilitarian", but also "limited", because it was generally used only for special cases: it leads to magic. This belief system was very important in the primitive era, and has also showed a remarkable capacity for survival, up to the present. Here we will just say this: The process of instituting religion, which we'll delve into later on, took magic from the center to the fringes of social usage, even assigning it an illegal status. The reason for this is that its very pragmatism was always prone to stray, in some instances, into quackery and fraud and, in others, into all sorts of superstition.

Anyway, it is convenient for us to remember that in the primitive era, magic was almost indistinguishable from religion, for the simple reason that the same individuals adopted one attitude or the other, according to circumstances. Also, those who practiced magic "professionally" generally were wise men or women also highly proficient as herbalists. So much so that it is advisable to call the wizard-medicine man of the primitive tribes the Siberian honorific title of "shaman", in order to differentiate him from the marginal and oftentimes fraudulent sorcerers or witches of later epochs.

Insofar as the type of attitude we find more compelling -the religious one- William James said, over a century ago, that regardless of what else it might imply for the (modern) believer, it always means approaching the divinity with a solemn, grave attitude, and never through curse or jest.[29]

I do not think that this attitude has changed much since primitive man. Reflecting on the origins of religion, Eugenio Trías says: "Religion is born simply by an awakened and lucid awareness of that Greater Power that, as death bears witness, does not yield or bend by any action or expression of human beings…religion, instead of trying to master the sacred, prostrates itself at the feet of mystery, dismayed by the realization of our extreme poverty in the face of those superior powers."[30]

Religion, then, was born as recently as the arrival of our ancestors to high self-consciousness and to articulated language, maybe 50,000 to 40,000 years ago, but in any case much later than morality, which may have had its feeble stirrings in the australopithecine groups, but came into its own in the hominids, roughly 2.5 million years ago. If the conditions for religion have anything to do with the evolution of language, then those conditions may have taken a crucial step some 350,000 years ago.

Notwithstanding the enormous differences in the origins of morality and religion, when our ancestors arrived to high self-consciousness, they incorporated their system of morality and justice into their new magic-religious vision of the world, thus beginning the enduring association of two social disciplines with vastly different origins and functions, as one is for regulating communal living, and the other for explaining the world and man's relation in it.

The reason for this association seems to be that, at some point of development, the mythological "explanation" came to include not only the cosmic and biological levels of phenomena, but also the social one. When that happened, the new but powerful magic-religion embraced the old and austere morality. The meeting of these two different social disciplines had various consequences, the following two being the standouts:

1.- Making behavioral norms sacred intensified the conservative trend within each group, meaning that it increases the difficulty of modifying them in response to changing circumstances. It also caused the norms of a given group to diverge from those of others, until the differences could reach levels which made "negotiating" among groups difficult.

2.- Making them sacred also fostered a wider observance of the moral norms, but at the price of making them more arbitrary and less accessible to common sense.

Nevertheless, we should not rush to label the consequences of the association of these two disciplines as inconvenient or undesirable: Firstly, it enjoys universal validity in all societies, except among certain philosophers or in very advanced societies; Secondly, because there seems to be something in the human mind that disposes us to look for stability of certain basic beliefs, many would welcome that certain concepts, God for one, were unshakable.

I think this characteristic of the human mind is best expressed by the Argentine philosopher Miguel Angel Virasoro:

"(In view of the way we behave and feel)…it seems necessary to think…that human consciousness has two aspects, dimensions, or directions: one of them immediate and changing, attentive to what occurs and influenced by it; and the other distant and unchanging, an existential witness of the individual and the world…this unfolding of consciousness produces a tension toward transcendence (that he calls abyssal)…since man has the intuition to be essentially free (…for that "something" that tenses, supports, and animates all his or her being), even if he or she is constrained by his or her circumstances in the world…whose collateral transcendence (he calls it phenomenological) he or she also feels…This inner tension makes man a dramatic being, since his or her biological activity becomes affected by a benevolent and idealizing purpose (zenithal or archetypical transcendence)."(31)

In order to channel this tension, man proceeds, as we have seen, to regulate his or her behavior adopting moral values that we can define as: Existential relationships of man with the others and his or her world that enjoy a consensus in his or her society, and have been transformed over the course of history. Each individual can use these values in order to ponder how desirable, convenient, or compulsory are the various courses of action that he or she has available or are possible, when confronted with important situations.(32)

2.6.- Panorama of Humanity 10,500 years ago

Some 10,500 years ago, when the last Ice Age had ended and the human species, with no near relatives remaining, had occupied the last accessible region of the continents, its numbers may have totaled some 7.5 million (33). This is estimated by the territorial area needed for the hunters and gatherers of the Upper Paleolithic to subsist at that cultural stage. We can say that, at that time, humans' state of affairs were as follows:

1.-   They had ascended to high self-consciousness and their moral systems allowed them to live in clans or hordes, grouped in tribes, where their basic rights were mutually respected, and resources for individual development were equitably distributed. Equality existed as a fact, forced by their harsh circumstances. Outside the tribe, there was little solidarity: They probably respected the lone voyager and may have helped strangers in danger, but reacted to any group that would appear to be a menace to their territorial rights by deploying defensive forces, carrying out punitive raids, or even waging war with extermination purposes. As such, within the solidary groups there was a much better social life that the "war of each one against the others" that Hobbes had imagined, but outside the tribe the situation also differed enormously from the "Arcadian world" that Rousseau imagined, though the adjective of "noble savage" I think would be very appropriate for most of the individuals living at that time.

2.- As a consequence of their arrival to high self-consciousness, they had acquired a belief in their own mortal souls and had imagined larger, longer-living souls or *anima* for various cosmic, meteorological, and biological phenomena, and with them structured myths "explaining" the world and their position in it. The resulting magic-religious system was so prevailing, even in the social aspects, that morality became associated and included in it, and some of its norms acquired a sacred status, as did also other social aspects of their private and public lives.

3.- During this last stage of the Paleolithic, say between 50,000 and 10,000 years ago, humanity became divided into races, basically one for those who had remained in Africa, another for those who had migrated to Europe, and a third for the ones who had ventured into China. One Siberian branch of the latter peopled the Americas. The "common monogenetic original form" endured only in the Bushmen, the Papuans and Melanesians, and the Aboriginal Australians. Articulated languages also divided at roughly the same slow pace as the racial aspects, and with them some more or less superficial aspects of the systems for morality and justice also diverged. The latter was emphasized by the diversity of mythological "explanations" that emerged in the shape of new magic-religious systems.

Chapter III.- The Neolithic Revolution and The First Civilizations

3.1.- Early Human Population and Ecological Impact

We will endeavor to visualize our species', *Homo sapiens sapiens,* increase in number and ensuing ecological impact, from about 65,000 years ago to the dawn of civilization. Why do we select that period?

We viewed in chapter 1, section 3 that our subspecies originated in Africa during the Third Ice Age, between 200,000 and 140,000 years ago: they then proceeded to slowly people that Continent. Their oldest remains out of Africa, found in the Syria-Palestine region, date from a little later than the onset of the Fourth Ice Age, 108,000 years ago, during its first moderately cold stage. Those first migrants, however, did not display any particular drive and shared the area with our Neanderthal cousins.

The Fourth Ice Age ushered in its first very cold stage 73,000 years ago, reached its coldest spell 65,000 years ago, and warmed up again to moderate cold 57,000 years ago.

The traditionally arid parts of the African Continent received plenty of moisture during the coldest stages, so the Sahara turned green. By the time a new migration left Africa 65,000 years ago, they were reaching an upper cultural level. We know that because, quoting Olson: "Their stone tools were smaller and more sophisticated. They worked bone and antler into carefully predetermined shapes. They wore jewelry made from shells, bones, and animal teeth. They covered their dead with red ocher and buried them in graves. Most telling of all, they created art, something humans had never done in the past." [1] Obviously, as we saw in the previous chapter, those Africans were ascending to high self-consciousness, to articulated language, and to the adoption of magic-religious beliefs. They were to spread to the rest of the world, invigorated by these cultural advances.

Excluding the Neanderthals, what was the estimated human population some 65,000 years ago? If we take into consideration that modern man's population in Eurasia was then negligible, we only have to account for Africa. Its population cannot be estimated on the basis of one inhabitant per 10 sq. kms. (3.86 sq. miles) that experts use for the last portion of the Upper Paleolithic, when the hunting techniques reached their peak, but rather a density 3 or 4 times sparser. Then, if Africa has an area of 30 million sq. kms., its population can be estimated at around 750,000 human beings at that time.

We have already mentioned that experts' best population estimate for 10,500 years ago, i.e the year 8,500 B.C.E (before the common era), when all humanity was still at the hunter/gatherer cultural level, but already occupying all accessible continents, was roughly 7,500,000. The best estimate for 5,000 years after that, i.e for the year 3,500 BCE, when Neolithic peasants in lower Mesopotamia and the Nile delta were establishing the two earliest civilizations the population of the whole world may have doubled to 15 million, probably evenly divided between sedentary farmers, seasonally migrating herders, and nomadic hunters and gatherers.

Two thousand years later, i.e. by the year 1500 BCE, when the Sumerian and Egyptian civilizations had run their initial course, wheat farming had extended to the west as far as the Atlantic coast of Europe and to the east down to the Ganges Great Plain; sorghum and rice cultivation was allowing the Chinese to attain civilization; and corn, bean, and potato farming were getting underway in the Americas. The world population then may have reached 25 million.

This data enables us to calculate the growth rate of modern humans' numbers in early times:

YEAR B.C.E.	EPOCH	Population in Millions	% Increase per Millennium
63,000		0.75	
	Upper Paleolithic		4.2
8,500		7.5	
	Neolithic		14.9
3,500		15	
	Early Civilizations		29.1
1,500		25	

What can this very tentative tabulation tell us? To begin with, that the population remained constant during hunters and gatherers' years at the Paleolithic cultural level, because the crawling 5% per thousand years pace can easily be explained by a slow territorial expansion until all accessible continents were peopled. That is the reason underlying the highly concentric morality of the humans of that era: strongly solidary at the clan or horde level, less so at the tribal level, but hostile to any group that could pose a menace to their territorial control, save for the occasional lone traveler or persons in danger. Here we have harsh, nature-imposed population control.

From the year 8,500 BCE on, modern humans were able to free themselves from those shackles, albeit to a certain degree, as evidenced by the increase of only roughly 15% per thousand years during the 5 millennia of primitive agriculture in some regions, through the year 3,500 BCE. During the following two millennia, up to the year 1,500 BCE, the rate rose to 30% per thousand years thanks to the irrigation systems of Lower Mesopotamia, of the Nile river valley and delta, of the Indus river basin, and the new agricultural practices in China and the Americas.

Humans' most noticeable impact during those early times was caused mainly by their great capacity for and versatility at venturing and adapting themselves to living and thriving in a great diversity of terrains and climates (as we saw in chapter 1, incise 4). Their most significant ecological impacts were:

1.- Between 60,000 and 40,000 years ago, peoples of the "original trunk" navigated over wide marine stretches, initially reaching New Guinea and then Australia, where they introduced a wild dog –the "dingo"- which was to deeply modify the marsupial native fauna.

2.- Between 45,000 and 35,000 years ago, peoples from the Middle East migrated into ice-cold Europe, competing with the Neanderthal man, whose species became extinct, as we have already mentioned.

3.- Between 12,500 and 10,500 years ago, Amerindians -descendants of Siberian peoples- entered the Great Prairie of North America, where they participated in the extinction of mammoths, camels, and horses.

4.- Between 8,500 and 5,500 BCE, wheat and some vegetables spread throughout the Middle East and surrounding regions, together with domesticated goats, sheep, donkeys, and pigs. Human densities then reached around 1 inhabitant per sq. km., modifying the flora and fauna of the region. Farmers were yet unable, however, to settle and cultivate the lower Mesopotamia plain nor the delta and valley of the Nile, because of the dense thicket of vegetation still covering them and their large fauna.

5.- When those first farmers domesticated the bovine species, they could use two castrated bulls (oxen) to pull a plow for making a continuous excavation or furrow. The purpose was to sever the roots of native vegetation, thus clearing many areas of very fertile soil for sowing wheat and vegetables. This allowed them to settle lower Mesopotamia and Egypt for agriculture from the year 5,500 BCE on, and by 3,500 BCE human density in those fertile valleys may have reached 10 inhabitants per sq. km.

6.- Between 1700 and 1500 BCE, the Sumerian and Egyptian civilization, then at the decline of its first stage, and the Indus Valley civilization, which had emerged 1,000 years before, were invaded by barbarians of Iranian peoples from Central Asia (Hurrites, Hyksos, Coseans, and Aryans) who had domesticated the horse, harnessing two to a one-axis war chariot, which gave them a military advantage over the armies of the civilized states. In China, by that time, an ethnic group of warriors, the Shang, acquired the domesticated horse from the Iranians and formed the aristocracy of the first Chinese civilization, which began around the year 1750 BCE.

Thus, around the year 1500 BCE, conditions were in place for the economic and military superiority of Eurasia (except its northern taiga and tundra zones) and North Africa over the rest of the world. This has been effectively explained by Jared

Diamond (2): The only equine that could survive the sting of the tse-tse fly in sub-Saharan Africa was the zebra, which has proved to be impervious to domestication. Australia became isolated again after the last great thaw, with only its marsupial fauna, modified by the dingo. In the Americas, the Indians participated in the extinction of the horse and there was no bovine native species that could be domesticated.

3.2.- The Social Aspects of the Neolithic Revolution

Here we will address mainly the Neolithic of the Middle East, which later expanded to Europe and India, but we must take into account that, at later times and independently, similar social processes took place in China and in the Americas.

First, let's review the technological advances achieved during the first stage of the Neolithic, between the years 8,500 and 5,500 BCE, following the order and numerical sequence given by V. Gordon Childe(3):

1.- A primitive agriculture of wheat and some vegetables developed: polished stone shovels were used for digging holes for seeds, and hoes of the same material for reaping sheaves of wheat.

2.- Medium-sized animal species, i.e. goats and sheep, were domesticated, and fed straw when pasture was scarce. Later on, donkeys were domesticated for transportation and pigs for their meat.

3.- Houses were built, generally made of adobe walls, rubble masonry foundations, and thatched roofs, for sheltering the increasing population. Silos for storing grain were also erected. (4)

4.- Baskets and sacks of strong vegetal fibers were fashioned for transporting grain from fields to silos. Later on, ropes were made with these fibers to control domestic animals.

5.- To heat water for boiling vegetables and meat, baskets were lined with mud and, later, evolved into ceramics for many kinds of pottery.

6.- People learned to spin sheep wool into thread and then weave it for manufacturing cloth and blankets for the increasing population.

Account for this technological progress, we shall now endeavor to ponder population growth in an area including medium and higher Mesopotamia, the non-desert parts of Syria-Palestine, the western part of the Iranian plateau, and all of Anatolia up to the Caucasus mountains, an area of roughly 2 million sq. kms. (770,000 sq. miles). In the year 8,500 BCE it may have been peopled by some 200,000 hunters and gatherers, but the spread of the agricultural population may have increased it tenfold by the year 5,500 BCE, to some 2 million. What happened to the social fabric of societies in that area? The answer seems to be that it had become very significantly stratified: A ruling class had emerged, composed of chiefs and shamans or warriors and priests, while the majority of the population became sharecroppers or landless peasants.

This Neolithic population lived in politically independent villages or cluster of villages, with no cities. Even if archeologists have found and intensively studied two massive compounds of houses, one in the southern Anatolian plain, called Çatal-Huyuk, and the other the Jordan valley in Palestine, called Jericho, they weren't cities in the proper sense, due to their lack of specialization. What has been unearthed there can help us answer the following question: Why did that portion of humanity -and others in its wake- begin its march toward the production of food, which would eventually elevate it to the ranks of civilization and to the present?

The answer is not as obvious as it seems, because on average, humanity undoubtedly suffered a toll in the process: Human remains from that time on show signs of disease, deterioration, and violent death, some for ritual or sacrificial reasons. Besides, the ruling class was a privileged elite that had to be supported, so life must have been hard and tough for many. Then, why start to change activities?

Part of the answer may be: because of the benefit of numbers. If it happened that during those 3,000 years between 8,500 and 5,500 BCE, the population in the Middle East grew tenfold, but that 90% of the population increase was composed of sharecroppers or landless peasants, we can compare the before and after situation as follows: If we consider that the class of warriors and priests equaled in numbers the hunters and gatherers living in that area before, then the inevitable conclusion is that the net gain was the existence of the new "proletariat". Thus, their condition might not seem unduly harsh in this light, if the alternative is their non-existing.

Clearly, none of the individuals who began agricultural practices could have imagined the long term consequences. However, both they and those who followed somewhat later could appreciate the phenomenon –albeit at a small scale and in the short term- and the convenience of having relatively certain food staples, despite their various disadvantages: They soon noticed that domesticated plants and animals were more prone to catch diseases than their wild counterparts, and worse, that some could be contagious to their human keepers. In the end, the advantages prevailed and human groups settled to tend to their crops and herds. The change from nomads to settlers was basic for all further development.

The most important change that led toward a stratified society and may not have seemed so at the onset, was women's seclusion in their husband's home, mainly at night, once every head of a family had his own house. Even if it was a patriarchal family and an old father and his married sons shared a big house, each son had his own hearth or home fire. This led first to the recognition of sons by the paternal line, then to private property, first of the house and farming implements, then of any animals, and, lastly, to the property of the land. Those properties were then passed down from fathers to sons, and after some time not only properties but also the social position and standing were inherited, be it that of chief or shaman, warrior or priest. Eventually, the ruling class closed itself to marriage to "the lower ones", and became a caste.

The fact that chiefs or warriors made up the ruling class of the new stratified societies tends to seem natural to us, because we realize that it should have been even more necessary then to seize a territory and retain it, than it was during the hunting and gathering stage, because part of their land was now cultivated for their food staples. What might not be as clear is why should the shamans or priests be part of the ruling elite? The answer is because magic-religion was increasingly staking a greater claim within human groups since, as we have seen, it explained the meaning of life and the world to individuals with higher consciousness and also governed their morality system. We talk about chiefs and shamans, warriors and priests, as if they were always different individuals, but we are actually referring to functions, which, at least at the beginning, could have been executed by the same person.

Religion was so important that some scientists think some events as significant as was the domestication of bovines for the expansion and development of the Neolithic culture, may have had a religious origin: In the Çatal-Huyuk area, wild bulls of the *auroch* species were captured for a religious rite purpose, but over time people began to become familiar with them, probably also started capturing cows and calves, and after a while using them as a source of milk and meat, and harnessing their pulling power.[5]

Inconsequential as it might seem to us moderns, another factor which could explain man's entering the food production and settlement stage may have been the need that these groups had for performing religious representations and ritual practices: Caves were unavailable or not large enough in many places, so when the first houses and silos were built, the idea of building house-temples to fulfill those needs might have been born. In order for us to better realize the need Neolithic man had for making religious representation, we must delve deeper into what we saw in chapter 2, section 4, in the sense that their imagined spiritual world was being built by dreams or visions, which acquired consensus in the whole group.

In this aspect, neurology has made such progress that scientists now have a much more precise idea about in which circumstances we have dreams and what they involve: They have found that a sleeping person first falls into a deep sleep, which then alternates four or five times a night with restless spells of "rapid eye movement", when dreams happen. [6] Dreams and visions can also be induced in an person who is partially or fully awake, by altering his/her consciousness through a variety of factors, such as frenetic euphoria, a combination of fatigue and fear, an illness which takes a person to the brink of death, and/or inhaling or drinking hallucinogenic or stimulating substances.

Science has also made great strides in determining, in some measure, the structure of dreams and visions with an altered consciousness: Although the subject or plot can vary from person to person and always unfolds in his/her cultural setting, it seems that all hallucinations, due to our neurological structure, have the same general format, divided into three or four stages: in the first stage, simple linear geometrical figures prevail; in the second, the figures may transform into persons, animals, or objects; in the third all figures swirl in an eddy or vortex or at least pass through a narrow tunnel or passage, eventually emerging into a more calm or quiet space, but with the figures of the second stage acquiring very peculiar shapes, like surreal combinations of humans and animals or animals and objects. (7)

Taking into account the universality of these visions of altered consciousness, anthropologists are beginning to feel convinced that this is how primitive peoples could have imagined "the other world", and why they came to believe in it with such staunch faith: For the simple reason that everyone could, to a certain degree, experience the visions of the shaman, the chief, or that of any other seer, if they also entered in altered consciousness state. It is under this criteria that the cave paintings of the Franco-Cantabrian Paleolithic could be interpreted, aided by the interpretations based on anthropological studies of Bushman or San art, in southern Africa.(8)

The figures that were finally emerging from the consensus of the groups of the Paleolithic were assigned a symbolic meaning, which is why painting them on cave walls or molding them into clay figurines became imperative: This way, during the ensuing hallucinatory experiences, subjects would have visions of the sacred symbols approved by consensus. Later, in the settled Neolithic, the sacred symbols had to be sculpted into large figures or painted on the walls of the house-temples, as the inhabitants of Çatal-Huyuk and Jericho did. Thus were born religions that the later monotheistic ones would disparage as "idolatry" or, less severely, as "polytheism".

3.3.- The Second Expansion of the Neolithic

The second series of technological advances identified by V. Gordon Childe, which set the stage for the second expansion of the Neolithic between the years 5,500 and 3,500 BCE, include the following (9):

7.- The second level or stage of agriculture, which included selecting new varieties of wheat for hotter or colder climates, cultivating more vegetables, constructing irrigation ditches, terraced hills to prevent soil erosion, and domesticating fruit trees, such as grapes, olives, dates, and figs.
8.- Copper metallurgy, developed first in Anatolia, which very successfully substituted many stone weapons and tools.
9.- The potter's wheel and boring bow, which helped enhance the quality of ceramics and carpentry.
10.- The domestication of the bovine species, mainly for harnessing two oxen to pull the plow.

11.- Fluvial navigation, using a mast for sails and also oars, in the Euphrates, Tigris, and Nile rivers.

As we saw in chapter 3, incise1 (p 5), the Neolithic farmers were finally able to settle the lower Mesopotamia plain and Nile river delta and valley aided by the oxen team. However, expansion was also taking place in other directions:

Toward the east of Iran's semi-arid plateau, around the year 4,000 BCE, Neolithic peoples finally reached the Indus river basin in northwest India, where Pakistan is now. By the year 2,500 BCE, a new civilization would be born.

Toward the west, from its base in the Anatolian Peninsula, agriculture and animal husbandry expanded to the Balkan Peninsula, and from there to the Danube river basin, settled around the year 5,000 BCE. The native European peoples that adopted these technological advances, rising thereby to the Neolithic cultural level, differed linguistically from the rest of the European peoples. Hence, we have to call them "Aryans" or "Indo-Europeans". Some Aryan groups headed towards the east, occupying the Ukrainian prairie and southern Russia, and from there reaching Central Asia around the year 3,000 BCE, where, roughly one thousand years later, they domesticated the horse.

Other Aryan groups expanded toward the west, reaching the Atlantic coast around the year 4,000 BCE. From then up until around 2,500 BCE a Neolithic culture developed in much of Western Europe, with members erecting many monuments utilizing large rocks (megaliths) or building earthen mounds over tunnels and chambers, all with religious or sepulchral purposes.

These western religious monuments -chiefly those discovered in the bend of the Boyne river in Ireland and the island of Anglesey in Wales- show, even more so than their Middle East counterparts, an aspect of the religion of the Neolithic that will persist to this day: A three-tiered world, the upper one being a "heaven" shared by celestial bodies and gods, an "earthly" level of men, animals, and objects, and a underworld level, which is the realm of the dead. These three levels or tiers are frequently united by a "vertical axis of the world", which intersects the hill's summit and the central chamber, whose access tunnel aligns with the sun's rays at the winter solstice. What's striking about this is that this design is replicated in many others very different parts of the world, such as the Temple of Inscriptions in Chiapas, Mexico[10] and in many stories of Aztec personages traveling to "the other world", published by Gutierre Tibon [11].

3.4.- The Ascent to First Generation Civilizations

We have seen how, around the year 5,500 BCE, Neolithic farmers, with the help of a team of two oxen pulling a plow, started to settle the fertile plains near the rivers in the lower Mesopotamia, an area of 72,000 sq. kms. (28,000 sq. miles); and how they also settled in the Nile valley and delta, a combined area of some 36,000 sq. kms. (14,000 sq. miles).

Some 2,000 years later, around the year 3,500 BCE, those fertile lands may have reached a population density of 10 inhabitants per sq. km. (26 per sq. mile). If so, then there were 720,000 inhabitants in lower Mesopotamia, which we will herein call Sumer, for the language of its early settlers, and some 360,000 in what we'll now call Egypt. Those dense agricultural populations needed a number of hydraulic works for irrigation, so they were in dire need of a central authority who would direct the entire society. That need pushed them to ascend to the level of high urban culture or "civilization", first in Sumer and then -some 200 years later- in Egypt. This phenomenon unfolded as follows:

In Sumer, six city-states emerged, each with some 120,000 inhabitants. In each one, its elite of warriors and priests built a command and ceremonial center: the first six cities on this Earth. They directed the public functions, exercising authority over all the villages encompassed in the area, which paid them "taxes", either in goods, such as grains or artisan objects, or contributing with work gangs assigned to public works, such as canals, dams, roads, forts, or temples.

The same quantum leap from a Neolithic agricultural village to civilization was repeated another five times all over the world: in Egypt shortly thereafter, followed by the Indus river basin, northern China, Mesoamerica, and the Andes. Three new technological breakthroughs developed independently in each of the six cases - hence we can say that they are "concomitant" with civilization- and were identified in this order by V. Gordon Childe.[12]

12.- Solid monumental architecture, at first for the command and ceremonial centers, and later culminating in pyramids, towers, and walls.

13.- Ideographic writing, in order to register taxes: Sumerian cuneiform [13], Egyptian hieroglyphics, Indus script, Chinese script, Mesoamerican codex, and Andean quipus, the most primitive of the six, used only as tax register.

14.- The accurate determination of the astronomical length of the year.

In the special cases of Sumer and Egypt, Childe identifies another two technological advances:

15.- Deviating dams from rivers and irrigation canals.

16.- One and two axis carts, with solid wooden wheels, pulled by one or more oxen teams.

In the following pages we will endeavor to understand how the magic-religion of the Neolithic underwent modification in the Sumerian and Paleo-Babylonian stage between the years 3,500 to 1700/1595 BCE and during the Old and Middle Kingdom stages of Egypt between the years 3,300 and 1674/1552 BCE, as well as in the intermediate and peripheral areas of Syria, Anatolia, and Crete, in their own ascent to civilization.

We must first try to imagine that during that enormous period of time -almost two thousand years- both areas, Sumer and Egypt, lived almost totally isolated from one another, though they must have known of each other's existence, mainly through Syrian, Anatolian, or Cretan intermediaries. The fact is that they had no substantial influence on each other, at least consciously, though their technological advances slowly passed between them.

This isolation is the reason why their particular visions of the world were closed in on themselves. Each was isolated, though to a different degree, almost absolutely in Egypt but less so in Sumer, as it was always receiving an influx of Semitic immigrants and was in contact with Iranian nomads.

The kind of religious mentality shared by members of both societies, and which would appear in all first generation civilizations, can be called "collective magic mentality" because they kept "soldering" in the same mythological explanation the cosmic, biological, and social levels of existence, as they had inherited it from their Neolithic and Upper Paleolithic ancestors. But in their new civilized conditions, the priestly chaste had made a more extensive job, covering the new multitudinous and stratified social phenomena and linking them with the biological and cosmic ones in the most coherent and plausible ways they could find. To reinforce their refurbished myths, they tried to represent that new divine world in an impressive form, with sculptures and paintings in the temples and by putting them in scene in multitudinous rituals.(14)

In order for us to comprehend the strength of that mythological explanation of the world, we can contemplate the case of Egypt, whose early political unification gave any pharaoh in his reigning term an immense political-religious prestige. When the Old Kingdom reached maturity during the IV Dynasty the large pyramids were built for three of them, not only as sepulchers but mainly as a proper and dignified stair or "escalator" for his soul to ascend to the God Rah fire chariot, the Sun. For this reason they were covered by a brilliant white mortar and looked like gigantic dies in the sunlight. (15)

In Sumer, the Gilgamesh epic deeply explores the relationship between the human and divine worlds, the Tower of Babel of Paleo-Babylon age, being a pragmatic intent for uniting those two worlds.

Other "excesses", in view of the modern point of view, which fostered the "collective magic mentality" were: the construction of the Chinese Great Wall, apparently at first more for keeping out the evil spirits than the barbarians; The human sacrifices of the Aztecs, to assure that the sun kept its course (16); The assignment of the property of the best lands to dead Incas.

The relationship between men and gods at this stage of cultural evolution was almost entirely propitiatory. Let us hear how Karen Armstrong describes it:
"People normally experienced the sacred as an immanent presence in both the world around them and inside themselves...They were all subjected in a cosmic order which included everything and kept it alive...Sacrificing animals was a universal religious practice in ancient times. It was a way of recycling the diminished forces which kept the world alive. They had a strong conviction that life and death, creativity and destruction, were inextricable interwoven. People realized that they survived only because other creatures surrendered their lives in their benefit, so the animal victim was honored for its self-sacrifice. Since there could not be life without such death, some imagined that the world had begun to exist as a result of a god sacrificing at the beginning of times." (17)

This world of first-generation civilizations isolated from one another in the Middle East was so stable that it may have lasted much longer than the two millennia that history asserts, so we should ask ourselves: what made them change their ways and accelerated their ascent toward higher civilization? The answer is far from simple, but the slow changes that historians detect could have been partially triggered by discrepancies between what religion, for all as coherent as priests tried to make it, may have led them to expect, and what really happened, both in the natural or human world. When such a discrepancy occurred, changes in religion, even if only of emphasis, had to be made, with the inevitable loss of political-religious credibility.

Better documented is another cause: barbarian invasions at the end of this period in the Middle East. They were the Iranian peoples who had domesticated the horse in Central Asia around the year 2,000 BCE, and who, between 300 and 500 years after that, shook the Sumerian-Babylon and Egyptian civilizations to their foundations and completely destroyed and superseded the Indus River one.

3.5.- World's Overview around the Year 1,550 BCE

We have estimated the world population by this year at 25 million, distributed as follows:

In Mesopotamia, the area being cultivated had increased to 125,000 sq. kms. (50,000 sq. mi.). With the aid of its hydraulic works it may have had a population density of 30 per sq. km. (78 per sq. mi.), for a total of 3,750, 000 inhabitants. Egypt was more fertile and better administrated so its density might have stood at 60 per sq. km. (155 per sq. mi.) for 2,250,000 inhabitants. Another 3 million people could have been living In the intermediate area of Syria, Anatolia, and Crete, for a grand total of 9 millions in the Middle East.

In India, the Indus River civilization was being decimated by the Aryans, but agriculture had been introduced to the very large and fertile Ganges Plain, so coupled with South East Asia it may have had a population of 5 million.

Meanwhile, the sorghum and rice agriculture in northern China was giving birth to a new civilization, which with the remainder of Asia may have totaled 4 million inhabitants.

Europe's central and western portions -entering the Bronze Age- could amount to some 2 million inhabitants, with roughly the same numbers for Africa and the Americas, almost all in the hunter and gatherer stage, though two small areas were developing agriculture. These three continents, then would account for 7 million.

New technological breakthroughs of the Childe series (18) were:

17.- Around the year 2,800 BCE metallurgy of a copper and tin alloy developed in Anatolia. The result, bronze, was much better, chemically and mechanically.

18.- At about the same date the inhabitants of the isle of Crete were founding their Minoan Civilization, not spontaneously but as a result of partaking in the maritime leg of trade between the Sumerian and Egyptian civilizations. They developed the first merchant marine, transporting eastern Mediterranean Egyptian wheat to the Syrian coast and carrying back Lebanese cedar timber.

19.- Around the year 1900 BCE the structural arch allowing large indoor spaces was developed in Paleo-Babylon.

20.- As we have seen, Iranian peoples of Central Asia had domesticated the horse around the year 2000 BCE, and circa 1700 BCE one of those peoples, the Hurrites, attacked Babylon with one-axle chariots pulled by two horses.

So we have a world that around the year 1550 BCE was populated by some 25 million humans, and some of them had already passed through a period of "collective magic mentality", whose credibility had been shaken by invasions of better armed barbarian peoples (This type of mentality was going to be repeated mainly in the civilizations that were going to develop in the Americas). The Middle East peoples were about to enter into a more dynamic period, driven by the cultural advances of the two earliest civilizations and the recent breakthroughs of the bronze metallurgy, marine navigation, and domesticated horses.

3.6.- Working Hypothesis

Although the level of certainty in humanistic sciences is low and one cannot generally talk of rigorous proof, I think it convenient that I state clearly the hypothesis that I am trying to propound while offering a panoramic view of history in the following chapters, if for no other reason than to make it easier for the gentle reader to draw his or her own conclusions. The hypothesis is as follows:

1.- That morality, being so anciently rooted in the hominid genre and having such a firm biological mechanism of reinforcing feelings such as guilt, disgust, shame, and remorse, conserves in all cultural and geographic circumstances a huge common core and a variable periphery, dictated by history's fancy.

2.- That even if that common core of human morality is not anchored in the objective reality of the world, it is firmly in line with, and stems from, the living interrelations of human groups. Studying the history of humanity, we can assess it, by and large, from the following two perspectives: a) It has been good enough to carry humanity to its present levels of power and complexity; and b) It does not guarantee us that we can wend our way with our huge power to the future for as long as we do not anchor it in objective reality.

3.- That the magic-religious sentiment is very recent, maybe as recent as half a hundred thousand years. That it is a consequence of our ancestors having arrived to high self-consciousness. That its foundation is our sense of awe at knowing we have a will and can have a purpose. That it is our way of acknowledging our extreme want and weakness in front of the world's phenomena and that in order to provide ourselves with an explanation we concoct a "theory of the world" of the mythological type that has to be represented.

4.- That since the magic-religious mythological explanation encompassed all phenomena -from cosmic and biological to the social levels- it was necessary to incorporate morality within the religious vision of the world. This association would inject a new rigidity to morality and somewhat distort its original purpose, which was simply to outline the best way for humans to interrelate in groups. From then on, however, it was subject to supposedly divine commandments

5.- As we proceed with our overview of human history, we will see that: a) in both friendly and hostile interactions among different human groups, the core morality proves very stable, so much so that time and again it serves as the bedrock to establish relations; and b) on the other hand, the religious aspect –or "theological"- in particular, will tend to be divisive and to flare into conflict. But we will also see that it can be stopped short and undergo radical modification, something which will never occur with morality.

Chapter IV.- The Arrival to Second Generation Civilizations

4.1.- The Crisis of Propitiatory Polytheism in the Bronze Age

Around the year 1550 BCE, the Middle East arrived to a critical level of growth, similar to the one it had arrived at two thousand years before, when villages in the fertile valleys grew in number and such a crowding ensued that they needed a higher political organization. The same thing occurred in 1550 BCE, when all the socio-political entities in this area started to impinge on one another and could no longer ignore the rest, because they already formed a mosaic of sorts.

The time when they, and particularly Babylon and Egypt, could think of themselves as unique worlds was over, and they were forced to recognize not only each other, but also the entities that had cropped up in their vicinity. These were: the many principalities in Syria, the Hittite and Mitanni kingdoms in Anatolia up to the Caucasus, and the Minoans of Crete. These were joined by two neighbors of Babylon: the warlike Assyria to the north and Elam to the southeast, on the Persian Gulf's Iranian coast.

We will not concern ourselves with all that transpired in the 400 years between 1550 and 1150 BCE in Egypt's New Kingdom, the middle-aged Babylon and their warlike new neighbors. Suffice it to say that during this Bronze Age, international relations began through the establishment of commercial routes, both maritime (the Minoans) and by land (mainly by the Syrians, with horses and donkeys, since there weren't domesticated camels yet). Wars also started and the first battles fought, both on land and at sea.

We will instead focus on the changes that the "collective magic mentality" experienced, mainly in the manner its faithful will come to see the world and reassess the individual, which will occur at the end of the period. First we will see the slow change of perspective become noticeable in the two more peopled and advanced regions, Babylon and Egypt.

Three circumstances occurred in lower and middle Mesopotamia, as early as in its first Sumerian stage, which led to their grasping the ethnic or "nationalistic" aspects of religion. This means that if the primitive gods had been assigned functions related only to cosmic, meteorological, biological, and social phenomena, as soon as they ascended to civilization, the gods also had to be assigned ethnic or nationalistic functions, for the following reasons:

First, because they had seemingly always been divided into roughly six sovereign states, so even if they shared most gods, each state was partial to a certain one.
Second, very early in history there was migration of Semites into the Sumerian area, which in turn was attacked by Iranian nomadic peoples. All of them had their own protector deities and contributed new mythologies.

Third, there were neighboring states, Elam in the southeast coast and later Assyria in the northern highlands, who warred and even conquered Babylon.

These events forced everyone to reevaluate the relative power of the gods, mainly those with ethnic or nationalistic assigned functions.

In contrast, Egypt was invaded by barbarians only at the end of a long period of isolation, so it apparently embarks on its New Kingdom stage of the Bronze Age and on international relations little changed. However, it so happened that the impact of the new plurality and diversity of the world that they were forced to accept affected the Egyptian ruling class more than it had the Babylonians. The policies adopted by the pharaohs bears this out: They decided to march forward and confront the new world outside their borders, so as to not be caught unawares again, in two directions:

First, to forestall a possible invasion by African peoples, they began to "colonize" the Nile south of the First Cataract, the Nubian region of present day Sudan.

Second, they began the military conquest of the Syrian region, starting, obviously, in its southern part. When they reached the central part they clashed militarily –the first war in history- with the Hittites of Anatolia, who had invaded the northern part of Syria for other reasons

The spiritual jolt that the Egyptian governing class had to assimilate was the fact that the world was much larger and multifarious than the one their ancestors had come to believe in, in their almost cloistered isolation. This shock made the high class Egyptians try to imagine a more universal and overall divine world than the one described by their mythological narrative and which by then seemed, at least to some, too parochial or provincial. One of them, it so happens, was no less than a pharaoh, Akhenaton, who reigned between 1353 and 1336 BCE. During those 17 years, he imposed the first monolatry in history, with the Sun's disk as the only god, as evidenced in the ruins of his palace at Tell el 'Amarna (1). At his death, the priestly caste reinstated the old theological order.

Around the year 1230 BCE, an unknown catastrophe occurred in the eastern Mediterranean. Historians have yet to learn if it was geological or political in nature, but they know that it wreaked havoc on the socio-political order in that region. Some of the events may be those narrated in a later era as "the Trojan War". One of the most severely affected populations were the Pelasgians of the southern coast of Greece, who had acquired civilization from their contacts with the Minoans of Crete and formed the Mycenae kingdom circa 1450 BCE. Around the year 1200 they fled their country by sea, cast out perhaps by invading Greeks, and sailed to southern Anatolia where they took part in the destruction or plunder of the Hittite kingdom. Some then sailed to the coast of Syria, where they began forming the Phoenician people. Another branch of the Pelasgians or "sea peoples" attacked Egypt in 1175 and were repelled by the royal navy. Records refer to them as "pelest". They finally settled in the southern Syrian coast, naming that country Pelestine or Palestine, and would be called "Philistines" in the Bible.

Around the year 1150 BCE, the two largest states -Egypt and Babylon- entered an era of decadence in which all possessions were lost and they divided into two or more administrations. Consequently, their appeasing, polytheist type of religion, with two criteria for assigning functions to gods, one phenomenal, the other ethnical, also plunged into a profound crisis.

4.2.- The Birth of Two "Axial" Peoples [2]

Around the year 1130 BCE, when the initial effects of the catastrophe were over, two new peoples made their entrance into history: the Hebrews and the Greeks. They did so at a time when all the Middle East was passing through a severe socio-political crisis, which would last another four centuries. On the other hand, three other very important technological advances were beginning to be put to use at the time of their genesis as peoples, but not until the end of the "Dark Ages" would they be extensively utilized and make a socio-political impact. As per the Childe sequence [3]:

21.- Iron metallurgy first developed in Anatolia, near the Caucasus, around the year 1500 BCE. The furnace consisted of an excavated vertical hole in a steep clay slope, uncovered at the top and with a blast hole at the bottom. It was filled with charcoal, fired, and, when hot enough, iron ore was poured into it. Soon came the realization that the stronger the blast, the purer resulting metallic "sponge" was, so the main invention was a hand or foot-operated bellows, made of cowhide. The "sponge" was reheated in a forge and hammered on an anvil to pound off the molten cinder out of the hot malleable mass.
This technique was invented by the Hittites, but the large-scale export business was developed by their Phrygian successors, whose king Midas (725-695 BCE) was so rich that the Greeks invented the myth that what he touched turned into gold.

22.- The phonetic alphabet was developed by the Phoenician people on the coast of Syria, with only 20 symbols for letters (at the beginning for syllables), in comparison with the hundreds or thousand of symbols that ideographic writing required. This invention was so important that all existing alphabets derive from it, from Hebrew and Arabic, written from right to left, and Greek, written at first in both directions -in "boustrophedon" or "as the ox plows"- to Roman, among others, written from left to right.

23.- Again, the Phoenicians started the first trade for luxury goods. First they exported objects made of glass, material invented by the Babylonians, and then a red ink or tincture used to dye very fine woolen capes. They obtained it from a mollusk that the Greeks called "foinix" and the Romans "purple".

The two new "axial" peoples which formed in this region had visions of the world so original, that when they developed themselves three centuries later they originated new civilizations of a higher or "second" level. Both visions, even if very different one from the other, agree in reevaluating the individual. Let's see their respective new visions of the world:

Historians think that the Hebrews were groups from the southern part of Syria, "the land of Canaan", that took advantage of the withdrawal of the Egyptian army in the year 1145 BCE, refused to be subjugated in the coastal area, urbanized to a small degree, either by the Philistines in the south or by the Canaanites in the fertile area to the north, and retreated to the mountains.

There in the mountainous interior, they may have received groups of desert dwellers known as "habiru", who contributed with monolatrous religious ideas, possibly derived from Egyptian monolatrism. The newly formed Hebrew people organized in twelve tribes and agreed to worship and venerate just one god, who could not be represented in any form or figure, but who lived inside a "covenant ark", which was carried in formal procession from one tribe to another. Around the year 1125 BCE, the Hebrews won a battle over the Canaanites, thus assuring their permanent socio-political existence. (4)

The Greeks were Indo-European peoples who had entered the Balkan Peninsula from the north in the middle of the second millennium BCE in three waves: Aeolians, Ionians, and Dorians. They had entered into contact with the peoples of Mycenaen culture, a branch of the Minoan civilization of Crete, in the coastal lands of modern Greece. The Greeks knew of, or maybe even took part in, the Trojan War, which took place circa 1230 BCE. When "the sea peoples" retreated from the coastal areas, the Greeks substituted them and organized themselves into small states ruled by warrior aristocracies. Gradually, they acquired a seafaring vein, which would become their main hallmark once developed.

4.3.- Gestation Period in the Dark Age from 1150 to 750 BCE

The period from 1150 to 750 BCE is one of relative darkness in the Middle East and the Eastern Mediterranean areas, as the largest civilized entities, Mesopotamia and Egypt, were in decadence during those four centuries. The former was divided into the Chaldean state -the lower and central most densely populated area- and the warlike kingdom of Assyria in the highlands. Egypt was divided into Valley and Delta states, and later reunified under foreign Libyan and Nubian dynasties.

This absence of "great powers" allowed many small peoples to forge their own traits, with the most significant changes occurring in the Syrian and Greek regions.

The Syrian area was in the process of dividing into three regions with distinct cultural peculiarities: the south was home to Canaanite and Philistine urban centers on the coast and Hebrew tribes in the mountains; the central coastal area harbored the seafaring Phoenician city-states; and the new kingdom of Damascus sprung up in the midnorth.

The Phoenician cities engaged with the Greek world and extended their trade and colonization activities to the western Mediterranean, with the powerful aid of their phonetic alphabet and their luxury goods.

The Hebrews, settled in the mountainous interior, passed through their Judges period and founded a kingdom in 1020 BCE, with Saul, David, and Solomon ruling – in that order- from that date to 932 BCE. Archaeologists have found that the country was more primitive and poor than the Biblical narrative leads one to think. (5)

In the year 926 BCE, the Egyptian army razed the coastal Canaanite urban centers, only to withdraw. A new kingdom emerged there, which included both the ten Hebrew tribes of the central and northern mountains and the people of the coastal fertile area whose towns had been obliterated. This is the kingdom that the Bible calls "Israel", which soon attained a modest level of prosperity. Part of its population -the tribal and politically dominant one- was monolatrous or henotheistic, while the remaining portion -the coastal one- was polytheistic or idolatrous. In the harsh mountainous south, around Jerusalem, the small kingdom of Judah prevailed with a stricter monolatrous population. (6)

This difference in degree of monolatrous faith between the people of both kingdoms gave substance, two or three centuries after the events are supposed to have occurred, to the pious legends of the prophets Elijah and his disciple Elisha, Jews from the south who in a heroic stand fought the northerners' polytheism. In the most striking event, Elijah challenges 450 prophets of Baal and other Phoenician gods -on Mt. Carmel and before king Ahab- to a public showdown where both must ready the sacrifice of an ox and make it ignite by direct divine intervention. The prophets failed, while he succeeded: he caused the conductivity of a hilltop to increase by pouring barrels of water on the sacrificial site, causing a lightning strike! He then directed the angry mob of people to kill the 450 prophets. (1 Kings,18, 20-46)

The kingdom of Israel remained prosperous and in the year 853 led a coalition - with Damascus and the Phoenicians- against the Assyrians, whose army, not yet very powerful, was halted in the battle of Qarqar. But as the power of the Assyrian Empire increased, Israel, as well as the others, became a faithful subject, a state of affairs that lasted until 747 BCE.

Progress was very slow in the Greek region during this "dark age". During the early centuries, the people remained grouped in small communities ruled by warrior aristocracies, with almost purely agrarian economies. However, since their territory had access to the sea aplenty and was in such close proximity to the Middle East, the cradle of civilization, these factors helped spur the pace as soon as they embraced the following breakthroughs:

The most consequential was maritime navigation. Not only did it yield an economic edge, it also forced their societies to be more egalitarian. Their productive capacity soon specialized in cultivating those agricultural staples which could be exported - like wine and olive oil- and in making artisan objects that could be sold abroad. They would then transport their products and gainfully barter them for all the other goods they needed. This "mode of production" tended to equalize the farmer with the upper class, as he would also function as a sailor and a soldier at times, thus diminishing the importance of the warriors as such. From then on, a man was more valuable to his "polis" if he knew how to navigate, to deal in trade, and to speak foreign languages.

Another technological advance was iron metallurgy, learned from the Phrygians through the "polis" they had founded in the Anatolian Aegean coast. Yet another was the alphabet, learned from the Phoenicians. It was adapted to their Greek language, initially written in "boustrophedon", but later from left to right.

These advances also influenced the Greeks' religious beliefs and practices, which, up until then, consisted in representing natural forces and their impact on human lives in a rich mythology, where characters frequently interacted with humans, and vice versa. The ritual practices for reenacting those beliefs "…compelled the Greeks to revive their fears and face them, and proved to them that it was possible to transit in safety to the other side."[7]

So it happened that around the year 750 BCE, two peoples, Hebrews and Greeks, were on the way to reevaluating the individual through very different social disciplines: The Hebrews by transforming the man-deity relationship, from being unilaterally appeasing, to a kind of pact or deal between each individual and the deity. The human considered him or herself under obligation to abide by a moral code in his or her private and public life, and the deity would protect him or her and his or her community, for as long as they remained faithful. The Greeks, on the other hand, were gradually transforming their society toward equality through their new "mode of production", based on maritime commerce.

During those four centuries between 1150 and 750 BCE, the Aryan civilization of northwest India had expanded through the Ganges Great Plain and the Heroic Era was coming to a close. In China, the new Chou Dynasty had passed its Feudal Era and was embarking on a divisive process.

4.4.- The Axial Period between the Years 750 to 500 BCE

Four people (8) are deemed "axial" by Karen Armstrong. That is because it is possible to trace in their history the transformation of their warrior type of morality to a type more attuned to social justice. Two of them -the Chinese and the Indians- would, generally, be excluded from the scope of our study, due to their being on the periphery or plainly outside the historic line that leads to the West; while two Iranian people, Medes and Persians, will be part of our story. For these reasons, we will only refer here to a summarized overview of the historic journeys trajectories of ancient China and India from the year 750 BCE on, and that of the Iranians from 1200 BCE on.

In China, even if feudalism tended to a division into fractional sovereignties, its members traded their warrior's code for that of the "respectable man". This change allowed violence to be cast in a ceremonial frame for a while, but after some time this new code proved insufficient and the moral milieu deteriorated. It was as a reaction to this situation that Confucius preached his ideal sociability philosophy. The political situation continued to deteriorate until it reached the "Warring States" epoch. Against this violence and selfishness rose six moralist "schools": One tried to base the behavior of those who exerted political and military power on justice; two of them preached harmony with nature by following "The Path" (Taoism); a fourth school was Confucian and conditioned the legitimacy of any governing entity to obtaining a "Celestial Mandate"; a fifth school was legalistic; and a sixth, logical.

In India, the Vedic religion transformed itself from having a warrior's morality to another that tended to the non-violence, founding destiny in the *karma* doctrine or the reincarnation of souls, and practicing the spiritual introspection. All this caused the birth of moral religions, as Jainism and Buddhism and led Hinduism to the inclusion of the chaste system, and toward the personalization and representation of the divine.

The Aryan or Indo-European peoples who had settled in Central Asia -we may now call them Iranians- domesticated the horse around the year 2000 BCE for its use in stockbreeding, pillage raids, and combat. Some of the Iranian peoples invaded civilized areas between the years 1700 to 1500 BCE. Some time between the years 1200 and 1000 BCE, the remaining peoples received the preaching of a prophet named Zoroaster or Zarathustra. He convinced them that Mazda was the supreme God, master of all other spiritual beings, reason why He transcended the world. Nevertheless, the existence of evil in the world convinced Zoroaster of the presence of an Evil Spirit, and from that he deduced that it was the duty of the faithful to promote good with his or her behavior and avoid and combat evil.

Around the year 1000 BCE, two Iranian peoples migrated south from Central Asia, settling in what we now call the Iranian plateau: The Persians traversed most of it and settled in its southern part, establishing contact with the Elamites. The Medes settled in the northern part, establishing contact with the Assyrian Empire around the year 850 BCE, first serving in the army as mercenaries, and then put in charge of maintaining communications between Assyria and northwestern India through the so called "Khorassan Route".(9)

Around the year 640 BCE, the Persians took advantage of the destruction of the kingdom of Elam by the Assyrians and occupied those lands as vassals of the Empire. Meanwhile, the Medes organized a semi-independent kingdom around 650 BCE, first ruled by Phraortes, then in 625 by Cyaxares, who forged an alliance with Nabopolassar of Babylon and others. Together, they took and razed the capital city of Ninneveh in 612 and defeated the last Assyrian army in 605 BCE.

Once having reviewed this, we will focus on the ethical thinking of Hebrews and Greeks, as both currents would converge into Christianity, thus forming the foundations of Western Civilization. For both peoples, these 250 years marked the ascent to maturity of their main cultural characteristics, albeit for very different reasons, since there were few contacts between them. That ascent brought about their being the founding fathers of two "second generation" civilizations in Arnold J. Toynbee's series: The Syrian-Iranian, the former name encompassing Hebrews and Phoenicians and the latter Persians and Medes; and the Greco- Roman Civilization.(10) First, we will examine how the definitive features of the Jewish religion became entrenched and then the beginnings, crisis, and maturity of Greek philosophical thought.

4.5.- The Forge of Monotheism in Israel

In the waning years of Jeroboam's reign in Israel, circa 750 BCE, a prophet by the name of Amos appeared in Judah. He believed he had been given a divine mandate and began to preach in the northern kingdom of Israel. He mainly railed at the animal sacrifices made by many locales' idolatry practices, but he also condemned government agents' neglect in assisting the poor, the corruption of many royal officials, and the king's servility to the Assyrian Empire, which he thought was dangerous, as it could easily turn against them at the least carelessness or provocation.(11)

The next prophet, Hosea, was an Israeli who preached against immorality and idolatry after Jeroboam's death, probably from 745 BCE on, when there was a rapid succession of rulers, until a usurper ascended the throne, in 735. He revised the policy, rebelled against the Assyrian Empire, and was defeated and killed in battle in 727. The towns were razed, all but Samaria, capital city of the northern kingdom. Part of the population (13,500 according to an estimate (12)) was uprooted and exiled. Samaria fell in the year 722.

Seeing the disastrous end of their northern neighbor, the rulers of the kingdom of Judah applied themselves under King Hezekiah (727-698) to follow God's commands, banning all hilltop animal sacrifices as practiced in idolatry. They also began to collect in the royal library of Jerusalem the components of the first two books of the Bible, Genesis and Exodus, in their two versions: "J" for Jehovah from the south and "E" for "Elohim" from the north, both written, for the first time, in Hebrew phonetic alphabet script. Karen Armstrong says that for those early Biblical writers: "...human life was not confined to the mundane, but had a transcendent dimension, that shed light on the most deeper meaning of events and gave them a paradigmatic significance", and she adds: "But nobody imagined that J and E were definitive texts". (13)

A few years before the reign of Hezekiah, circa 737 BCE, two other prophets began to preach in Jerusalem: one "minor" named Micah and one "major" named Isaiah. Both made it very clear that what was truly evil about idolatry was that "its superstitious propitiation of the gods" could serve as an excuse for "persons neglecting their responsibilities in their private or public behavior" (14). "First" Isaiah, so called because there were later additions to this book, already reflected his conviction that God was not simply a sacred being for Israel, but the Creator and Ruler of the world, completely above and removed from all humanity.

Both prophets are also famous for the modern controversy raging on if they thought that Judaism should be a "universalist" or "particularist" religion, according to their respective visions of the ideal future. Some verses say of the Messiah that "... he shall judge among many people, and rebuke strong nations afar off; and they shall beat their swords into plowshares, and their spears into pruning-hooks: nation shall not lift up a sword against nation, neither shall they learn war any more." (Micah 4:3). This can be said to mean either Israel's absolute military supremacy or the vision of an idyllic pacifism. Other verses, though, are more nationalist and bellicose, claiming vengeance for Israel. (Micah 7:8-20).

These pacifist visions, springing from the belief in a powerful but good and just God, were hard to rationalize in the terrible world in which the Assyrian Empire was reaching its supreme military might, by dint of steel weaponry and chariots. Assyrian religiosity was strictly propitiatory: the might of a god was measured by the success of its faithful.

In this sense, Isaiah also endorsed God in the magic powers contest, by assuring that He would defend Judah if its people kept their faith, as the Assyrian Empire was only His "instrument". This false confidence was a factor in King Hezekiah's unwise decision to join an anti-Assyrian coalition in 705, the year Sargon II died. His successor, Sennacherib, razed Judah in the year 701, with Jerusalem being the only city spared, owing to an epidemic that weakened the Assyrian army.

The next king of Judah, Manasseh (687-642) was a loyal vassal of Assyria and allowed the cult of its deities even within Jerusalem. The ultimate price for this crime was paid by his son, assassinated in 640 by the rebelled rural aristocracy, who installed an eight-year-old boy, Josiah, as king. By then, Assyrian power was ebbing, having been expelled from Egypt by a native rebellion led by Psamtik, and also having retreated from Palestine, whose coastal areas were occupied by the Egyptians. In the year 632, Josiah, then 16, declared himself a faithful follower of Jehovah and in 622 began work on remodeling the Temple. In the course of those works, priests "discovered" a new book of the Bible, subsequently called by the Greeks "Deuteronomy" or True Law. In all probability the priests themselves fashioned it, as it was the first book of the Bible that was not only a collection of oral traditions or the preaching of a prophet, but had been composed at the same time it was written. Josiah embraced it and embarked on his religious reform.

The "deuteronomist" priests not only forbade the worship of other gods in both Judah and the abandoned Israel, but also created a new judicial structure for the kingdom, with a semblance of a court unconnected with the monarch. In addition, they "nationalized" theology and passionately emphasized the importance of justice, fairness, and compassion, even more so than Amos and Hosea. (15)

But the Great Reform ended badly, since Judah could not adapt fast enough to the shifting political and military tides of those times: In 612, a coalition of Medes and Babylonians had destroyed the capital of Ninneveh, and in 609, Necho, the second pharaoh of Egypt's Saite Dynasty, entered the coastal lands of Israel intending to help the last Assyrian army. Josiah tried to intercept him, but was defeated and killed in the first encounter.

In 605, Nebuchadnezzar ascended the throne of the New-Babylon Empire, and so Israel became a sort of chip gambled between him and Necho. In 597 young king Joachim was exiled, with 8,000 subjects, to Babylon. Ten years later
Judah rebelled: Jerusalem was razed, the temple destroyed, and another group of 5,000 people were exiled, followed by a third group in the year 581 BCE.

One of the few who remained in the ruins of Jerusalem was the prophet Jeremiah, who had opposed the rebellion and almost paid for it with his life. After those frightful events, the people realized how correct his preaching on the conflict had been: Things should be seen as they are and reality -however painful and terrible- must be faced.

Meanwhile, those exiled to Babylon were able to preserve their community as far as beliefs, education, and religious practices. They could even pass judgment on their own internal affairs. Soon, they were prosperous since they were located "at the center of the world". Nebuchadnezzar's architects, for example, were implementing the 24th and next-to-last technological breakthrough in the V. Gordon Childe series (16): They were constructing aqueducts to irrigate the famous woods above the artificial hillock or "Hanging Gardens" inside the city.

Two additional factors contributed to the exiled Jewish community's elevating their religious culture to unqualified maturity: One was the visions of the prophet Ezekiel, which gave them the -let's say- psychological framework for having a motivation to preserve their beliefs in those trying circumstances. The other was the magnificent work done by the priests or Levites -called "P" by modern scholars- who gave the collected narratives of the books of Genesis and Exodus their final form as a complete and coherent history of the world since the Creation up to the arrival of the "chosen people" to the "Promised Land". In doing so, they availed themselves of many stories of Sumerian-Babylonian mythology, but always giving them a benevolent twist.

Later, they complemented the two basic historical books with those of Numbers and Leviticus, which together with Deuteronomy composed the five books of Jewish Law or Pentateuch. The main novelty was that the regulations of ritual purity and the dietary laws were made compulsory to all, as if the loss of the Temple had made priests of every one of them, and had to live isolated from the rest of their Babylonian neighbors. In order to make that separation honorable, all were under the obligation to maintain a high ethical level and a warm empathy toward all individuals outside of their communitarian faith.

In the year 539 BCE, Cyrus, king of the newly founded Persian Empire, conquered the New-Babylonian Empire, thus putting an end to the 3,000-year existence of states built on the "first-generation" Sumerian-Babylonian Civilization. A few years later, in 525, his son Cambyses conquered Egypt, thus ending the independent existence of the main state based on another very old "first-generation" civilization. The Persians and their cousins, the Medes, had a monotheistic religion which followed the teachings of Zoroaster, which is why they immediately recognized Jews' freedom upon their returning to Judah, those who wished to do so, and living there as faithful Persian subjects.

The return of a portion of the Jewish population to the Holy Land was painful and deceptive in several ways. Under the leadership of Nehemiah and Ezra, the returning community settled apart from their native neighbors, who did not observe the law as befitted Levites, because one century after their return "Jerusalem was a little run-down town in an anodine corner of the Persian Empire". Consequently, "...the returning exiles were not at the vanguard of world events, but lived in obscurity; their struggle for survival had become more important than the search for a new religious vision."(17)

4.6.- The Democratizing of Greece between 776 and 506 BCE

In the middle of the 8th century BCE, the Greeks emerged from their "dark ages" and consolidated their organization into city-states called "polis" -most with access to the sea- either in the Peninsula, in the isles, or in the Aegean coast of Anatolia. Their basic "mode of production" was the seafaring trade, which had a significant egalitarian effect, barring those who were slaves. The main socio-political event was the struggle by farmers, oftentimes sailors or soldiers, to gain political rights and vie with the warrior aristocracy for power.

Over the course of the following century, 7th BCE, three types of (ancient) democracies emerged from that social crisis, the Spartan, Corinthian, and Athenian being the most representative. With them, the Greeks would forge their greatness. Spartan-style democracy was the most egalitarian towards its citizens, since everyone, including the two kings, lived in the same barracks. But it was also the most restrictive, based as it was on the slavery of the Helots, descendants of their Messenian neighbors (resoundingly defeated in 670), who accounted for more than half of the Spartan population. The Corinthian type of democracy was more based on seafaring commerce: from the year 655 on a "tyrant" ruled in favor of fostering the common people's good and maintaining the warrior aristocracy at bay. The Athenian mode of democracy, which would eventually attain more greatness, had its beginnings around the year 621, and we will examine it in greater detail below.

All the other "polis", dozens of them, adopted one or another type or model of democracy, or a combination thereof. The most notorious effect everywhere of egalitarianism was military might, as from the moment a man was also a citizen he could be called up to the army or navy and would have to be willing to defend the institutions of his polis. This marked how the first disciplined infantries in history were formed: they were made up of heavily armed soldiers (*hoplites*), who would advance until it engaged the enemy army directly and fought it as one. Similarly, the disciplined crews of the warships were composed of sailors who could row in synchronization in pursuit of an enemy ship and, once alongside, board it. This was the real foundation of democracy.[18]

Notwithstanding the political division inherent in the "polis" system, the Greeks felt that they shared the same culture and language. That was the rationale behind their forging a number of pan-Hellenic or collective institutions in the 7th century. Chief among them were the Olympiads, the Delphi Sanctuary, and Homer's epic tales; each embodied some aspect of their collective mentality. The Olympic games, of a religious character, trace back to the year 776 BCE in Olympia in the Peloponnesus. They allowed the rulers of the many polis to exchange ideas and, also, forge heroes in peaceful competitions honoring the gods. The Delphi Sanctuary, founded circa the year 750, had been ascribed the power of communicating with the gods by means of an oracle or answer delivered through a priestess known as the Delphic Sibyl, capable of falling into a trance; this system afforded the chief priests some control over the answers being delivered. The Iliad and the Odyssey, the great epic poems of Homer, native of Anatolia's Aegean coast, who composed them around the year 750, made the ancient human and divine archetypes accessible to the Greeks, by clearly and beautifully describing extreme situations and circumstances that had probably happened 500 years before and been handed down by oral tradition.

Some 100 years later, around the year 650 BCE, Hesiod modified the terrible Homeric mythology, in an attempt to show that divine purposes represented "an effort to achieve more clarity, order, and definition."(19) During the social crisis, he also recommended aristocrats curb their pride and direct their thoughts to justice: hence, his works were very beneficial and well received.

Athens launched its reforms in the year 621, with Draco -whose name even today is applied to laws that are harsh and difficult to abide by- appointed as arbiter between the classes. However, if allowances are made for his want of tact, he achieved two things: First, the aristocrats held on to political power, but circumscribed by what the law ordered or permitted; Second, their performance could be contested, they were financially accountable, and they had to disclose their judicial rulings.

This primitive model of democracy functioned clumsily, so in the year 594, Athenians called in a real politician, a wise and learned man named Solon to govern them. He proceeded to correct the social fabric in depth, proposing and instituting an agrarian reform, which prohibited large estates, but allowed wide differences in property sizes to spur efforts. Then he instituted the "state of law", which meant that the polis involved itself in resolving quarrels between citizens; this also meant a kind of secularization, since it signaled that citizens accepted their share of responsibility in managing public affairs.

Solon retired in 560. In its wake, there was a partial relapse to an aristocratic mode of government, but the majority wanted a return to democracy. In the year 508, Cleisthenes reclaimed the power for the people and the following year they supported him in force to crush an aristocratic coup of state attempt. As a result of this triumph, the "isonomic" or "equality before the law" type of democracy, for all free and native adult males, became firmly implanted in Athens the year 506 BCE.

Athenians, like all other Greeks, continued their quest for religious experience by practicing "the Mysteries" (i.e. Eleusian or Dionysian) in order to prepare for facing the intractable, dark problems of existence. At the same time, they began to try to apply reason to understanding the phenomena in the world, as Tales of Miletus and others started to try to identify the Earth's component elements.

4.7.- The Persian Wars

Darius ascended to the throne of the Persian Empire in the year 521 BCE, after a dynastic crisis, and proceeded to organize and give it its definitive size. His territorial acquisitions included: a) Introducing agriculture and civilization, in the year 520, to the portions of Central Asia irrigated by the rivers Oxus (now Amu-Darya) and Yaxartes (now Syr-Darya); b) Incorporating the heavily populated Indus river basin (today Punjab and Sind, mainly in Pakistan) to the Empire; and c) Conquering the barbarian Thrace (now European Turkey and Bulgaria). His main three policies for organization were: 1) Toleration of the cultural and religious uses and practices of each people. 2) Decentralization of the administration of the enormous Empire into 20 "Satrapies", which meant almost "kingdoms", with sufficient autonomy. 3) Establishing a communication network: constructing "caravan-serais" or "khans" at one day's journey intervals for the newly domesticated camel, charting caravan routes with army protection, and supplying each inn with food and pasture, which travelers could pay for.

Visualizing this huge Empire as if it were just another country among many would be a mistake, since it included the populations and territories of what had been the first three "first-generation" civilizations, plus all intermediate and surrounding areas. Its total population may have numbered some 25 million, and if we take into account that the whole world in the year 512 BCE may have had some 75 million human beings, we will realize that the other 50 million were living in areas as remote to them as the rest of India or Europe, or in areas they didn't even suspect existed, like China, Sub-Saharan Africa and the Americas. We will then grasp that for their inhabitants, as well as their rulers, the Persian Empire was not "a country", but virtually the entire world.

Compared with that behemoth, the Greek world was a trifle, with a population estimated at under one million, including all the colonized areas, like the Aegean coast of Anatolia, Sicily, and the southern third of Italy.

In this light, the balance of force, quantitatively speaking, seemed decisively to favor Persia. But Greece had just experienced the birth of a socio-political system - egalitarian democracy- which imbues the societies that adopt it with tremendous strength, in comparison to societies that have "fractures", like social stratification by class or a diversity of national or religious loyalties. So, in this other light the balance was in favor of Greece. However, nobody knew that then as never before had there been a confrontation of military organizations with such characteristics.

That is why the Persian Wars are so important: First, we have to take into account that, up until 2 centuries ago and stretching back over 23 centuries, they marked the beginning of human history. Second, the first historian on record, Herodotus, studied them, in order to understand what had transpired. That marked a major departure from all chroniclers before him, who had simply written or sculpted what they were told. Third, they were -and still are- a kind of "history lab" for what we already pointed out: It marked a confrontation between quantitative and qualitative factors, so we can still gain benefits from their study.

Having said all that, the narrative of events can be summarized in a nutshell: All the Greek polis on Anatolia's Aegean coast had become subjected to the Persian Empire sometime after the year 547 BCE, when Cyrus defeated and incorporated the Kingdom of Lydia. It had been such a rich and prosperous country that its capital,

Sardis, was the site were the first money in history was minted -the 25th and last technological breakthrough of the V. Gordon Childe series (20). The coastal Greek "polis", particularly the Ionian ones, had never been very content under Persian rule: hence the local Satrap's suggesting to Darius the conquest of Thrace. He proceeded to do so by marching into Europe with an army, in 512, conquering Thrace, and then proceeding north into Sarmatia (present day Rumania and Ukraine). All this was done to give the Ionian polis "colonies" to trade with, an arrangement that kept them happy for a while.

The consolidation of democracy in Athens came about in 506, however, causing a swelling of pride in their Ionian cousins in the Anatolian polis. One of them, Miletus, birthplace of the first philosopher, Tales, went so far as to adopt the democratic system in the year 500. This was a flagrant rebellion against the Empire, so they mounted a surprise assault on the Persian Fleet, capturing it. Athens felt obligated to help them in their rebellion, so it deployed its fleet, whose men teamed with the Milesians to try to take Sardis. The fortress resisted, however, and, on their way home, the Persian cavalry attacked the combined army, decimating it. The Athenian survivors re-embarked and sailed for home in 497. It took three years for the Persians to reassemble their fleet: Ready in 494, they took and razed Miletus, massacring its defenders and selling survivors into slavery.

Now, the only thing pending was to punish Athens, for having aided the Ionian rebels. Darius sent a select army of 25,000 professional soldiers to the Sardis Satrap, weighing anchor during the summer of the year 490 and landing at the beach near Marathon, 42 kms. (26 miles) from Athens. The polis sent a hastily assembled army of all its able-bodied citizens, some 10,000, to fight them.

The battle basically consisted of a frontal clash in which the disciplined and heavily armed Athenians massacred the Persians, advancing upon them as a solid block. After several hours of this, the Persians fled in disarray to the safety of their ships. The battle toll: 6,400 dead Persians, against 192 Athenians, a ratio of more than 30 to 1. (21)

Darius was unable to exact revenge for this defeat, dying four years later, in 486. But his son Xerxes, after crushing revolts in Egypt and Babylon, proceeded to raise an enormous army of some 250,000 men, as he envisioned occupying all of Greece. Ready in 481, he marched with his men to Sardis. Simultaneously, he had ordered his Phoenician, Egyptian, and Anatolian subjects to send warships and transports to supply the army. Estimates put the number of ships that he received for both tasks at 1,200.

Meanwhile, in the year 483, Athens had carried the motion of its leader Themistocles of tapping their new capacity to mine silver to defray the costs of buying wood and to build a fleet of 300 warships.

In the spring of the year 480, the huge Persian army crossed the strait of Hellespont from Anatolia to Thrace, and slowly advanced through Macedonia, entering Greece from the north into Thessaly. This advance spurred the Greeks to the "miracle" of seeing representatives of all the polis attend a pan-Hellenic conference. The Athenians had consulted the Oracle at Delphi, which had said "only a wooden wall will resist". That was interpreted by Themistocles as meaning that the 10,000 Athenians had to serve in the war fleet and lead all the other fleets contributed by the polis. The Spartans provided only a small quota (300), but were put in command, led by their King Leonid, of the land-based force, some 10,000 *hoplites* strong.

The war strategy agreed upon called for Leonid's army to defend the Pass of Thermopylae, and Themistocles' navy to block the Persian fleet from outflanking it by sea. The clash occurred in June and the Greeks were able, at first, to stop the entire Persian army in its tracks and prevent the fleet from outflanking the battlefield. However, special troops eventually found a way to make a flanking advance through the mountains, threatening to surround the defending Greek army. At that point, Leonid ordered all the army units from the other polis to quickly retreat, while he and his 300 Spartans fought a last stand against the Persian army for a few more hours, until all had perished.

Themistocles returned to Athens with his fleet and had the entire population evacuated to the neighboring island of Salamis. He positioned his fleet behind it, in the straits, where they could maneuver and have an advantage over the larger fleets of Phoenicians and Egyptians serving the Persians. Xerxes arrived in August with his army, razed and burned an empty Athens, and called his fleet in. Arriving in September, it soon waged a decisive naval battle: The pan-Hellenic armada sank and burned the better part of the Phoenician fleet, a sight that prompted the Egyptian ships to flee.

In autumn of that year, 480, Xerxes ordered almost 200,000 men to withdraw, since feeding and outfitting them in Greece was impossible without the fleets. He only left some 50,000 select soldiers, seemingly enough to keep most of the polis into submission.

That scenario could very well have played out had not the Spartans -realizing the danger they were all in- contributed a 10,000 strong force -that joined up with the 10,000 Athenians and 20,000 from all the other polis, like Corinth- assembling an army almost as large as the select and efficient Persian army. The decisive battle was fought at Plataea, near Thebes, in the summer of the year 479, resulting in a resounding pan-Hellenic victory. This forced the Persians to immediately evacuate the Greek Peninsula and later Thessaly and Macedonia as well. In Europe, their presence was reduced only to Thrace.

Thus, the Persian Wars' main operations came to an end. The ensuing years merely saw naval expeditions, the recovery of some islands, and the evacuation of Thrace. Formal peace was signed 30 years after Plataea, in 449.

4.8.- The Golden Age and the Peloponnesian War

The Persian Wars were also very important in unleashing a sense of euphoria among the Greeks. They would in time, however, learn that euphoria has two sides: a constructive one, driving them to achieve a 50-year Golden Age between 479 and 429 BCE; and a destructive one, plunging them into a terrible war, given the name "Peloponnesian" by Athenian general and historian Thucydides. Fought between the Athenian and Spartan Leagues, it lasted 25 years –from 429 to 404- and was so bloody that it caused Greece to fall into a void of creativity that she was never to overcome. (22)

The Golden Age is famous for the heights that Greek architecture, sculpture, and painting attained, becoming "classic" in the process. That remains outside our focus, as we will concentrate instead on what Karen Armstrong tells us about how the new genre of "tragedy" changed the Greeks' view of the world.(23)

In his work *The Persians*, Aeschylus succeeded in rousing a feeling of empathy among the audience towards the defeated Xerxes' pain and confusion. In his *Seven against Thebes*, he presents a world cleaved between the old, irrational religion and the fact that one cannot completely be rid of it. In his *Orestiad*, he captures the painful passage of the Athenians from their old familial and tribal loyalties with its blood vengeance ethics, to the new division of the polis into "demos" or quarters and the justice meted out by courts. Lastly, in his *Eumenides* or *Furies* he shows that even when the new democratic virtues of moderation and balance of power have gained the upper hand, horror for crimes committed is still very much alive.

Sophocles showed, in his tragedy *Antigone,* that "…firm beliefs and clear principles do not necessarily lead, in an infallible manner, to a positive result", as well as that "…man…was the lord of all the things he commanded and seemed to be invincible… were it not for the macabre fact of death, which clearly evinces his authentic helplessness". On his famous work *Oedipus Rex*, Armstrong says: "With his self-inflicted auto-mutilation he reaches the limits of knowledge, further out than what can be spoken or perceived, almost a parody of the mystical knowledge".

Euripides in his work *Medea* showed that "reason was being converted into a frightening weapon, since it could lead people to a moral and spiritual vacuum and, if skillfully used, could find convincing reasons for perpetrating cruel and perverted actions. He presents a woman who convinces herself to commit a horrible crime, but his audience could see in it an allusion to the protracted debate in the Athenian Assembly which … had thrown the Greek world into the Peloponnesian War." In his work *Bacchantes*, written in the year 406, a few months before his own death and two years before the end of the catastrophic war, he represents his polis, Athens, in the collective role of the women of Thebes, maddened by violence, marching behind their woman leader, holding high the severed head of her son.

As a final commentary regarding that terrible war among brother peoples, we can point out the following: If in the year 479, when the Persian Wars were practically over, both Athens and Sparta had kept their pride in becoming heads of leagues in check and invited all the other polis into an egalitarian and democratic political structure, the Greek world might have grown into a larger, more powerful unified country. As it happened, each of the leading polis imposed its conditions on the smaller members of each League, sowing hatreds and disloyalties that finally ended in the catastrophic war. There would be another two attempts to spread democracy in the Ancient World, but they would come courtesy of two other peoples: Macedonians and Romans.

4.9.- Greek Philosophy (24)

We've seen how starting in the 6th century, Tales of Miletus and others began to study the world as it was. This initial attempt was strongly fostered by the democratizing process, because of the importance new citizens attached to having their voices heard and their positions embraced by the ruling assemblies of their polis. In order to do so, it was necessary to have a command of the topic and also to be able to express it clearly and persuasively: in other words, to convincingly speak in public. Consequently, many citizens proved willing to pay for receiving instruction in both. The demand for learning was met by teachers for adults called "sophists" or sages.

As part of their profession, the sophists began to pose themselves general conundrums, such as the distinction between the natural and the artificial, to determine what was hard-wired in our character and what had to be learned. This tendency toward intellectual analysis gave prestige to the notion that virtue was knowledge, and every man could learn to practice virtue.

But since they also taught rhetoric or the art of speaking well, many sophists fell in the bad habit of saying that any position could be defended if one had the required skill to present it convincingly. Due to these excesses, the common citizen began to lose confidence in the sophists and in reasoning itself.

Socrates reacted precisely against this bad habit, dedicating his life (469-399) to firmly anchoring "Sophia" in the truth and in the good, describing himself as a friend or *philo* of that Sophia. His method was called "mayeutic" or "childbirth", because it was a strategy for gleaning the right answers from his interlocutor as a result of the answers he gave to the series of questions that Socrates posed to him, set out in such a manner that the other man had to ponder each concept and statement, causing the truth to be drawn as finely sieved material. If the issue was important, then the truth was akin to gold nuggets.

At the end of his life, a confused and upset Athens, which had lost virtually all its men in a war that proved futile, could no longer stand the truth that Socrates proclaimed and condemned him to death. He accepted his fate serenely, which secured him a spot in history books for all posterity.

Plato (427-347), his student, proposed a world of ideal Forms that men should intuitively recognize, and that would serve as a model or paradigm of conduct in this imperfect world. In his Academy, students were trained in geometry as an exercise for learning abstract concepts, followed by more rigorous dialectics, which could induce states of altered consciousness, similar to mystic experiences. All those exercises were intended as a means for a person's soul to accede to the immutable and eternal world of ideal Forms, perhaps thus ridding itself of the worst effects of suffering and death.

In his later works Plato tried to imagine the universe as the fulfilling of an intelligent and logical plan, which all men could comprehend if they applied to it with logic and dedication, as a kind of anticipation of the scientific method, only including also the spiritual or mystic aspect.

This thinking led Plato to propose ideas that were very difficult to put into practice. As an example, in *The Republic* he proposes an absolute monarchy so severe that the ruling philosophers and the defending warriors would carry out their functions with such dedication and disinterest as to not have families or properties of their own. The state would take care of their housekeeping and of their biological reproduction by means of eugenics. The common people could have their own families and private goods, as they had no power to wield.

Aristotle (384-322), his student, returned philosophy to earth, grounded by his study of biology, his collection of the basic laws of as many polis as possible, and his captivation by processes of change. He would go on to study ethical and social issues, always analyzing them by applying reason. Case in point: in political science he proposed what could be called a restricted democracy, granting voting rights only to those in possession of means and education -a "mesocracy". As an aside we might add that all modern founding democracies began this way.

On the religious front, he accepted Plato's ordered universe, at the center of which he envisioned a changeless Ultimate Cause, which did not particularly care for the human race. In regard to the Olympian pantheon, their mythology seemed to him suspect of having been misunderstood, but he acknowledged that this popular form of understanding religion could prove useful as a divine deterrent ensuring compliance of polis' laws and norms, since they fostered certain behavioral attitudes and feelings.

It can therefore be said that Aristotle laid the philosophical foundations on which the West would build the scientific method almost 2000 years later.

4.10.- First Confrontation between the Working Hypothesis vs. the Historical Events before Alexander's Exploits

In two of the cultural transitions we have reviewed -the first from the hunter/gatherer stage of the Upper Paleolithic to the farmer/herder stage of the Neolithic village world, and the second from the latter to the "first generation" civilizations- morality underwent significant modification indeed, apparently at odds with our hypotheses. But if we focus on those changes in morality, it becomes evident that they stem, in turn, from the profound qualitative and quantitative changes in social, political, and economic structures that human groups witnessed in the course of these two transitions. Now, we can endeavor to explain what transpired:

The change in morality consisted in the weakening of the group solidarity, concentrating now in the patriarchal family, with private property and inheritance, becoming weaker in the tribal, regional, and national circles. If we examine this morality change we will see it more a change in relationships than in contents, for the following reasons:

High social solidarity within the clan or horde was due to the high degree of dependence among members for defense and feeding, i.e. for survival. As soon as that dependence waned as a result of food being produced and of defense being in the hands of a minority of warriors, the reason underlying that strong solidarity began to weaken.

Another fact to consider is that as the new group solidarity was weaker it was also much widely spread, comprising tens of times more people in the Neolithic, and hundreds or thousand more in civilized states.

Allowing for all of the above, I think that we may tentatively conclude that even if several relational aspects of morality were affected in those two transitions, its content varied little or not at all, because its foundation continued being "the normative system most convenient to favoring the survival and development of human groups."

Can we extend this conclusion to the periods of the Bronze Age from 1550 to 1150 and to the Dark Age from 1150 to 750 BCE? We must remember that wars came into being then, waged both on land and sea, and that slavery became organized on a large scale. I think it can be extended, if we take into account that wars were an anomaly, compared to the lengthy periods of peaceful commercial relations. Proportionally to the number of people, these eras may have been less bloody than the tribal territorial fights. And as far as slavery is concerned, it may seem less despicable if we view it as the alternative to killing the vanquished men.

Before we continue focusing on morality, let us take a look at what happened with religion, in the course of those same transitions.

The primitive animism of the clans or hordes of the Upper Paleolithic unavoidably suffered conceptual modifications when passed down to the various Neolithic worlds. One reason was that it now had to rationalize the new phenomenon of social class stratification. In addition, the celestial hierarchy necessitated modification, favoring those gods in charge of bringing rain and those who were patrons of a certain ethnic o regional group.

This type of conceptual modification was accompanied by a change in relationships, as shamans ascended to priests, becoming one of the two ruling classes. Also, new sedentary living habits allowed novel forms of depicting religious mythology, abandoning the cave in favor of the temple, and developing monumental sculpture.

When some large Neolithic groups gained first-generation civilization status, the ensuing conceptual, relational, and artistic changes in religion reached their pinnacle for the following reason: Now the priestly caste had to present, in a single comprehensive and plausible mythological explanation, all known phenomena, from cosmic and biological, to social. We saw how this ushered societies into the "collective magic mentality", which yielded works and practices at odds with modern man, like huge towers, pyramids, and human sacrifices.

We saw in the Bronze Age, from 1550 to 1150 BCE, that religions had to beat a retreat once they lost credibility through their increasingly apparent contradictions when predicting or controlling events, the most glaring being those related to the invasions by the barbarians, who later became the ruling warrior and priestly caste.

This disavowal of the polytheist religions, coupled with the technological advances in iron metallurgy, phonetic writing, and marine navigation, brought about the birth of two "axial" peoples, Hebrews and Greeks, who would reassess the individual in very different manners, both having their "gestation" period in the Dark Age up to the year 750 BCE.

Having thus arrived to the period of evolution -for both morality and religion- that Karen Armstrong calls "The Axial Period from 750 to 500 BCE", we reviewed the changes that occurred in other "axial" people, like the Chinese, Indians, and Iranians, how monotheism took hold in Israel, and the democratization of Greece. What did we learn from these events?

That all mankind shares a proclivity to revert to the ancient course: that morality serves to ensure better living standards within our group. If a society swells to a very large size, i.e. China and India, it then develops a new, more adequate system of morality. If you live in a highly advanced, complex, and competitive world, as the Hebrews and Greeks did, then you develop socio-political systems, either moral codes of "divine revelation" or democracies, that better serve the circumstances of a people.

The Persian Wars represented a "trial by fire" for both systems: First, monotheism triumphed in the formation and organization of the Persian Empire, and, second, democracies prevailed in defending their democratic institutions against that huge neighboring empire. We then examined the twin wakes left by the resulting euphoria: the constructive one in their Golden Age, and the destructive one in their Peloponnesian War. Lastly, we saw the quest for truth embarked on by philosophical thinking, and the tremendous paroxysms it went through.

Hence, from prehistory to the 6th century BCE the working hypotheses stands: Morality remains the core of the mainstream system for improved group living, but religion undergoes change to accommodate a coherent and plausible explanation of the world and of man's fate.

Chapter V.- Hellenism and Christianity up to the Barbarian Invasions and the Emergence of Islam

5.1.- The Origins of Hellenism and the Western Mediterranean

In this chapter we are going to proceed with our journey across another 1,000 years of history, from about 350 BCE to 650 ACE, but we will cast our net over a wider geographical area. We'll include not only the Middle East and the coastal countries of the Eastern Mediterranean Sea, but also coastal countries to the West - today's Tunisia, Algeria, and Morocco in North Africa. In Europe, we'll focus on the Italian and Iberian Peninsulas and initially what was then known as the Gaul. We'll address Britain and Germany a little later.

The most significant socio-political phenomenon during this timespan and in this region will prove to be the sizeable progress of a second-generation civilization which, as we have seen, was born in Greece. It would become known as "Hellenism" when adopted by people of different cultures, as happened with the Syrian-Iranian civilization, extended and developed by the Persian Empire, the Romans in Italy or the barbarian peoples in North Africa and Western Europe.

The unfolding of the geographic expansion of the Greek or Hellenic influence can be classified as twofold: One advanced mainly by peaceful means and the other by military ones. The former began with the founding of colonies in the Western Mediterranean and ended with the Persian Wars. The military one began with the conquest of the Persian Empire by Alexander the Great's army, endured throughout his Seleucid and Ptolemaic successors, and prevailed during the Roman Empire. The previous Roman Republic was also, in part, a product of peaceful Hellenic expansion.

In the Dark Age, from 1150 to 750 BCE, the Western Mediterranean, which includes the Italic and the Iberian Peninsulas, the south of France and Northern Africa (Tunisia, Algeria, and Morocco), was in a cultural level similar to the farming and herding Neolithic, only more advanced, since its peoples had received the copper and bronze metallurgies and were receiving the iron one.

Around the year 825 BCE civilization began in two parts of this area, one in the central part of Italy, where the Etruscan people ascended to high urban culture, and the other in northern Tunisia, where the Phoenicians of the Syrian coast founded their colony of Carthage. Around the year 750, as we saw, The Greek colonization began in the southern third of Italy, Sicily being divided between Greeks and Phoenicians.

Between the years 750 and 475, the Phoenicians extended their colonies to the coasts of Numidia (Algeria), Mauritania (Morocco), and Southern Spain. The Greeks extended their colonies to the coasts of Southern France and Northern Spain.

Fostered by all this commercial activity, the Etruscans rapidly enhanced their cultural level, reaching that of their Greek and Phoenician neighbors. In Andalusia, the Iberian kingdom of Tartessus began a modest ascent.

When the Persian Empire was formed and the Persian wars fought, Phoenician colonies became independent in their new state of Carthage. The Greek colonies formed several polis -Syracuse, Naples, Sybaris, and Taranto. In central Italy, one of the Etruscan cities, Latin-speaking Rome, overthrew its monarchy and organized a republic. Here a new social discipline, public accord embraced as law, began and was so momentous it warrants our attention.

From the year 475 on, Rome's social classes -patricians and plebeians- engaged in political quarrels that were resolved not in an authoritarian way, nor by violent revolution, but by negotiating their differences until they reached "sacred" accords, which were scrupulously upheld and put in written form.

This new discipline gave Rome such might, that it soon conquered Latium, the Latin-speaking area. It not only subjected its peoples: it negotiated peace treaties that included trade regulations and army draft quotas. In this manner, the region under Roman law kept growing. In the year 380, an already strong Roman Republic began to wage war and incorporate some of the neighboring Etruscan cities, followed by the barbarian Sabinians, Umbrians, and Samnites, negotiating peace treaties with each upon their defeat. By the time these wars ended in the year 290 BCE, Roman law extended through all of central Italy, for even the northern Etruscan League of cities negotiated a treaty with Rome, which was, by then, a power to reckon with.

The Carthaginians, meanwhile, also developed their state, but under the rule of the great seafaring merchants, whose commercial maritime routes reached Guinea in Africa and the North and Baltic seas in Europe. In the Mediterranean region, they acquired Sardinia, Corsica, and had colonies and allies in southern Spain.

5.2.- The Emergence of Macedonia and Alexander the Great's Exploits

As we saw, when Xerxes' army invaded Greece from the north in the year 480 BCE, it traversed a poor and little populated "kingdom" called Macedonia. That country kept growing and developing, increasingly absorbing more culture from the Greeks, until they finally adopted their language.

After the terrible Peloponnesian War of 429-404, when Athens and Sparta collapsed, the north-central polis of Thebes prevailed militarily from the year 371 on. Twelve years later, in 359, Philip II ascended the throne of Macedonia, and proceeded to expand it, incorporating Thrace eastward to the Anatolian Straits, and westward to Epirus, across the Adriatic Sea from the heel of Italy's "boot".

In addition, Philip strengthened his realm until it could deploy two and then three 6,000 men phalanxes, which fought in ranks of 6 men deep and 1,000 wide. With this backing and much diplomacy he was able to gradually impose his "hegemony" over the majority of the Greek polis. Not even the famous "Philippic" orations of Demosthenes in Athens could stop him, until in 338 he defeated a coalition army, led by Thebes, in the battle of Chaeronea.

Philip was murdered in the year 336 and his 20-year old son Alexander, who had been Aristotle's disciple, succeeded him. Greece revolted but Alexander soon defeated the coalition army and razed Thebes, an event that persuaded the rest to submit. He invited all to reinforce his army for the conquest of the Persian Empire, which his father had planned to do and he resolved to execute.

Philip was murdered in the year 336 and his 20-year old son Alexander, who had been Aristotle's disciple, succeeded him. Greece revolted but Alexander soon defeated the coalition army and razed Thebes, an event that persuaded the rest to submit. He invited all to reinforce his army for the conquest of the Persian Empire, which his father had planned to do and he resolved to execute.

In the spring of the year 334 he crossed the Straits between Europe and Asia with an army of some 30,000 Macedonian and Greeks, and in the Granic river defeated the combined army of the Persian Satraps of Anatolia. Alexander proceeded to incorporate what we can now call "his empire" both the Greek polis of the Aegean coast and the former kingdoms of interior Anatolia. The Persian Shah Darius not interfered with these activities, but assembled an enormous army of some 250, 000 Asian men in northern Syria.

Early in the year 333, Alexander crossed the Taurus mountain range and in the battle of Issus defeated the enormous army of Darius III, who abandoned his harem there and his treasure in Damascus.

For the rest of the year, Alexander conquered with part of his army the coast of Phoenicia, achieving the capitulation of Byblos and Sidon, but had to leave his army to mount a siege on Tyre by land and its fleet by sea, until it was razed.

Alexander then headed to Egypt, where he founded his new capital city, being recognized both as pharaoh and as a god. His new empire already included all the lands with access to the eastern Mediterranean Sea: Greece, Anatolia, Syria, and Egypt, which would remain under Greek or Roman rule for the next 1,000 years, until the Arab conquest. But instead of consolidating these territorial gains, offered to him by Darius III as a ransom for peace, he ordered his entire army to march to northern Mesopotamia. There, he defeated an even larger, but more unwieldy army, self-styling himself the new Shah of the Persian Empire, since all the remaining Satraps recognized him as such.

Alexander did not accept a mere formal rule through the Satraps, but insisted in submitting with his army, now reinforced with large contingents of Persian cavalry, all the territories of the Iranian plateau, Central Asia, and the Indus river basin. He spent five years doing so, through the year 326, returning to Mesopotamia en 324, and dying the following year. His Empire was divided between his Macedonian generals, as we will see below.

With all this, Alexander consummated two different feats, which would modify the later history of large parts of Asia and the Mediterranean area:

First, he made the complete Hellenization of Anatolia, or Asia Minor, as present-day Turkey was then known, inevitable. The entire region was covered with polis, autonomous in their internal affairs although subject to paying taxes, and with various vassal and independent kingdoms, like Armenia.

He also assured the semi-Hellenization of Syria, with its new capital city of Antioch and many other Syrian-Hellenic polis, but also that of some native kingdoms culturally difficult to assimilate, like those of the Hebrew and Nabataean peoples.

Even if its new capital city of Alexandria became the largest and richest city in the Ancient World, Egypt's Hellenization was the most superficial. The reason was that most of the rural population never integrated into polis, but remained landless peasants, dependent either on the Hellenic government or on the Egyptian priests or landowners.

Second, he also effected a substantial Hellenistic penetration in Mesopotamia and Iran, but through Persian institutions. Parthian warriors recovered those lands in the 2nd century BCE, two centuries after their Greek conquest.

Lastly, the Hellenistic penetration reached places as remote as Central Asia and present-day Afghanistan, where the Greek-ruled kingdom of Bactria was organized, and even Northwestern India, where the kingdom of Menander existed for a time. Those Greco-Buddhists realms had an influence in molding the philosophy of Mahayana Buddhism, which would later expand to China, Tibet, Mongolia, Korea, and Japan.

5.3.- The Cultural Components of the Hellenistic World (1)

Besides Macedonia itself, which continued to function as a kingdom, Greece, organized in new leagues, and several kingdoms in Anatolia, there were two main successors to Alexander the Great's Empire:

One was the Seleucid Empire, which at its foundation by Seleucus included part of Anatolia, Syria, Mesopotamia, Iran, Central Asia and the Indus basin. The latter was lost in the year 315, Central Asia around 250, Iran in 155, and Mesopotamia in 125. The Empire was thus reduced to Syria, which in the year 64 BCE became a Roman province.

The other Empire was founded by Ptolemy and included Egypt, southern Syria, Cyrenaica, Cyprus, and parts of the southern coast of Anatolia and islands in the Aegean Sea. It entered the Roman orbit in the year 30 BCE.

The Hellenistic world thus included all the lands of the Eastern Mediterranean and the Middle East. Its main socio-political characteristic was that it consisted of two huge monarchy states with populations of the most varied cultural origins, interacting with one another. Our interest is mainly in its religious composition, so will review some aspects of the situation that resulted when the Macedonian realm consolidated and how they evolved until the Mediterranean world was absorbed by the Roman Empire, while new Persian dynasties were established in Mesopotamia and Iran.

In this Hellenistic world there were, basically, three types of religions:

First, there were the ancient polytheist religions of Mesopotamia and Egypt, and its derivates in Syria and Anatolia, which during their long evolution had kept their appeasing character. Since the Persian conquests, two centuries prior to the arrival of Hellenism, they had lost their "official" status and were transforming into popular "salvation" religions, in a form that we will see below.

Second, there were two monotheistic religions, very different from one another: One of them, Judaism, whose people, as we saw, had lost their sovereignty three centuries before, but whose prophets and priests had written an impressive book that all believed was divinely inspired. It told the history of the world, the entrance in it of the "chosen people", and pointed to a final destiny, hotly discussed if being in this world or in "the next".

Another monotheistic religion, albeit with a dualistic tendency, was the Iranian one, reformed by Zoroaster, and whose faithful were the Mede and Persian peoples, united under the Achaemenid Dynasty. This religion continued to be professed in the Iranian Satrapies under Alexander and the Seleucids, and again became "official" under the Parthian and Sassanid native dynasties.

Third, there was also the Greek religion known as Olympian or Homeric. Its problem lay in its diminishing scope of validity, after having received two almost simultaneous blows: First, the development of philosophy, which claimed for itself the right to know about the nature of the world and human behavior, by means of rational analysis of facts, as the only path to truth. Then, the end of the polis' sovereignty transpired, which caused its popular religious cult to disappear to a large extent.

This was, by and large, the situation of the Hellenistic world around the year 300 BCE, when it entered into full religious effervescence. At the same time, many people resented the drastic changes brought about by living in huge monarchy states in whose political operation the common man had little or no say, as all important decisions were taken in Alexandria, Antioch, or Pergamum. Finally, it was also in those cities where most of the literary and scientific activities took place, although the Platonic Academy and the Aristotelian Lyceum continued to function in Athens.

It was at that time that two new currents branched themselves off the main trunk of philosophy. Both were "endo-axials", since they sought inside the individuals the behavioral norms that could guide man's actions in the new circumstances. Both held that "man is the architect of his own destiny". The people who adopted these philosophies were known as either "Epicurean" or "Stoics".

The emergence of these two normative proposals and the swift adoption of one of them, Stoicism, by a substantial part of the Hellenistic world, including, eventually, the ruling class first of the Republic and then the Empire of Rome, signals, in my view, one of the clearest corroborations of the predominance of the moral sense in humanity, in comparison with the more superficial and fickle religious sensibility.

Although the Epicurean philosophy appealed only to the high-class intellectual elite, it is worth describing, possessing as it did characteristics that now strike us as very "modern". Moreover, some of its tenets were embraced by other popular ideologies. Its founder, Epicurus (341-270), was a Greek from the island of Samos who wanted to wipe out religious superstition, which he had personally suffered: He tried to structure a completely naturalistic vision of the world, in which mysteries had no place. Of course, he chose to ignore many aspects of how the world worked, but denied that the gods had any hand in it: He insisted that if those figments of man's imagination had any existence at all, then they would be part of our world.

Regarding his moral proposal, he suggested that the only criterion for good or bad behavior was our own emotional reactions to what we planned to do or had done: they were good if they gave us pleasure and bad if they pained us. Since much in this world depends on serendipity or causes beyond our control, we should try to live a sedate, retiring, and respectable life. To do so, one should try to avoid stressful and troubling situations until attaining a state of "ataraxia", that may translated as relaxed or imperturbable.

In a positive slant, he recommended *carpe diem,* meaning to make the most of each day, of every moment, or of every opportunity. In order to be in a position to do so, one should be disciplined, always maintaining a friendly, empathetic disposition toward others, in order to receive from them, in turn, similar treatment. (This is a version of the Golden Rule, also espoused by Confucius.)

By all of the above, Epicurus proposed that man was the measure of everything else, subjected only to his own free will, albeit dependent on a whole system of physical and social needs. Man, then, has to decide his, or her, own course of action, according to the purposes, aims, and goals that he/she sets out for him/herself.

Zeno (350-260), the founder of Stoicism, was a Phoenician from Cyprus who moved to Athens, where he founded a school. The cornerstone of his teachings was to refrain from the superfluous and act decisively and with composure in the face of pain and suffering. Both attitudes -*apatheia*- were intended to minimize those instinctive emotions that overcome us in certain circumstances. Later on, Roman philosophers, like Seneca and Epictetus, would sum up this proposition by saying *abstine et substine,* meaning "abstain and bear".

The Stoic view of the world saw the universe as one huge being, whose immanent control was rational and linked to its physical, psychic, and ethical components. From that functional structure stemmed physical events and human history, both results of an inexorable chain of causes and effects that had a fixed purpose.

From this vision of the world, the Stoics concluded that each individual had a specialized natural role to play in society, since each man has a deep sense of self-acceptance which makes him or her cling to existence and strive to survive. This deep sense gradually extends from the individual to include family, kinship, tribe, political community, and, eventually, all humanity. So, according to the Stoics, a person possesses both the right to be a member of a community and the duty of behave in a manner benefiting it. By doing so, they recognized and supported a strong moral imperative.

The content of that moral can be summarized as man's duty to live in harmony with nature (as Lao-Tse also recommended), to abide by the universal order, as divinity dictates, and identify with it. By behaving in this manner, a person can break free of the shackles of social rank and status, thus allowing the intrinsic value of each human being to be recognized.

5.4.- Political History of the 3rd, 2nd, and 1st Centuries BCE

During the 3rd century, the Seleucid and Ptolemaic Empires virtually maintained their early configuration, fostered international trade, and maintained prosperity. More or less the same could be said of Macedon and Greece. In contrast, the Western Mediterranean saw a time of tremendous confrontations among three different emerging powers:

First, the Greek polis in the southern third of Italy, militarily backed and led by Pyrrhus, king of Epirus (now Albania) and nephew of Alexander, confronted a growing Roman Republic which, as we saw, had extended its public accord-based law treaties to the central third of Italy. After two "Pyrrhic" victories, he suffered a definitive defeat, which meant an unqualified triumph for Rome, confirming as it did the loyalty of the people in the central third of the country and incorporating the polis of the southern third to the Republic. This territorial expansion put Rome at odds with Carthage, as they now shared a common border in Sicily. After a protracted First Punic War, in which the Romans had to construct and deploy a war fleet, they gained the rest of Sicily plus stripped Carthage of Sardinia and Corsica as well.

The fight did not end there, because Carthage, led by the Barca family, strengthened its dominion in Spain, where Hannibal built a formidable army for fighting the Second Punic War. In the year 218, it crossed the south of Gaul and the Alps, entered northern Italy, where the Romans had recently subjected the Gauls, and Hannibal soundly defeated them. He kept advancing and winning battles through central and southern Italy, until 216, when he completely annihilated the Roman army in the only "perfect battle" that history records.

It seemed that the end had come for the Romans, but her magnificent institution of public accord-based law permitted them to defend their capital city and to rebuild an army, led by Scipio and deploying the strategy developed by Fabius: Never facing Hannibal in battle, but attacking his base in Spain and then in Carthage proper. There, Hannibal –denuded of his army- was finally defeated by the Romans.

During the 2nd Century BCE, the balance of power tipped against the Hellenistic monarchies and in favor of Rome, which defeated and incorporated Macedonia (168), then Greece and Carthage (146) and was bequeathed the kingdom of Pergamum, in Anatolia. The Seleucids, who in 200 seized Palestine from the Ptolemaic empire, were defeated by Rome in 188 and then lost, as we have seen, Iran in 155 and Mesopotamia in 125, with Syria as the rump state.

Those 2nd Century triumphs, relatively easy for Rome, in the long run spelled its demise, because they irrevocably damaged the quality of its political system, which had so strengthened its society. The damage was produced by the huge power and riches the easy conquests bestowed on many Roman military officers and senators, who "acquired" many large land properties, worked by slave labor in the shape of prisoners of war. This new system slowly forced the small rural properties out of business, severely eroding the middle class, also a purveyor of merchants and entrepreneurs.

When the Gracchi brothers tried to arrest the damage by attempting to pass land reform legislation in the Senate, they were assassinated one after the other by the plebs, aided and abetted by the rich and powerful. Thus, the middle class, core and cornerstone of the democratic system, slowly eroded, until it ceased to exist.

The 1st Century BCE saw the *triumvirates,* or three men pacts, emerge in the upper echelons of the Roman Republic, usually composed of a victorious general, a skillful famous senator, and a very rich entrepreneur, first Marius and Sulla; then Pompeii, Crassus, and Caesar; and lastly Marc Anthony, Lepidus, and Octavianus. The pact always ended in an internecine fight; the last man standing was named Imperator in the year 27 BCE, with the name of Augustus.

By then, the Roman Empire included all countries along the Mediterranean Sea coast, in the East: Greece, Macedonia, Anatolia, Syria, and Egypt, and in the West: Italy, Gaul, Spain, and North Africa. Their only civilized neighbor was, to the East, The Parthian Empire, which included Mesopotamia, Iran, and parts of Central Asia.

5.5.- Cultural Evolution in the 3rd, 2nd, and 1st Centuries BCE

The religious effervescence we have referred to had been caused by: a) The loss of validity or credibility of polytheist religions; b) The social trepidation and turmoil brought about by the political change of peoples having members of a minority of a different cultural extraction as rulers; and c) The mingling of one set of religious beliefs and practices with another.

Many reacted to all these changes in ways vividly described by Pierre Lévèque, in referring to the Greek people: "This fervor was even greater among the people, overwhelmed by the social crisis, vexed by the vicissitudes of a tormented history, uprooted from their traditional beliefs. Since they could not find comfort in wisdom, the yearning for salvation became a torture, and the masses could find tranquility only in emotional, even ecstatic, cults, that achieved for the believer a personal and direct contact with the god chosen by him or her."[2]

This is how the notion of "the salvation of the soul" of each individual after the death of his or her body began to emerge in the Greek world. In a sense it was "borrowed" from Iranian beliefs in the spiritual survival of heroes, and from the Greek philosophical ideas of the relationship of the spiritual part of the soul (*nous*) with the divine. This new religious concept of "salvation" had a marked effect on the social behavior of the Greek, Anatolian, Syrian, and Egyptian peoples. With the demise of the official polytheist cults, individuals had to associate with others willing to believe in the same divine formula for salvation, without much regard to their social rank or status, ethnic origin, or gender. As such, Hellenes and Orientals, freemen and slaves, and men and women mingled inside those cultural communities or brotherhoods.

¿Which formulas of divine salvation were adopted? Judaism and the Iranian religion of Zoroastrianism led the way towards reducing the number of acting deities until there were just two or only one. They were also forerunners in establishing the condition that, in order to merit salvation, the faithful had to abide, in private and public behavior, by a moral code and, also, had to observe and practice the ordained rituals, some of them shrouded in mystery. The most popular dramatis personae were the goddess Isis and her brother-husband Osiris, known also as Serapis, in addition to other gods like Demeter, Ishtar, and Aphrodite.

In Palestine's Jewish community, certain socio-political events took place in the 2nd Century BCE, that yielded a new concept which would be as important to Christianity (and later to Islam), as the aforementioned concept of "salvation". This new concept was monotheism's obstinacy in prohibiting its faithful to participate in any kind of sacrifices, ceremonies, or rituals before any pagan god or human personage making a bid for deification.

The events unfolded as follows: Between the years 320 and 200 BCE, southern Syria, which included Palestine, was ruled by the Ptolemaic dynasty of Egypt. It was so tolerant that the Jewish community in Palestine had no problem being its subjects, with the one in Alexandria even being assisted by the Court in translating the Bible into the Greek language -the so-called "Version of the Seventy" or *Septuagint.* In the year 200, the Seleucids seized southern Syria from the Ptolemaic kingdom, but were defeated in 188 by the Romans in Anatolia. Seeing this, their Iranian subjects soon showed their disaffection.

The new Seleucid king, Antiochus IV Epiphanes, decided to strengthen the unity of his Empire, which was threatening to fall apart, by forcibly trying to Hellenize his Syrian subjects. To do so, he indulged Hellenic institutions, even in Jerusalem, where the people rebelled in the year 167. This sparked a revolt by the Jewish people of Palestine, led by the Maccabee brothers, which did not end until 30 years later, when one of their sons, John Hyrcanus, was proclaimed king.

That Jewish kingdom was made a Roman vassal by Pompeii in 64 BCE and reduced in size. The last vassal king was Herod and in the last year of his reign, circa 5 BCE, Jesus was born, according to the Gospels.

By then, the messianic branch of Judaism was in a state of acute frustration, since it could not imagine how the promised Messiah would contrive to defeat the Roman powerhouse, which was reaching its climax. This is why the most extremist simply abandoned all plausible historical solutions and embraced an eschatological vision of the future. "At the end of time" everything would be put right by direct divine intervention, when the dead would be resurrected and judged, together with those still alive: Would all men be judged or only those of the chosen people? Would the righteous go to Paradise or to a Heavenly Jerusalem? And would the condemned go to the *Gehenna,* the *Sheol,* or burn in eternal fire? Nobody could answer those questions with any assurance.

Meanwhile back at the Academy: During the 3rd Century, it took the position -under Arcesilaus- of accepting only intellectual knowledge that had reasonable odds of being truth. During the 2nd Century, under Carneades, it denied the existence of both the ideal world of Plato and the inexorable chain of cause-effect of the Stoics, thus closing all avenues to dogmatic certainty. Although the Academicians acknowledged that the universe was an interconnected and organic whole, and that nature is coherent in its forces and processes, they denied that the existence of either a provident god or an anthropomorphic god could be surmised from all this. Carneades added that, even if a substantial part of the forces that rule the world are natural, meaning external to man, the internal human forces that spring from their own free will also exert an influence on it.

Panaetius of Rhodes (185-112), who introduced Stoic doctrines to Rome in the Scipionic Circle, considered convenient, spurred by these attacks of the Academy, to dismiss and invalidate astrology and divination. He also relaxed their strict control over the presumed evil effects of instinctive actions, and agreed to approve the achievement of the aspirations prompted by those emotions. With this, Stoicism entered a humanistic period.

Nevertheless, in the decisive clash that could have preserved Roman democracy, had the Gracchi brothers prevailed in protecting the small rural properties against the big land and slaveowners, Panaetius aligned Stoicism against the Gracchi and on the side of the Scipios and other rich owners.

During the 1st Century BCE, Posidonius (135-55) and Cicero (106-43) gave Stoicism its third face, the first one anchoring it in nature and humanism, in an effort to counter the religious movement that preached belief in "the other world". He introduced factors such as cultural environment, climate, and diet into history, instead divine interventions. Cicero was the great syntheses maker and divulgator of Greek knowledge in Latin language writings, and contributed with his notion of natural rights.

5.6.- The Upper Roman Empire

Historians call the "upper" portion of this Empire the time when this political body operated at a high commercial level, which allowed it to maintain a large urban structure. This period, however, saw a gradual social deterioration that proved irreversible, due to the gradual erosion of the small rural landowner and producer, who also supplied many merchants and democratically motivated army conscripts. The diminishing numbers of the middle class caused the army to become mercenary, which meant it became more expensive to maintain and less efficient in combat. That situation also led the army to hire barbarians, which, in turn, meant a stronger barbarian military pressure in the European borders of the Empire: the Danube and Rhine rivers.

Formally, Rome was still a republic and the Senate functioned, but the chief executive and judicial official, the "emperor" or chief of the army, was also given the functions of lifetime consul, popular tribune, and even high pontiff. All of this practically made him a monarch, albeit bereft of hereditary rights. That's why he usually "adopted" as his successor the member of his extended family or close political circle with the best ability to command the army.

In that period there were four adoptive "dynasties", as follows:

Between 30 BCE and 67 CE, the Julius-Claudius Dynasty: which included Augustus, Tiberius, Caligula, Claudius, and Nero.

Between 67 and 96, the Flavian Dynasty: which included Vespasian, Titus, and Domitian.

Between 97 and 193, the Antoninus Dynasty: which included Nerva, Trajan, Hadrian, Antoninus Pious, Marc Aurelius, and Commodus.

Between 194 and 235, the Severus Dynasty: which included Septimius Severus, Caracalla, Heliogabalus, and Alexander Severus.

At the onset of that 265 year period, i.e. immediately before the birth of Christianity, the rulers of the Roman Empire began to display an interest in giving beliefs some uniformity and, moreover, to cults' religious practices. But they encountered the following problems:

Firstly, "The Olympians were frozen in their Homeric postures…while the society that had once cast them in its own image evolved to new levels of awareness and morality"[3]. Secondly, the God of the philosophers, whether Plato's Ideal Mind or Aristotle's Prime Mover, could be a persuasive intellectual concept, but had the disadvantage of never having had a popular cult and, therefore, completely lacked religious appeal.

On the other hand, although science had made great strides in its qualitative aspect of forms and functions, and in studying the changes and evolution of matter and life, it lacked quantitative techniques almost entirely. One main reason for that is that their numeral system did not position columns in powers of ten, which the Hindu invention of the numeral zero would make possible. In this fashion, science left so many things unexplained about the universe, that forgoing religions was not considered feasible.

The only option remaining was the celestial vault, which impressed everyone, from the philosophers down to the common people. Here, the problem for the Romans was that the Mesopotamians and Egyptians had already laid claim on the heavens, and that, later, their Persian neighbors established a solar cult. They would eventually adopt it, but the Roman rulers wanted something more practical for now, that strengthened the patriotic duty of the citizens and emphasized the figure of the emperor. For that, they turned to the Stoics.

The Stoics had the great advantage of espousing the monist principle of the unity between the divine and the human, which virtually everyone in the Hellenistic-Roman world shared. In view of this, it was only necessary to try to find some congruence between the ancient mythologies, the new philosophical ideas, qualitative science, and astronomy. It was, indeed, a very difficult task, but the Stoics solved it by resorting to a new technique in the study of texts that they called "allegorical reading" or "of the underlying sense". According to this, one part of the text could be read in a literal sense and others in philosophical, poetic, or ideological senses. (This technique would be received very gratefully by the monotheists, as it would permit them to read their sacred books with a semblance of congruence.)

In due time, the Stoics delivered to the Roman rulers what they so urgently needed: One universe, one divine principle, one morality, one law, and one state. At its head was a personage whom the Senate could deify –if he had been good- upon death or even while still alive, i.e Augustus. It only anathemathized those that ended a Dynasty badly: In Commodus' case, they decided he had been "...more cruel than Domitian, more impure than Nero".

5.7.- The Origins of Christianity

Jesus' preaching, which probably took place between the years 25-28 of the Common Era, when Tiberius was emperor, was performed in the apocalyptic and messianic framework of that branch of Judaism that considered "the end of time" imminent. It produced both the zealots, who ended up rebelling against Rome, and the Essenes, who practiced a communal life alienated from the rest. Jesus differed from the former in his pacifism, since he described the Kingdom as coming from Heaven, an event that would presumably occur in that same generation. He differed from the latter in not isolating himself, but preaching openly to all faithful Jews, urging them to obey the Law of God sincerely and in a charitable manner, without hiding behind a punctilious but detached ritual observance, as the Pharisees did.

Even if Jesus' preaching sparked a movement limited only to the Jews in Palestine, it acquired intense drama when the high-level priests of the Temple of Jerusalem and their Pharisee followers succeeded in making the Roman authorities intervene. Heading them was Pontius Pilate, and the priests convinced him that if Jesus proclaimed himself "the Son of God" and in fact, king, they said, then it could mark the beginning of a rebellion. Pilate then agreed to have him flogged and crucified.

Jesus' followers continued to go and be accepted in the Temple, until they internalized the conviction that their Master had been resurrected and began to hail him as the promised Messiah, at first only in the synagogues of the Hellenized Jews who visited Jerusalem. In the process, they also concluded that many ritual aspects of the ancient Law had been abrogated and that the Temple was going to be destroyed, as Jesus had prophesied. When they began preaching that openly, they were condemned by the priestly establishment, with one of them, St. Stephen, being stoned to death, probably in the year 34.

Saul, an Hellenized Jew from Tarsus, Anatolia, who had witnessed the execution and taken note of the proclamations of Jesus' followers that had seemed blasphemous to him, as to many other Jews, was converted by a vision he had on the road to Damascus, which blinded him for a time. Once cured, he moved to Antioch, the Syrian capital, arriving there in the year 35 or 36. He presented himself before St. Barnabas, who led a group of Jews followers of Jesus there.

When both of them realized the open disposition of many gentile "clients" of Judaism -Syrians, Anatolians, and Greeks who knew and accepted Jewish monotheism, but were not willing to practice the strict rituals of the Law- they decided to preach the Good News to them and accept anyone who would recognize Jesus as the Messiah into the group.

This decision strained tensions between the group in Antioch and the one in Jerusalem, led by St. Peter, St. John, and St. James. At the end of the year 38, they reached an agreement and decided that neither circumcision nor the rituals would be compulsory for gentiles who accepted both Jesus and Biblical monotheism.

So, St. Paul and St. Barnabas returned to Antioch and preached both to Jews and to gentiles, expanding the group with converts of both religious extractions. By the year 40, they were called "Christians", from the Greek name for Messiah, "Anointed" or "Christ", that Jesus had been given. Thus, a new religion was born, 12 years after the death of its founder. This religion would go on to conquer the Roman Empire and then serve as the "cocoon" for the birth of two "third-generation" civilizations: The Western, Catholic or Roman (later, part of it Protestant), and the Eastern, Byzantine or Orthodox.

The preaching of Christianity was done mainly by St. Paul in Anatolia and Greece, expressing his doctrine in his famous letters or epistles. The Jerusalem apostles had to flee the city as soon as the militant zealot party began to prevail. St. James died in the confrontation. They preached in Syria, in Egypt, and in some cities of southern Italy. The apostles all used the same strategy: First preaching in the synagogues, until the Jewish community became divided; then strengthen the group of those who accepted Jesus as the Messiah with converted gentiles who had also embraced the Biblical Monotheism.

St. Peter preached in Rome itself, where he founded a Christian community. He narrated his memories, which one disciple, St. Mark, registered in writing. St. Peter perished in the year 64, during Nero's persecution.

Some 10 years after the destruction of the Temple of Jerusalem, circa the year 80, St. Matthew wrote another gospel in Syria that tells something about Jesus' infancy. A few years later, St. Luke, a physician of Hellenic culture, wrote his gospel, following it with the Acts of the Apostles. Finally, around the year 95, St. John recorded his memories and expounded the doctrine of the preexistence of the "logos" or word of Christ that had lived with the father "since the beginning". Some disciple of his, probably at Ephesus, later wrote the Apocalypse around the year 105, or maybe a little later.

As is often true with beginnings, during the first 100 years -say until the last rebellion of the Jews in Palestine in 135- Christianity grew very slowly among the non-Jewish community. It meant a strange view of divinity, consequential, personal, and even historical, as compared to the immanent and impersonal view of the Stoics, highly esteemed by the Roman authorities, as it was disposed towards monarchical absolutism and the deification of the emperor. This meant that, besides its strangeness, Christianity also involved a political risk for the middle classes, and more so for the higher ones. For this reason, during this initial period, the majority of converts to Christianity were slaves and people from the lower classes, from the cities more than from the rural areas, and almost solely in the eastern portion of the Empire.

Notwithstanding this, early Christianity began to acquire some features which strengthened it and made it more appealing: In the first place, it formed mutually binding communities through their practice of charity and respect to all. This was because of their steadfast belief that the behavior of each individual in this world would be judged and rewarded or punished in "the next". In this way, good and justice would prevail in the end, regardless of how harsh and unfair his or her earthly circumstances had been.

Once the rest of the population was becoming convinced of the morality of those brotherhoods, they ceased to insist that the Christians practiced repellent rites in their gatherings. On the other hand, they admired the simple formula for their "salvation" in their personalized monotheism. By then, there were only two other obstacles to overcome: That the Hellenic culture consider their theological beliefs acceptable and -the most difficult one- that a way of reconciling Roman patriotism with the beliefs and practices of Christianity could be found.

The city of Alexandria attracted a number of Christian converts trained in philosophy, who began to demolish the first obstacle. The first was St. Justin the Syrian who together with a disciple began to give rational structure to Christian theology, based on a compendium of the four gospels, written or translated into the Greek around the year 140. They tried to plead the truth of it according to the rules of logic, although their premises were still weak and defensive. St. Justin later went to Rome, where he died a martyr.

Around the year 190, the Athenian St. Clement followed him to Alexandria, and forged a wider and more coherent theological structure: He framed the faith in the revealed mysteries of Trinity, Incarnation, and Revelation together with the philosophical concepts that interpreted them in a rational form. He used the resulting syntheses to teach the Supervisors (*Episcopos)* or Bishops, who by then headed all Christian communities in most Provinces in the eastern part of the Empire, and a few in the western part, like Rome, whose bishop had been accorded some kind of primacy. Sometimes several bishops gathered in synods in order to present a common front against heresies or doctrinal deviations, such as those of some ultra-Christian factions who wanted to abolish the Old Testament, or to combat Gnosticism, a pessimist doctrine, elitist and dualist, also derived from Judaism.

Between the years 210 and 250, Origen, an Egyptian, was the most prolific Christian apologist, excommunicated in 231 by a synod for the neo-Platonist slant he gave to the doctrine regarding the preexistence of Christ's soul. Notwithstanding, his manner of interpreting the Old Testament from the Christian point of view, and of reading the whole Bible according to the philosophical rules and techniques, were basic contributions for emerging Christianity. There was a dire need for this in the 3rd Century, when the Church was forced to confront that "the end of time" was retreating to a remote and indefinite future. Hence the need to prepare for a long militancy in this world, instituting "means of salvation" called "sacraments".

The last rival religion of Christianity in the minds of the Empire's higher classes was Neoplatonism, given definitive and classic form by the Egyptian Plotinus between the years 250 and 270, when he had access to the higher echelons of power in Rome. It was transcendent metaphysics to which one could arrive to inner individuality only through arduous intellectual and moral training. That doctrine synthesized all spirituality that was possible to deduce by pure reasoning, as per sophisticated philosophical techniques. The weakness of this doctrine was its virtual inaccessibility by the popular classes, which is why it never took root among the people.

5.8.- From Military Anarchy to the Triumph of Christianity

The demise of the middle classes in Italy, caused by the crushing of the small rural owner and producer by the large estates worked by slaves, and which began when the policies of the Gracchi brothers failed to be adopted in 123 BCE, had its dramatic denouement 350 years later, during the reign of emperor Alexander Severus. An army entirely composed of mercenaries, as expensive as it was inefficient, demonstrated during its barbarization how difficult it was to control, first by assassinating the great jurist Ulpianus in front of the emperor, and later killing the emperor himself on the Rhine border, in the year 235.

During the Military Anarchy, as the terrible period between the years 235 and 270 is known, parts of the Empire became independent, German barbarians made inroads in others, and at times there were several "emperors" simultaneously trying to rule in one part or another of the Empire.

At last the army, from their leaders down to the last foot soldier, realized that they were destroying the source of their income and their social stability. From then on, they were willing to follow and obey a series of honest and patriotic emperors, such as Aurelian, Probus, and Tacitus, who in the years 270 to 284 tried to put the Empire back on track with its old structure, but found themselves stymied by the following reasons:

Trade had plummeted in volume, so the size of many cities, Rome among them, was shrinking, while new slaves were very difficult and expensive to obtain, and had been declining in numbers and productive importance, mainly in Italy. As a result, the Imperial Government was collecting less tax money each time, not nearly sufficient to pay the army, increasingly necessary both to hold the Germanic barbarians at bay at its European borders, and to defend its Asiatic borders against the new Sassanid Persian Empire, who had already defeated and imprisoned a Roman emperor.

All these problems were summarily tackled by Emperor Diocletian, who ascended the throne in 284, implementing the following three great and necessary reforms in the imperial structure:

First, he realized that the Empire could not be governed from Rome, because the weakness of communications was dwarfed by the size and nature of the problems to be addressed. So, he decided to establish two new administrative capital cities: One for the less embattled Eastern region, in the Straits connecting the Black Sea and the Mediterranean Sea between the Balkan Peninsula in Europe and Anatolia in Asia. Its name was Nicomedia and he made it his own residence.

To govern the Western region, he picked a brother-in-arms and Illyrian named Maximian, and urged him to settle in Milan, where he would be nearer the legions defending the upper Danube and Rhine borders. He also decided that both should receive the title of Augustus from the Senate and that each be granted the right to name a successor, who would bear the title of Caesar, to aid them in their administrative functions, and also to avoid succession wars. He asked his Caesar to reside in Antioch and in Alexandria, to help him run Syria and Egypt, while Maximian Caesar was sent to reside in Treveris (now Trier), on the Rhine border, to help him oversee Gaul and Britain.

Second, at the Provincial level he separated administrative and military affairs, which until then had been assigned to a single individual. From then on, the military chief would be independent, receiving his orders from the imperial commander. And the administrative chief would have the paramount task of collecting the required taxes by enforcing whatever measures need be to do so. Each district in his jurisdiction was taxed a certain amount, and its inhabitants had to pay in a mutually binding form, raising it amongst themselves. If the peasants in an area could not or would not pay, then their status changed to vassals of a lord, and he became, then, the one in charge of paying the taxes.

For almost 20 years, these measures were enforced, achieving the desired results, but in the year 302 Diocletian realized that what he had structured was some kind of a tax-squeezing machine without a "soul", incapable of motivating the population to act spurred by patriotism. So, it became necessary to implement a third reform, emphasizing the divine status of the Augusti. The main problem was how to handle the issue of the Christians, who by then accounted for more than 50% of the Anatolian population, about 40% of that of Syria and Egypt, and between 25% and 30% of the inhabitants of Greece and the Balkans. In contrast, there very few Christians in the Western region, perhaps as little as 10% in Italy and 5% or less in other areas.

Galerius, the Caesar of the East, was convinced that the solution was to persecute Christians until they accepted to make sacrifices to the emperor, which Diocletian agreed to in 303. As was to be expected, many Christians refused to do so, thus beginning a bloody persecution in the Eastern part of the Empire. In the West, Maximian applied the decree half-heartedly, and his Caesar, Constantius Chlorus, practically ignored it. In 305, Diocletian abdicated, but the new Augustus in the East –Galerius- didn't relax the pace of the persecution, backed by his new Caesar, Daya. A few days before he died in 311, Galerius published an edict of tolerance, which Daya did not enforce. In the West, Constantine, son of Constantius Chlorus, defeated Maxentius, son of Maximian, in 311, and together with his brother-in-law Licinius, proclaimed the Edict of Tolerance for all Christians, in Milan, in 313. Licinius marched to the East, defeated and killed Daya and put and end to all persecution against Christians.

Regardless of their own personal religious convictions, that probably remained pagan to the end of their days in both instances, Constantine and Licinius realized that by accepting and advancing Christians as the new backbone of the Empire, they were introducing a new divine being as authority. Since their Christian subjects adored the one and only God as Creator, Provider, and Judge of the entire universe, it stood to logic that that included all peoples and their monarchs as well. Both Augusti found themselves compelled to accept that proposal, as they considered it less damaging than prolonging the persecution that had so bloodied the highly Christianized East.

Meanwhile, philosophers, thinkers, and members of the high class saw with dismay what that was happening: That a new criterion of "revealed" truth was being introduced, that the Christians were convinced that they had absolute primacy over any of the criteria for truth and certainty forged in its long history by Hellenism.

However, it was true that the best Christian thinkers acknowledged that faith could not contradict the natural order studied by science and philosophy, as it was also God's creation.

Those two questions -political and intellectual- marked the beginning of the rift between Constantine and Licinius, the former zealously promoting Christianity in the West and the latter attempting to balance his policies in the East between Christians and old-world Hellenists. The rupture between the Augusti occurred in 324, when Constantine marched to the East, defeated Licinius and later had him killed.

Constantine, now the sole emperor, decided to work with the Church's hierarchy from inside Christianity, but then he realized that the Church's members were not absolutely sure themselves what their theological beliefs were. Since the Imperial Government could not contemplate those discrepancies, he called on his "minister of Christianity", bishop Osius of Cordova, to convene an Ecumenical Council, which assembled and held its sessions in Nicaea, near Nicomedia, in the year 325.

Most of the attending bishops were from the Eastern part of the Empire, and they were divided into three "Patriarchates": Nicomedia, Antioch, and Alexandria, with only one -Rome- recognized for the West. The main theological problem was the "dogma", or official belief, of "the nature" of Jesus Christ: The bishops possessing a more Hellenistic culture followed the path indicated by St. Clemens, in the sense of the pre-existence of Jesus Christ for all eternity. The more advanced group among them, led by St. Athanasius, Patriarch of Alexandria, proposed, as per the Latin apologist Tertulian, not only two but three "persons" in God: That of the Father, the one of his son Jesus Christ, and a third, an interaction between the two, called "the Holy Spirit or the Holy Ghost". But the three were "of the same substance".

It so happened that in one of the districts of Alexandria, Arius, a native of Libya, preached around the year 321 a stricter monotheistic version, similar to that of the future Islam, saying that only the Father was God, but Christ, the Word, had been created in time and sent for "the salvation" of men.

Although Athanasius' proposal was approved by an overwhelming majority during the Council's sessions, Arius and a small group of followers, fellow Libyans, did not yield. Then, in its final Act, the Council enacted an abstract of the Christian Doctrine as a whole: the famous Creed, which defines "orthodoxy" or correct doctrine.

Constantine kept supporting Christianity and he completed the construction of his new capital city on the European side of the Bosporus Strait in 336. His successors maintained, somewhat tepidly, his pro-Christianity policy, except for his nephew Julian, who in his short reign in the years 360 to 363 tried to reinstate Paganism to legal equal footing. He was followed by the Valentinian Dynasty, blatantly committed to favoring Christianity. Its faithful gave the Empire absolute loyalty in military and administrative matters, notwithstanding that they reserved their worship only for God.

Even with this caveat, they ideologically propped up the government, since their religion taught that all authority comes originally from God, and this tenet gave it a "catholic" or universal vision, that was well embraced in the Empire for its cosmopolitan structure. This aspect of Christian public morality simply built upon that of the Stoics.

5.9.- The Officialization of Christianity and the Barbarian Invasions

By then, the Germanic barbarian peoples were assembling at the Empire's borders, ready to penetrate its military defenses at the slightest sign of weakness. To the north of the lower Danube, in present-day Romania and Ukraine, the great Gothic people had settled. A portion of them, the Visigoths, or western Goths, had converted to the Arian variety of Christianity.

In the year 374, several hordes of Mongol peoples, the Huns, crossed the river Volga at its closest point with the Don and attacked the eastern Goths or Ostrogoths, defeating and making them their military slaves. In light of this, the Visigoths crossed the lower Danube and asked the Empire for asylum in 375, settling in present-day Bulgaria. They were so ill-treated by the Roman army, however, that they rebelled in 378, and when Emperor Valens appeared with his legions to submit them, the Visigoths made military history by soundly defeating the Roman infantry with their cavalry and killing the emperor, in the famous battle of Adrianople. From then on, for more than a thousand years, cavalry would decide field battles.

Amidst those terrible circumstances, the Hispanic Theodosius ascended the throne. He would be the last man to reign over the entire Roman Empire. As his first order of the day he quelled the Visigoths, thwarting their taking any important cities, and negotiated their peaceful settlement more to the west, in today's Croatia.

Meanwhile, under the leadership of "the three Cappadocians", St. Basil and the two St. Gregorys, Fathers of the Eastern Church, all of Christianity's dogma, morals, and rites became totally infused in the literary and philosophical thinking of Hellenic culture: from then on, that culture would operate only as a vehicle of the new religion. The Fathers and all the bishops were convened by Theodosius to a Second Ecumenical Council, in Constantinople in 381. In its sessions, Christianity was made the official religion, pagan cults were banned, and the Olympic Games, as a pagan practice, were suspended, held last in 393. Of more interest for our purposes, however, are the doctrines and deeds of the so-called five Fathers of the Western Church.

The first was the zealous activist St. Ambrose, elected by the people as bishop of the new capital city of Milan. After a hotly contested dispute with the pagan senator Symmachus, he prevailed with Emperor Gratian to have the Altar of Victory removed from the Roman Forum. In 388, Theodosius marched to northern Italy to fight a pretender to the throne and settled in Milan. While there, a rebellion broke out in the eastern city of Thessalonica in 390 and, exasperated, he ordered the army to massacre civilians as a lesson to the other cities. When St. Ambrose learned of it he denied Theodosius access to the Church and to the sacraments, and did not readmit the emperor to the Eucharist until he acknowledged his crime and did public penance. This event was of fundamental political importance to the later history of the West, as it signalled the formal division of political power into two independent spheres: The secular ruler was invested with what in Latin is known as *potestas*, meaning the power to manage and ordain in the military and administrative sphere; in the hands of the hierarchs of the Church lay the power of *auctoritas*, meaning the moral right to define what is good and evil, permitted or prohibited, according to the Law of God. In the Middle Ages they would be known as Temporal and Spiritual Powers, and in modern times the Executive, Legislative, and Judicial Powers.

The second Father of the Western Church seems to have been, like St. Ambrose, from Pannonia (present-day Austria): St. Hieronymus (Jerome). He made a priestly career as a reformer of morals in Italy, and by the year 380 he realized how dire most of the clergy's cultural level was. Analyzing the problem, he concluded that the most pressing need was their access to the Holy Scriptures, for no Latin translations existed. Announcing his decision to devote the rest of his life to solving this problem, a women's committee raised the money so he could go to Palestine and establish monasteries for translators there. He acquired the oldest originals he could find of both the Old and New Testaments in Hebrew, Aramaic, and Greek. Shortly before his death in the year 420, he finished his Latin version of the Bible, which is called "Vulgate" and was immediately adopted by the Church.

The third "Western" father, St. Augustine, although a contemporary of the previous two, was from a very different part of the Empire, from Hippo in North Africa (present-day Bona, in Algeria). His family was well-to-do, so he was able to study rhetoric, literature, and philosophy, mainly neo-Platonic, which convinced him of the objective existence of a spiritual reality. In Carthage, he ventured into Manichean Gnosticism, which had been preached by Manes in the Persian Empire between 237 and 277 and had also made inroads in the Roman Empire. Later, however, he became convinced it was too much of a fantasy and abandoned it. Then, he went to Milan and, under the guidance of Ambrose he converted to Christianity in 386. Augustine concluded that the immense distance between God and man had only been overcome through Incarnation, which had freed us from Original Sin. This doctrine was contested around the year 400 by the Briton monk Pelagius, who proposed that man is born in a state of innocence, and that his perseverance in virtue depends on him/herself, a view very similar to that of the Stoics and of modern times. Nevertheless, Augustine managed, around the year 412, for the Church to accept his doctrine. By then, the city of Rome had been sacked by the Visigoths, and his pagan friends mocked him by saying that the Romans' adoption of Christianity had doomed it, by weakening them significantly. Augustine decided to devote the rest of his life to proving how false this accusation was: He consented to be named bishop of his native Hippo, where he proceeded to write the book "The City of God". In it, he pushed the envelope of the strict separation of the affairs of "this world" - secular, temporal, or earthly ones- and those of "the other world" -spiritual and moral ones. In this way, outcomes of victory or defeat are not measured by the results in "this world". He proceeded to demonstrate this through his knowledge of past empires: it should be measured by the good conduct of men, who must always be charitable and preserve faith and hope in times of adversity. Despite the fact that this recommendation would increasingly make people turn to divine intervention, it also helped to avoid despair and loss of morale in the centuries of cultural backwardness that followed.

Before viewing the feats of the last two Fathers of the Western Church, we will see the socio-political events which occurred in the interim: Indeed, the Western part of the Empire would soon disappear: When Theodosius died in 395, no one would ever again restore the unity of command of the whole Empire: He divided it between his two sons, Honorius and Arcadius. The Visigoths that he had settled in Illyria (present-day Croatia) soon were tempted to enter Italy, but Honorius placed its defenses at the command of Vandal general Stilicho, who held them back. To be able to do so, however, he had recalled various legions from the Rhine border. German barbarians took advantage of this situation when the surface of the river Rhine froze over in early 407: A huge wave of five peoples, Franks, Suevi, Alani, Vandals, and Burgundians overwhelmed the defending legions and invaded most of Gaul. That was the end of the territorial integrity of the West, because the occupied lands would never be recovered, and the barbarians soon turned themselves into warrior aristocracies ruling the Romanized population. Honorius ordered Stilicho assassination for vain suspicions, so when the Visigoths led by Alaric attacked the north of Italy in 409, there was nobody who could hold them back: They sacked Rome in 410 and marched further south, where Alaric died. Honorius had moved his court to Ravenna, in the Po River delta, inaccessible to cavalry, and negotiated with the new Visigoth chief, Ataulphus, the evacuation of his people from Italy, in exchange for giving him his sister Gala Placidia for a wife and accepting his forming a "federated" kingdom in southern Gaul and northern Spain. His proposal was accepted and was a fait accompli by the year 414. By then the Franks, pagans still, had settled in northern Gaul, while the Burgundians, who converted to Christianity, did so in southeast Gaul. The Suevi, the Alani, and the Vandals settled in Spain from north to south. The latter also ventured into North Africa in 428, took Hippo in 431, where St. Augustine had recently died, and entered Carthage in 439.

Meanwhile, the Eastern part of the Empire was relatively peaceful, since its rulers could buy the barbarians off the Danube border. Nevertheless the Provinces of the old Syrian-Iranian culture -Syria and Egypt- began to show political restlessness: The cause was that the massive Christianization had the secondary effect of breathing new life into the native Semitic and Hamitic languages -Aramaic and Coptic. It was in those languages that the ascetic and monastic ideals of those peoples' Christian religiosity was expressed, and from those ideals two new nationalisms arose, in the form of heresies regarding, again, the nature of Jesus Christ, which was the most complex part of the new religion and the one less appreciated by those ancient peoples, who were less interested in philosophical concepts.

The spark was ignited by Nestorius of Antioch, for it was when he went to Constantinople that the Church hierarchy realized that he preached that Christ was two persons, one divine and one human. In order to officially debate that thesis, the Third Ecumenical Council was convened in Ephesus in 431. It condemned Nestorius without the presence of the rest of the Syrian bishops, and proclaimed the dogma of just one person in Christ but with two different natures. The next churchman to rebel was the Patriarch Dioscurus of Alexandria, as in a consensus with other Egyptian bishops he proclaimed the theses of "monophysism" or that Christ had just one nature. So, the Fourth Ecumenical Council had to be convened, in Chalcedon in 451, which condemned this doctrine and again proclaimed the dogma of one person with two natures: Jesus Christ was "Truly God and truly man". The Egyptians grudgingly accepted, but in the next century they would succeed in forming their own, separate Coptic Church.

Meanwhile, the Huns, under their great King Attila, had subjected all the Germanic peoples outside of the old Roman borders, and in 451 Attila felt his confederation strong enough to invade Gaul. Besides the three barbarian kingdoms that had formed, there still was a wide area around Paris under Roman administration. The official in charge was a cunning, patriotic general named Aetius. He reinforced his army by ordering the legions stationed Britain to concentrate in the Paris area, regardless of the fact that this evacuation had permitted the seaborne attacks of the Angles and Saxons of northern Germany to succeed. Aetius could convince the Franks, Visigoths, and Burgundians to present a unified front against Attila's army: The decisive battle was fought in the present region of Champagne in the year 451, and was truly very important, because the Huns and their Germanic subjects were fended off. Attila retired to the Danube plain, invaded the northern part of Italy in 453, but retired again and died the following year. That was the end of his powerful confederation of peoples, with each one going their own way.

This resounding victory was of little comfort to the Western Roman emperors because, by then, the Vandals from Carthage were attacking Rome by sea, sacking it systematically and paralyzing all maritime trade by the year 455. This was the *coup de grace* since from then on there were only shadowy emperors of the West "defended" by barbarian troops. The chief of the Heruli, Odoacer, relieved Romulus Augustulus of his purple tunic in the year 476 and sent it to Constantinople saying that it was no longer necessary, because he was going to be in charge of ruling Italy. Nevertheless, if that was the juridical end of the Western Empire, it was not yet the end of the Roman administration, because in the Paris Region a successor of the dead Aetius, named Siagrius, still held on, until the year 486, when the Franks, under Clovis, took that region and incorporated it to their realm.

5.10.- The West Sinks, the East Persists

So, by the year 486 the entire West had been subjugated by barbarian peoples, which divided it into "kingdoms" or warrior-controlled areas, while the East continued its practically normal life, with some barbarian pressure in the lower Danube, the powerful Sassanid Persian Empire as a neighbor to the east, and disaffection growing in its Syrian and Egyptian provinces. As in a sign of the times, the Ostrogoths entered Italy and Theodoric, their cunning chief, wrested the title of king from Odoacer in 493. But new political players were coming into being in Rome itself: the Popes of the Catholic Church.

Of the four original Patriarchates of Christianity, Rome initially was the poorer one and the one with less faithful, but its head gradually began gaining importance and authority in light of several circumstances. In the first place, it never let the other sees forget that it was the successor of St. Peter, leader of the Apostles, and as such had always had a say in Church affairs, both before and after its legalization, although it had hardly assisted, if at all, to the four ecumenical councils. Then came the demise of the political power in the West, which instead of weakening the popes had given them authority and prestige. As an example, in 453 and in absence of any imperial action, Pope Leon I marched to northern Italy to confer with Attila, and somehow negotiated with him the withdrawal of the Huns. Another example of how they could exploit their relative inaccessibility to Eastern Roman troops was their condemnation of the monophysism of Emperors Zeno and Anastasius, cutting off relations from 484 to 519.

So, when St. Gelasius ascended St. Peter's throne in 492 he reviewed the political-religious situation in the West and found: Italy, Spain, and North Africa were completely in the hands of barbarians who were Christians of the Arian sect, so there was little that could be done to influence those "kingdoms" and managing and aiding their poor and meager clergy was a daunting task. Britain was invaded by pagan Anglo-Saxons. Lastly, Gaul was divided into three "kingdoms": pagan Franks in the north, Arian Visigoths in the southwest, and Catholic Burgundians in the southeast. So, the strategy that the Pope and his advisors decided on was to try to convert the Franks to Catholic Christianity.

What he planned and succeeded in implementing was negotiating the marriage of Clotilda, daughter of the Burgundian king, to the pagan Clovis, with the goal of working on his conversion. Clovis accepted and when he became convinced that his wife's prayers had been an influence in his defeat of the Alamanni (All-men) tribes on the eastern side of the Rhine in 497, he consented to be baptized, together with all his nobles, at a riverside spot which later became Reims, where the bishop St. Remy also anointed him king. With his defeat and banishment of the Visigoths from Gaul in 507 and the subsequent inheritance of one of his descendants of the Burgundian crown in 523, all that had been Gaul, plus a part of Germany, became the Frankish

Kingdom. It was ruled from then on by Catholic kings, although frequently divided among the heirs afterwards.

At the same time, in 519, Justin, a Catholic who prohibited monophysism, ascended as Eastern Roman Emperor, and in 527 was followed by his son, Justinian, who was of exceptional importance. After crushing a rebellion in Constantinople and making peace with the Persians in 532, he sent his best general, Belisarius, to the North of Africa, where he destroyed the kingdom of the Vandals, proceeded to Italy and took Ravenna in 540. Unfortunately, an epidemic of bubonic plague made severe inroads in the Empire from 541 to 543 and weakened its drive to recover Roman lands in the West(4). Nevertheless, by the year 553 the Byzantines had occupied Andalusia and Cartagena in Spain and defeated the last Ostrogoth king in Italy. Also, their jurists had codified all the Roman Law in the famous Digest and their architects had constructed the largest dome in the world, the cathedral see of St. Sophia.

Proceeding now with the story of the last two Fathers of the Western Church, a few years before Belisarius entered Italy, in 529, still in the era of the Goths, a Roman noble, later known as St. Benedictus of Nursia, had realized that it was necessary for all the people, including the upper classes, to work, since slaves weren't available any longer and the population was diminishing, so no one was cultivating abandoned lands or maintaining the roads, the houses were deteriorating for lack of repairs, and even clothes were in rags. As was wont in that era, he found a religious way to remedy the situation, and founded communities of men dedicated to the service of God, willing to work abandoned land -sometimes even wooded- and to build their houses, make their furniture, weave their own clothes, lodge passers by, and give shelter to sick and disadvantaged people. Thus, the first of hundreds of "Benedictine Abbeys" was founded, which would eventually dot Western Europe, making manual labor respectable again, advancing existing technologies, and earning its founder the title of Fourth Father of the Western Church. The first abbey was the one at Monte Cassino, in Campania, which he himself headed, and the second was at Vivario, in Calabria, founded by Cassiodorus, ex-minister of Theodoric, like Boethius.

In 560, the plague took a severe toll on Europe, making it easy for another Mongol nomad people, the Avars, to enter, pushing the Slavic peoples into the Danube basin and the last Germanic tribe, the Lombards ("long-beards"), into Italy in 568, three years after Justinian's death. They settled in the north, mainly in Lombardy, but also in Toscana, and a few in the south, in Benevento, but they could not dislodge the Byzantines from Veneto, Ravenna, Rome, and the rest of southern Italy. When the military situation finally stabilized, the political map of Italy looked like a chessboard, a configuration it would retain up until the 19th Century.

In those very difficult circumstances ascended to the Papacy the year 590 one of the most notable men who had exercised it, St. Gregory the Great, a Roman of a well-to-do family and the Fifth and last Father of the Western Church. His most notable achievements were: He could implant some discipline in the clergy of all countries of the West negotiating with the local governments and sending supervisors; he imposed on them the rule of celibacy, which impeded the formation a parallel ruling priestly class, reserving the posts, in theory at least, for only those who had a vocation and aptitudes for it. Then, he decided that Christianity should not wait passively to be invaded by barbarians to convert them, but should send "missionaries" to the still Pagan peoples to do there the conversion. He selected twelve noble Romans, led by one later known as St. Augustine of Canterbury, and had them trained in manual labors in an abbey; then, he sent them to the northern part of the Frankish kingdom for them to learn the Germanic languages. When they were ready he send them to the country that was already being called "England", arriving to the Thames estuary in 597. There, the chief of the tribe of Kent ceded them the land for founding Canterbury Abbey, where they began their labor of teaching and converting.

The missionary effort continued after the death of St. Gregory in 604, proceeding from Kent to Wessex, Mercia, and Northumbria. There, they met with Irish missionaries: Ireland had been converted to Christianity by St. Patrick from the year 450 on, then missionaries were sent to Iona, in Scotland in 507, and after converting that country, entered England from the north, where they met with Roman missionaries around the year 650. The bishops of both currents met at the Synod of Whitby in 664, the Irish accepted the Roman way for dating the Easter each year, and the Irish hierarchy was recognized. Then, it was considered that the Christening of the British Isles was complete.

In Spain (Hispania) the Arian Visigoths converted to Catholicism in 589, recovered the Byzantine possessions in the southern part in 625, unifying politically the whole Peninsula, and in 654 they legislated the complete juridical equality between Visigoths and Celt-Iberian-Romans. That same year the Lombards of Italy accepted Catholicism, so the Arian sect practically vanished.

During the 6th Century, the Frankish Kingdom, which covered all of Gaul and part of Germany, had been divided into three or four administrations, depending, at times, on the number of heirs of the former king. During the 7th Century it was largely divided only into two parts: Neustria in the west, mostly Romanized and Christianized, and Austrasia in the east, which still included many Pagan Germanic populations.

Meanwhile, the Eastern Roman Empire was befell again by the bubonic plague in the years 580 and 595, and that, together with the stupidity and ambition of a general named Focas, who withdrew his troops from the Danube border to go to Constantinople to grab the throne, permitted the massive invasion of Slavic peoples into the Provinces of Illyria and Moesia (present-day Croatia, Bosnia, and Serbia). In view of such perfidy, Heraclius, the general in charge of the troops and the administration of Carthage, embarked his troops for Constantinople, where he defeated and killed Focas.

Once he was crowned, Heraclius proceeded to structure a profound socio-political reform, though geographically restricted to only Greek-speaking Anatolia and Thrace: He made an agrarian repartition of rural properties, as the Gracchi brothers had wanted to do in Italy more than seven centuries before, giving lands to the veterans of the army and reorganizing the provinces into military *themas.* In 616, when the reform was half-way done, the Sassanid Persians attacked, occupying the disaffected Provinces of Syria and Egypt, but making no dent in Anatolia. After a series of ups and downs, Heraclius defeated the Persians and its Avars allies, recovering the lost Provinces in 629 and concluding his great agrarian reform.

Only seven years after that, Arab warriors came out of the desert as if from nowhere, imbued with the new monotheist faith of Islam, and invaded and took definitively Syria in 636 and Egypt in 640. On his deathbed that same year, Heraclius would have felt reassured to know that the Arabs would never take his reformed Anatolia, and that his Sassanid rivals would lose not only half of their Empire, but the whole of it, Mesopotamia in 637 and Iran in 642.

So, in the second half of the 7th Century, the ancient Greco-Roman Civilization had completely ceased to function, substituted in Anatolia and in part of the Balkans by the new Christian Orthodox or Byzantine Civilization, but in the West a new civilization had yet to be born.

5.11.- Confronting the Historical Changes in Morality and Religion with the Working Hypotheses

We have to perform this analysis for about 1,000 years of history, from 350 BCE to 650 after the Common Era, although not worldwide, but only in the Mediterranean Basin and the Middle East. In that 1,000-year lapse, the world population increased from 95 to roughly 245 million. In the Mediterranean Basin alone, population increased from 27 to 55 million in the year 235, but then it is estimated to have decreased to 40 million by the year 650. The causes: disarray during the Military Anarchy, the barbarian invasions, and the bubonic plague. The region of the Empire which suffered the most was Italy itself, whose population probably shrunk by half between the years 235 and 650.

What can we say about the evolution of morality during those 1,000 years? If we examine, for example, the morality of Egypt's landless peasants during those 1,000 years we will notice very little change; not only then but also in comparison with the previous 3,000 years. Nevertheless, the little nuances of change in the behavior of the masses may be seen in greater relief if we examine those of their rulers, so let us proceed.

Before Alexander the Great's conquests, we saw that the entire Middle East formed part of "the only world" which was the Achaemenid Persian Empire. We also saw that the main policies of its organizer, Darius, were Tolerance, Descentralization, and Communications, which even to us moderns seem satisfactory, particularly given the brutal practices of their Assyrian predecessors. We have described the improvement in valuing the individual, which produced Monotheism among the Jews and Iranians, and Hellenism among the Greeks, by saying that civilization gained two new "second-generation" levels.

How did rulers' moral behavior evolve in those 1,000 years? We saw that the Seleucid and Ptolemy rulers of the Hellenistic monarchies had little legitimacy, since their subjects were of a different culture. Nevertheless, we noticed the willingness of those rulers to adapt themselves to their people's culture: It was evident mainly in Ptolemaic Egypt, as some Seleucid rulers tried to dictate a reverse cultural assimilation, which triggered the Maccabean Revolt among the Palestinian Jews.

What can we say of the public morality of the Roman Republic? Instituting the accorded negotiations between social classes and the peace treaties between peoples as the supreme law, would always be their pride and joy: It served them as the foundation for building the complex relationships that arise in large political units; it also follows similar structures of rights dating back since the times of the tribes and clans or hordes. That ascent to public morality began in 475 BCE when the Romans threw off the yoke of their Etruscan kings, and continued through the year 202, when they emerged victorious from the terrible Second Punic War: Then they had unified all Italy under an accorded Law. From then on, easy victories fostered large estates worked by slave labor in Italy, which crushed the small rural owner and diminished the middle class. Soon, the government went to "powerful men" who entered into pacts called *triumvirates.*

How do we classify public morality in the Upper Roman Empire? Overall peace, many peoples living together easily, formalized in legal equality for all. But not a democracy. On the contrary, increasingly more socially stratified, with slaves occupying the lowest rung. This crushing, unassailable socio-political circumstance pushed people to seek redress and justice in the rewards and punishments of "the hereafter", offered by the new religions "of salvation".

Continuing with morality, what changes occurred in the Lower Roman Empire and during the barbarian invasions? The most noticeable was that people continued reducing the scope of their relationships, to only their family, relatives, and community, and for most, civic awareness consisted only of the charity demanded by Christianity. For this reason, wide and generous, albeit simple, visions and attitudes, like those of a St. Benedictus of Nursia or a Pope St. Gregory I the Great, were few and far between.

How can we summarize the course of morality in those 1,000 years? If we judge it by the Egyptian villages, the change was imperceptible, but if we view it from the point of view of the behavior of the ruling classes, then changes transpired in the individual's range of relationships, widening when democracy prevailed and narrowing when there was insecurity. In neither case can we perceive substantial changes in the basic contents of morality.

In contrast with the aforementioned meager moral changes of the people of the Mediterranean Basin, which I believe are representative of the stability of conduct and behavior in the whole of humanity, their consecutive generations went through a series of profound, constant, and substantial changes in religion.

A short time before Alexander the Great's exploits, the religious situation in the Middle East was clearly defined: In the Achaemenid Persian Empire, monotheism, as Zoroaster had reformed it, prevailed, although polytheist religions continued holding sway among subjugated peoples. The Jewish people had put a more coherent Bible in writing while they were captive in Babylon and when the Persians liberated them, they were free to return to Palestine or remain with the diaspora.

Greece's Olympic religion had taken it, for a change, in two directions which foreshadowed little future for it: One, that religion had made them think about man's situation in this world, since if he/she could act autonomously on his or her own free will, it was also clear that he/she was also subject to forces or destinies that could not be controlled. Sometimes there was a sense of being more of a puppet, since when he thought he was about to achieve something, some power or fate pulled the strings. All this was magnificently expressed in the tragedies. In the other direction, they concluded that they had to study the phenomena of the world in a completely rational manner, so they began to study physical elements, numbers, and regular figures. Besides, their democratic system demanded they express what they wanted to their fellow citizens in a coherent and convincing manner. The combination of knowledge of the world and rhetoric took them to wisdom or *Sophia*. When some *sophists* abused their rhetorical skills, Socrates took it upon himself to anchor "philosophy" in truth and virtue, Plato soared to an ideal world, and Aristotle structured all knowledge in a rational method.

The clash of the two religious currents unleashed by Alexander the Great's exploits still resounds in our ears, so we will merely say here that, on the intellectual front, two important "endo-axial" or "inner value" philosophies emerged, those of the Epicureans and the Stoics, while on the religious front, all individual religions evolved toward "salvation". The initial inference was in this world, but then both polytheists and monotheists began to offer that "salvation" in "the hereafter". In this religious evolution, Judaism had an importance incommensurate with its number of faithful. The reason: the admiration elicited by its great book, which combined history, ethics and prophecy, and the fact of Jews being scattered far and wide allowed the book to be read in many places, once it was translated into the Greek language.

The history of Christianity's origin, its triumph, and its survival in the world of the barbarian invasions is of critical importance, as it merged the two great currents into one, though a clear priority was given to revelation over philosophy, since, as Tertulian asked, what does Athens have to do with Jerusalem?

This religious evolution ends with a surprising event: Two of the regions where Christianity first emerged, Syria and Egypt, uncovered in the course of their conversion a new nationalistic pride that they expressed in their Aramaic and Coptic languages, and later adopted simplified "heresies" from Christian monotheism, demonstrating a disavowal of the Greek Trinitarian lucubrations. Hence, when the Caliph Omar seized Syria in 636 and Egypt in 640, the Arabs were surprised at the overwhelming inclination of most of the people in both countries to adopt the simple monotheism of Islam. A similar thing occurred, although for different reasons, when the Arabs conquered the Sassanid Persian Empire, Mesopotamia in 637 and Iran in 642.

So the world of 335 BCE, still inhabited by a majority of polytheist individuals, although already adept at seen tragedy represented in the theater and at studying philosophy, proceeded nevertheless to adopt religions "of salvation". Then Christianity, prevailing over Neo-Platonism and Gnosticism, and embracing a good deal of the Stoic ethics, spread over the Eastern part of the Roman Empire and much later over the Western part. The West barely preserved Christianity during the barbarian invasions, shored up by dividing political power between Temporal and Spiritual, having the Vulgate Latin version of the Bible, and assuaged by "The City of God". Lastly, the Middle East, except for Anatolia, converted to Islam about the year 650.

What can we say transpired on the intellectual, political, and religious fronts in this region during those 1,000 years? As to knowledge of the world and political organization, there was an initial great leap forward, but then a retrogression that would plunge the West in a Dark Age for some 1,000 years.

Why didn't science and democracy prevail in this instance? In short: Because these societies were elitist. Was ancient democracy elitist? Yes, because the Greek system recognized only male free natives, so even extending it to the other polis of the League proved ineffectual. Rome could extend its accorded law over the whole of Italy, but we saw how it was overwhelmed by its own military success. What about science? I think that what they sorely lacked was an orderly numerical system for advanced mathematics, so they never went down the essential quantitative path.

So, if democracy and science were unable to prevail, the only road that lay open was religion. Within the religions, I think that Christianity was a worthy bearer of the Jewish and Hellenic traditions, revelation, and reason. In the West, the Five Fathers provided the necessary means to overcome the barbarism that was sweeping the region.

VI.- Infancy and Youth of the Western Civilization

6.1.- Birth of the Western Civilization

We saw that in the year 654, the Visigoths in Spain accorded legal equality to the Celtiberian Romans, that in the same year the Lombards in Italy converted to Catholicism, and that the Christening of the British Isles culminated in 664 at the Synod of Whitby. What about the Frankish Kingdom, which extended not only over the Roman Gaul but also over part of Germany? That vast territory, as large as the sum of all the other surrounding kingdoms, formed the core of what we now call "the West".

This Frankish Kingdom covered an immense wooded area of around one million square kilometers (nearly 400,000 sq. miles), bordered by the Mediterranean, the Alps, the North Sea, the English Channel, and the Atlantic Ocean. It encompassed the Low Countries, Rhineland, Bavaria, and Thuringia, but not Saxony. Its population may scarcely have numbered 8 million. The inhabitants of the western part, or Neustria, were Gaul-Roman christened to a degree, but those of the eastern part, or Austrasia, were mainly Celt or German Pagans. Their Merovingian Dynasty "kings" and warrior nobility spent their time fighting amongst themselves or cavorting about, leaving the administrative business in the hands of a "Palace Majordomo", one for each "kingdom".

In these obscure circumstances Pepin of Heristal became Majordomo of Austrasia in the year 679, with the "Palace" probably located in present-day Belgium or near the Rhine. He soon realized there was only one possible solution to bringing order to the huge chaos: Negotiating a formal agreement with the Catholic Church, whose organization he knew and appreciated, to help him manage the "kingdom" in his charge. In exchange, he offered to help in the missionary effort of converting his pagan subjects. In order to sweeten his proposal, he invited Berthair, Majordomo of the Palace of Neustria, to join him in his plan, but was soundly rebuffed. The dispute only worsened with a complaint presented by the Bishop of Reims against Berthair, so the Majordomos "declared war" between them. The decisive battle took place in the year 687 at the Tertry Wood, some 100 kms. north of Paris, where Pepin defeated and killed his rival. In view of his rising power, he was named Majordomo of both "kingdoms", and his proposal to the Church was officially accepted. Arnold J. Toynbee considers that event the starting point of Western Civilization (1).

Soon the Church began both its administrative collaboration and its missionary effort among the Pagan Germans, sending the Anglo-Saxon St. Willibrord in 694 as head of the first mission, which mainly spanned the land of the Frisians in the lower Rhine.

But clouds were gathering on the horizon, because the Islamic Arabs, led by the Caliphs of Damascus, were in the midst of their Second Expansion, reaching India in the East. In the West, they carried out a campaign in North Africa from 670 to 694, and invaded Spain in 711, a short time before Pepin's death in 715.

Selecting his successor was a thorny problem: First, Pepin was not a king and, second, he did not have a living legitimate child, but only a bastard one named Karl (from "churl") or Charles. But then, a grateful Church intervened to smooth things out, convincing the Merovingian royalty to accept his leadership. They agreed to name Charles the sole Majordomo in 720, urged on also by many Hispanic lords who had fled from the Arab conquest of the Peninsula. In 721, the Arabs crossed the Pyrenees and entered the southern part of the Frankish Kingdom.

Charles, who later received the cognomen Martell for his effective use of a mace in battle, proceeded calmly and deliberately to prepare his army, whose cavalry was the first in European history to have riders whose feet were held by stirrups attached by a strap to the saddle, itself fastened to the horse's thorax by a girth. Thus, the rider became an efficient fighting machine, as he could "stand on his feet" and handle his heavy sword, his mace or his lance with both hands.

By the time he was ready in 732, the Arabs had already advanced over half of France, so the decisive battle was fought almost at the river Loire, near Poitiers. It was a resounding victory for the Christians and a confirmation of Charles as undisputed leader. He kept fighting the Arabs until his death in 741.

Meanwhile, the Christian missions had enjoyed great progress in Germany under the leadership of the Anglo-Saxon, Rome-educated Winfrid, later named St. Boniface. He directed the founding of the Abbeys of Paederborn, Fulda, and St. Gallen, where the chief and leaders of the tribes received education that was then passed to the rest of the people. Once they were converted, they became full-fledged Frankish subjects. St. Boniface was named Bishop in 730.

The Arabs had also attacked the Eastern Roman Empire in two offensive wars, the first mainly naval, from 668 to 678, and had been stopped with the aid of the "Greek fire". From 711 to 718 they launched a second war by land, with the Arabs invading Anatolia and the Bulgarians Thrace, being narrowly driven away. In a bid to avoid new Arab attacks, the Byzantine Emperor Leo III the Isaurian tried to win over their friendship by strictly forbidding all pictorial or sculpted depictions of the Divinity. In 726, he issued an iconoclast decree, ordering the destruction of all images (icons) and crucifixes. That policy was condemned by the Pope in 729, and the Emperor was excommunicated in 731. Having done this, the Pope turned to the Lombards for protection against the Byzantine troops in Ravenna. They gladly obliged, but soon proved to be very annoying neighbors for the Pope, reason why he embraced the Franks after their resounding 732 victory.

In 741, Pepin the Short, son of Charles Martell, was recognized as the sole Majordomo, but by then he aspired to be king. In 747, he convened a national council, presided by St. Boniface, for reforming the clergy, and in 750, when the Lombards took Ravenna, seat of the Byzantine Exarchate in Italy, and the Pope turned to him for help, Pepin dethroned the last Merovingian king and had him and his only son tonsured and confined to a monastery in 751.

Now he only needed legitimacy, and asked for it openly: He wrote to the Pope offering to come to his aid in exchange for being anointed king. The Pope obliged and sent St. Boniface, by then called the Apostle of Germany, to Reims, where he anointed Pepin and his two sons in 752, in the presence of the nobility and the people. In 754 he received the visit of the Pope himself, Stephen II, who crowned him. Pepin then organized an expedition, crossed the Alps into Italy in 756, drove the Lombards from Ravenna, and confirmed the papacy in possession of it, as well as of the region of Latium around Rome. This alliance between the papacy and the Frankish kings would prove to be a constant in Western Civilization for a long time.

6.2.- The Carolingian Empire

Regarding the Empire of Charlemagne, eldest son of Pepin and who reigned from 778 to 814, we will address only those aspects that are relevant to our purpose, some not common knowledge.

In the first place, in the year 800, when Charles was crowned "Roman Emperor", his Empire legally encompassed all the lands of Western Christianity. From then on, a relationship was established with the Eastern Roman (or Christian, or Byzantine) Empire, and the partition of Italy was negotiated: To the West went the northern and central thirds -except for Venice and its lagoon- and the East appropriated the southern third and Sicily.

Of course, the nucleus and main component of Western Europe continued to be the former Frankish Kingdom, but now complemented with two thirds of Italy, plus the following acquisitions: In Germany were added Saxony in the north-east, marking the border with the Pagan Danish with a small fortified "March". Across the Great Danube Plain, still occupied by the Avars, a large and strong "Eastern March" or Ostmark —corresponding to later Osterreich or Austria- was established. To the west, the Brittany Peninsula was secured. Several border marches were established in a strip of land some 50 to 100 kms. south of the Pyrenees, in front of the Cordova Caliphate, called "The Spanish March". This huge territory, with an area of some 1,500,000 sq. kms. (about 600,000 sq. mi.), and a population of some 15 million, was administered by the Empire. There were, however, other areas which recognized the overall political hierarchy of the Emperor and whose religious and clerical affairs were managed by the Pope, like the kingdoms of the British Isles and the small kingdom of Asturias, which had survived Arab invasion in northern Spain.

So we can envision this heavily wooded large territory, very sparsely populated (about 10 hab./sq. km. or 4 hab./sq. mi.), practically bereft of communications, trade, or cities, as something akin to a political skeleton which functioned for a generalized Frankish-Roman-Christian fervor. It kept functioning during the reign of Louis or Ludovicus the Pious, son of Charlemagne, but, when he died in 840, the Empire divided among his three sons. Upon their death, circa 888, it broke into thousands of small parts, in what historians call "The Feudal Chaos".

The worst aspect of this imperial breakdown was that this time it also brought down the Catholic Church itself because, due to its alliance with the Carolingians, it had become practically one and the same administration. So the clergy also sank into the feudal chaos and the Papacy became a toy for the feudal lords in the neighborhood of Rome to play with.

6.3.- The Feudal Chaos (2)

Imagine a wooded area of some 200 square km., with its sides measuring about 15 kms (10 miles), peopled by some 2,000 peasants grouped in 400 families. Functionally speaking, the Carolingian Empire was divided into roughly 7,500 of these "cells".

How did they fend for themselves? In the center of the area would be a hill crowned by a stronghold, tower, or castle, where a petty lord and his family lived: if he was a layperson, we can call him a "baron". Seeking leadership and protection, the 400 peasant family heads looked to him. Since he alone was unable to provide it, he needed 20 men-at-arms on horseback at his beck and call, but how was he to pay them? There was no currency or trade activity. The only way was to assign each knight 20 heads of peasant families who would support him and his family with the product of some 100 hectares (250 acres) of land, given not in the shape of property but "in feud" or usufruct, "for having its fruit (or grain)". Then, each peasant became a vassal of the knight in a commendation ceremony of homage and fealty, saying to his new lord, in the presence of the other 19 peasants as witnesses, what he was under obligation to give and serve. Then the knight also said to each peasant that he was obliged to care, protect, and lead him and his family. In turn, the 20 knights became vassals of the petty lord or baron, in similar acts of homage witnessed by the other knights, specifying the military services he was obliged to render, including the number of squires and horses that he should bring and the times of the year when he would serve. The baron, in turn, vowed to protect and take care of each knight and his family's welfare.

This basic, fundamental structure could also be religious, with friars taking the place of knights, and an abbot that of a baron. In time, it expanded upwards, with the (250) petty lords of each of the (30) ancient imperial Provinces going en masse to the castle, palace or cathedral of a great lord who, if a layman, was a duke, marquis, or count, and, if clergy, a bishop or archbishop, to negotiate with him vassalage contracts, each stipulating his duties and witnessed by his "peers". Lastly, all the great lords got together, with the lays electing one among them as emperor, and the clergy, one of them as pope.

As we can see in this very streamlined picture of the multiple varieties of Feudalism, it basically consisted of two vassalage pyramids -one lay and one clergy- of five levels, with the lowest one, that of the peasants, common to both.

From a functional point of view, it can be said that power was exercised in polycentric form, each aspect of it as follows:

The judicial aspect was performed fully and autonomously in each of the feudal units at all levels, with each case judged by a jury composed of non-involved peers, and the lord acting as judge. After both parties were heard, an investigation carried out, and the case discussed, the sentence was meted out and then executed.

The legislative aspect practically remained unaltered: people applied the traditional law that had become imbued with Roman Right concepts and with tribal or national usage and customs that had evolved in each region.

The executive aspect consisted of planning and organizing common productive work, plus the defensive or offensive interventions ordered by the upper levels that be and deemed compulsory.

During the time that Western Christianity was a shapeless body, say between the years 888 and 955, it was attacked from the north by Viking seafarers, from the east by hordes of Hungarians on horseback, and from the south by Saracen pirates, but since it lacked a heart or brain it was difficult to kill, because only the "cells" destroyed in each attack would die, to be replaced by neighboring "cells" expansion. Thus, in instances of extreme socio-political disarray, feudalism fulfills its function of ensuring the survival of the society that adopts it.

6.4.- Overcoming the Feudal Chaos

Three events took place in 910 and 911, when the West was still in the midst of the feudal chaos, which would prove instrumental to the sustained ascent that its society has experienced, up to the present time, without any serious setbacks.

The first of them was, simply, the foundation of an abbey -Cluny in Burgundy- thanks to a ducal legacy. It so happened, fortunately, that it was provided with papal "immunity" from both lay and episcopal interference and, since the papacy was then practically inoperative, the Cluniac abbots and monks felt free to immediately return to the Benedictine Order's high standards of laboriousness and sanctity. This attracted more men of aristocratic backgrounds and produced a series of extremely able abbots and motivated monks. With this momentum, its new rule extended very rapidly to other abbeys who were willing to become "daughters" of Cluny, until one century and a half later it encompassed all Christianity and had permeated up to the Papacy. It was during this expansion that, on the technological front, Benedictine monks developed multiple plows mounted on wheeled structures and pulled by teams of horses equipped with comfortable collar harnesses, which allowed plowing the deep soil of recently cleared wooded areas, which then became wheat fields.

The second event was that the dukes of the northern part of present-day France, overwhelmed by the constant attacks of the Vikings, whom they called "Normans" and had already settled part of the coastal areas, offered Hrolf, their chief, in exchange for accepting to be christened, together with his men, to be recognized as a duke, like them, and a direct vassal of a descendant of the Carolingians who was recognized as king in the western part of the Empire. Hrolf accepted, the ceremonies took place, and thus the new Duchy of Normandy came into existence, whose dukes would prove to be very good, innovative administrators.

The third event consisted of the decision by the dukes of the central and eastern regions of the Empire, which now included Austria, Switzerland, Germany, the three Low Countries, and the eastern strip of France, to not obey the good-for-nothing Carolingians any longer, choose the one considered to be the most able, and name him Emperor. Their main objective was to coordinate their efforts to drive back and check the constant attacks of Hungarian horsemen. The first emperors channeled their efforts to founding cities and towns and building roads, but the third, Otto I of Saxony, vanquished the Hungarians in 955, remaking the Empire, now named "Holy Roman-Germanic".

After his victory, Otto went to Italy to reincorporate it into the Empire, but he found the papacy in such a deteriorated state that he thought it expedient to impose his authority on it, and stripped the papacy of its independent "Spiritual" Power. With these annexations, Otto brought about two-thirds of the old lands of the Empire back under his tenuous administration. The western part, although legally a part of the Empire (today western and central France) was left out of his realm, as the other dukes of those lands elected as "king of France" one of their own, Hugues Capet of the Paris region, who founded a new royal family upon the death of the last Carolingian, in 987. Nevertheless there was only one Western Christianity, although the emperor ruled only part of it, since not only France, but also the British Isles and the Kingdom of Leon-Asturias were an integral part of it, as well as other new lands as Christianization advanced. Although the papacy was fairly dependent on the Empire, the Church overall was being remade by the Cluniac Reform, as we saw.

The main additions to Western Christianity were barbarian pagan countries in central and northern Europe which had been compelled, either by military force or for obvious convenience, to allow the missionary effort. When the chief and his warrior nobility accepted baptism, a new kingdom came into the fold. Such had been the case of the Czechs of Bohemia since the Carolingian Era, and now befell the Poles in 966, the Hungarians in 1001, and a little later the Danes and Swedes.

In the south, Western Christianity was also gaining ground, making inroads into civilized countries: The southern third of Italy was wrested from the Eastern Roman Empire by Franco-Norman adventurers, and when the Pope condoned this action, it caused the formal breaking of relations between both Christianities in the year 1054, called "The East-West or Great Schism", which endures to this day. In the northern Iberian Peninsula, the kingdom of Leon-Asturias was joined by the newly-created kingdoms of Navarre, Aragon, Castile, and Portugal, which were gradually advancing their "Reconquista" over the Moorish petty states, into which the Cordova Caliphate had divided in 1031.

Another important change was that England grew culturally closer to the nucleus of Western Christianity, by virtue of its conquest in 1066 by a French dynasty, that of William, Duke of Normandy. He brought in his 12,000-strong army of French knights who deeply modified the socio-political fabric of England, as they received their land rewards or donations at the expense of the Anglo-Saxons with the imperative of not exercising judicial power in their domains, because William would do so in a centralized form. This is the origin of English Common Law and its later democratic breakthroughs. For this reason, this conquest would prove highly beneficial.

We can see that, by then, six centuries after having been thrown into the fray of the barbarian invasions, this new and forceful Western Christianity had only to recover its inherited division of powers in order to regain its socio-political quality as heir to the ancient wisdom. Recovery of the Spiritual Power was mainly the work of a man named Hildebrand, who since the year 1059 had been minister to two Cluniac monks who were elected pontiff and in 1073 he himself became Pope Gregory VII. In 1075 he "dropped his bomb": his Bull or Letter addressed to the Emperor, with copies sent to all the kings of autonomous administrations, that said, in essence, the following: That from then on, the Church was going to exercise anew its right to name priests, friars, abbots, bishops, or archbishops.

To us moderns, this seems very simple and straightforward, but if we take into account how the imperial and papal administrations had become entangled in Carolingian times, how every vestige of administrative structure dissolved during the Feudal Chaos and, lastly, how it had to be painstakingly restructured within the feudal order, we will then realize that the entire Clergy was a vassal of some superior lord. This historical precedent was compounded by the fact that the Church itself had imposed "the celibacy rule" on its church officials, still upheld. Then, in order to be able to occupy any post, from abbot up, any cleric had to receive his "investiture" from his lay equivalent. Still more: since the Church was by then the official collector of taxes, called "tithes and first fruits", then a very substantial part of them were handed over to the secular lords who exercised the Temporal Power.

Emperor Henry IV roundly refused to obey the *Dictatus Papae* and convoked a council in Germany to depose him, but Gregory answered by excommunicating him and writing to all the dukes in the Empire freeing them from their vassalage vow to the Emperor, and they soon agreed to rebel and prepared to fight him. Henry had to flee to Italy with only an escort and crossed paths with Gregory, who was en route to Germany, at the Canossa castle in February 1077. The Emperor performed penance outside in the cold, in what may be the most famous scene of all the Middle Ages, until the Pope relented and revoked his excommunication.

We cannot delve into it in depth here, but this quarrel, known as "The Investiture Controversy", was so fundamental and significant that it continued long after the death of both principals and was not settled with the Empire until the Concordat of Worms in the year 1122, and with the rest of Western Christianity until the IX Ecumenical Council the following year. It was the first council that had been convened after the Schism and it held its sessions without the attendance of the eastern prelates. So, by the end of the XI Century, western Europeans were ready to look again at what was happening outside, if not yet worldwide, at least in their neighborhood.

6.5.- The Crusades and the Birth of Bourgeoisie

The first part of the title refers to very famous events, but the second one alludes to a process that continues to be fundamental even to this day. In order to comprehend the importance of this social process, we can refer to our model of petty lordship of section 6.3: The mosaic they formed did not cover all available territory, but in the interstices between them, mainly at crossroads, small communities sprung up of people who were neither vassals nor protégées of anyone. The inhabitants of those villages were called "villains" in the feudal sense of being out of bonds. Their main means of subsistence was to journey searching for merchandise or buying it from passers by; so the little money there was circulated among them.

Nevertheless, it was not convenient for them to remain in such a precarious situation, so they tried to peddle merchandise to the people of the neighboring feudal units. To become a peddler, they had to negotiate with the baron (or abbot) the "privilege" or "liberty" of entering to barter merchandise in exchange, for example, of grain or animals. Gradually, barters evolved into monetary operations, at first using foreign coins, but later national ones.

In step with the development of agriculture, fostered by the technological breakthroughs we saw, population was increasing anew and the peddling business grew faster still by the use of, for example, mule pack trains or river navigation. Gradually, many towns increased their commerce and manufacture to the point that some were able to improve their defenses by erecting a wall around it. At that point it reached the level of "bourg" and its main tradesmen and industrial entrepreneurs received the appellation "bourgeois".

Robert Lopez holds the view that Western Europe was the only region in the world which, besides the ability of the peasants to migrate to resettle razed areas, also appreciated the importance of the merchants, of machinery and new technologies, and acquired the capacity to engage in local negotiations and initiatives, by reason of its successful political disintegration.(3).

As for the Crusades, their main cause was the change of leadership in the Islamic world from the Arabs to the Turks. The Turks were peoples of mixed Mongol and Caucasian races that settled in Central Asia, and had been converted to Islam from the 8th Century on. They then entered *en masse* to serve in the army of the Caliph of Baghdad, and finally seized secular power for themselves in the year 1055. A little later, and having already a strong base in Mesopotamia, they attempted what the Arabs could never accomplish: to engage and capture Anatolia from the Eastern Roman Empire. The Byzantine rulers had permitted the social fabric of small rural owners and producers that Heraclius had forged four centuries before, to fray. The Turkish army trounced the Byzantine forces in the battle of Manzikert in 1071, one of the most decisive battles in history, gaining with it more than half of the country we know today as "Turkey". They went on to conquer Syria and Palestine, harassing or barring the Christian pilgrims from visiting their holy sites. It was through these events that Western Europe learned what was happening.

In brief, the main circumstances and events of the First Crusade were: The Pope's preaching at a tournament of lords in the south of France in 1095, since he could not negotiate with the Emperor or the kings, because the "Investiture Controversy" was in course. As a result, the dukes of Western Christianity agreed to name the Duke of Lorraine as their leader, and everything unfolded in great disorder in 1097. They almost went to war with the Christian king of Hungary when traversing that land, and came even closer with the Byzantines, who closed the doors of Constantinople to them. Nevertheless, the Greeks realized that they could gain something from this unruly but brave and religiously motivated army, and agreed to lead them to the lands in Anatolia they still controlled and guide them in fighting the Turks, on the condition that all lands recovered in Anatolia were to be handed over to the Eastern Empire. The Crusaders would then be entitled to any lands conquered in Syria and Palestine. It was done so: the Crusaders warred their way through the south of Anatolia, returning it to the Greeks, and followed through northern Syria and the coastal strip that now is Lebanon, reaching Palestine and taking Jerusalem by assault in July, 1099.

Having fulfilled their vows, most of the dukes and their vassals immediately returned to their lands, with none having given thought to how the new Christian possessions were to be secured and maintained. The solution found by the lords who stayed on was to organize "professional" military units of priestly warriors, the famous military-religious orders of the Templars, the Teutonic Knights, and the Knights Hospitaller, the first two entrusted with terrestrial fortresses and defense, and the third to maintaining the sea routes open and manning the island fortresses.

The Second Crusade (1147-1149) was preached by a saint, Bernard of Clairvaux, who was giving the Benedictine Reform a second wind. He called to a new crusade urged by the Masters of the military orders, who explained that if the Christians did not take Damascus and kept that stronghold, they would end up losing all the territories in the Holy Land. Since the Investiture Controversy had already been settled, the saint urgently asked the Emperor and the King of France to go there. They did, but could not take Damascus and retreated.

In 1152, Frederic I of Swabia, "Barbarossa", very competent and convinced of the medieval mystic, became Emperor. He was very successful in Germany, where he directed the conquest of the northeast, the land between the Elbe and Oder rivers, against Slav pagan peoples. But on his Italian expedition he did not realize the great progress that the cities of the north had made, as centers for manufacturing cloth, weapons, and other artisan products. They sold the goods to the aristocratic republics of Venice and Genoa, who traded them in the Middle East for silk, species, and many other eastern items, taking advantage of the seafaring trade that the crusade's routes had opened. The Emperor treated the city's representatives as mere vassals and levied on them excessive taxes, so the cities, led by Milan, formed an Urban League, whose honorary leadership they offered to the Pope, who accepted. After arduous campaigns, the urban forces defeated the imperial army at Legnano in 1176. Barbarossa capitulated and accepted peace in which he promised to respect the cities' autonomy, in exchange for negotiated contributions. The Pope was so pleased, that in 1178 he convened the XI Ecumenical Council, in which he recommended similar arrangements to the kings of the other parts of the Western Christianity with their own cities. All this heralded the official entrance of the bourgeoisie into European politics.

Not much later, the Turkish Sultan of Egypt also seized Syria, thus surrounding completely the Crusades States and, in 1187, defeated the Military Orders and took Jerusalem. This caused the Third Crusade to be called forth. Barbarossa went there by land, reached Anatolia and died there. The kings of France, Philip Augustus, and of England, Richard *Coeur de Lion* sailed directly to Palestine: The first returned within the year and the second stayed and finally was able to pact a truce with Sultan Saladin, who kept Jerusalem but agreed to give free passage to Christian pilgrims. In the process, the Christians had built the fortress of St. John of Acre on the coast and seized the island of Cyprus.

In 1198, the throne of St. Peter was succeeded by Innocent III, the most politically powerful Pope in Church history. First, he called to and organized the Fourth Crusade, but when it was ready he ordered its leaders to sail not to Palestine but to Constantinople, and to enter there with the connivance of a Greek party in a dynastic dispute. His orders were readily executed and a little Eastern Latin Empire was formed. However, the Greeks formed around it three other "empires": Nicaea, Trebizond, and Achaia. This situation lasted only half a century. Second, he ordered a "crusade" against Manichean heretics in the south of France, which spilled blood and fire for two decades. Third, He convinced the kings of the five Christian realms of Spain to join forces and together with others he sent, fight the Emir of the Almohades, whose army was defeated in a decisive battle in 1212. Fourth, not everything transpired as Innocent wished: Philip Augustus had wrested the Duchies of Normandy, Anjou, and Aquitaine from the king of England, consequently nicknamed John *Sans Terre*. Then, Innocent authorized John to negotiate an alliance with the Emperor, and both their armies attacked France, but Philip defeated them in 1214. John returned humiliated to England and the great lords of the realm, both lay and clergy, took advantage of that and forced him to seal the Magna Carta in 1215, in which the king committed to sharing with them the government of the nation: this is considered to be the foundation of the Chamber of Lords and the beginnings of English democracy. Innocent died in 1216.

The drive of the Germanic world toward the northeast, launched by Barbarossa, was continued by two very different organizations: First, since the Teutonic Knights did not have any further role to play in Palestine, they received the Pope's authorization to redirect their activities to the coasts of the Baltic Sea, still inhabited by pagan peoples: They annihilated the Prussians, were driven back by the Lithuanians, and, farther north, subjected the Latvians. The other organization was the Hanseatic League, formed by northern Germany seaport cities, like Rotterdam, Bremen, Hamburg, Lübeck, and Danzig, following the Italian model. They developed an active trade with the Scandinavian countries and Russia, and colonized the Baltic coast, founding Riga in 1202 and Königsberg in 1255. The Danes and the Swedes participated in this movement, colonizing Estonia and Finland.

6.6.- The Medieval Apogee

The 55-year period from 1219 to 1274 is considered the Medieval Apogee of Western Civilization. In 1219, one of the most notable figures of that era, Frederic II of Swabia, ascended to the Imperial throne. The period also covered the entire reign of St. Louis, King of France, another notable, and culminated with the XIV Ecumenical Council, at which St. Thomas Aquinas' *Summa Theologica* was made official by the Church.

The Empire counted some 23 million inhabitants by then, 14 million to the north of the Alps and 9 million in Italy, now complete with its southern third and Sicily. Frederic II, called *Stupor Mundi* or "Awe of the World", had been born in Sicily and there, as an infant, learned to speak Arab and Greek and was so scarcely religious that he refused to join the ill-fated Fifth Crusade. When the Pope excommunicated him on those grounds, he brokered an agreement with the Turkish Sultan and succeeded in achieving Jerusalem's restitution, for which he was pardoned. He did not, however, fortify it and it was consequently lost again 20 years later. Nevertheless, his unshakable purpose of centralizing the administration of the entire Empire, as in southern Italy, put him on a direct collision course with the papal and feudal interests. Two political factions then arose: the Güelphs supported the Pope and the feudal way, and the Ghibellines the Emperor and centralization. The confrontation escalated into open war, and the Pope fled to Lyon, where he convened the XIII Ecumenical Council, in which Frederic was excommunicated again. The Güelphs provided enough money and troops to defeat and kill Frederic in battle in 1250. During the next 23 years, called the Great Interregnum, no new emperor was elected. Southern Italy and Sicily were broken off from the Empire and assigned to the House of Anjou.

France, in the time of St. Louis IX, had some 10 million inhabitants. The King proceeded to centralize justice in the Provinces of the "Royal Domain", to make peace with England and Aragon, and to lead the last two Crusades, the Sixth to Egypt and the Seventh to Tunis, both failing due to epidemics in the army. Louis died in his last crusade in 1270.

The population of the rest of Western Christianity at that period is estimated thus: England 4 million, Northern Europe 1 million, Christian Spain, which in 1266 had reconquered 90% of the Peninsula, 7 million, and Poland and Hungary 5 million, for a total of some 50 million, more than triple the population during Carolingian times. Its territory had more or less doubled.

St. Thomas Aquinas (1225-1274) performed systematic analyses of all the principles and cornerstones of knowledge of his time, as per the scholastic method, in order to structure a rational scheme of God, Nature, and Man. He succeeded in doing so by means of the herculean labor of reconciling and fusing in a new mold the two intellectual and cultural currents then available: The logically deduced knowledge of Hellenism, according to Aristotle's syntheses; and the dogmas of Revelation and the moral and cultic wisdom that had been transmitted by the Fathers of the Church. In order to posit the whole concept, he formulated a legal scheme covering all things: He put on the apex what he called Eternal Law or God's plan for the Creation of the World, unknown to us. From that Law, two other parallel ones derived: Natural Law, the rules for matter and life, as comported by divine disposition, and whose order we can learn through observation and study. The other Law parallel to it is the Revelation, which is that part of the Eternal Law that God has deemed convenient to let us know. Lastly and contingent on the two parallel laws are the human laws, legislated by those sanctioned by God, regardless of their being Christians. These laws cannot command anything in opposition to the other two, whence they depend.

This was Man's last great effort to try to reconcile his faith in "revelations" with the study of Nature. It succeeded only by virtue of the many things that were still unknown and a deliberate resolve to turning philosophy into the *ancilla* or servant of theology. During three or four more centuries, this model would still appear unshakeable and would inspire great literary works, the best known being Dante Alighieri's *The Divine Comedy.*

6.7.- The Late Middle Ages until 1360

In the year 1282, the men of the Spanish Kingdom of Aragon wrested Sicily - against papal orders- from the House of Anjou, which had its court at Naples. In 1291, St. John of Acre, the final crusader stronghold in Palestine, fell. That year, three Swiss cantons rebelled against imperial officials, clamoring for autonomy. From the year 1295 on, the King of England deemed prudent to accept the representatives of the bourgeoisie in Parliament, creating the Chamber of Commons, in order to negotiate taxes with them. The receipts allowed him to complete the conquest of Wales. Lastly, in 1296 a great legal and financial controversy broke out between the Holy See and the kingdoms of France and England over which "Power" had the right to tax each nation's clergy.

All these events signaled that the two main Medieval institutions -Papacy and Empire- were waning, and that the emerging powers would be the national monarchies, once they learned to find support in a strong bourgeoisie. This was the case in England, France, and in Aragon. In contrast, the still more prosperous bourgeoisies of northern Italy and the Low Countries could not form "national" monarchies, owing to the twin Papacy-Empire obstacle.

So, all this meant a deterioration of the medieval political structure and the beginning of the search of another order to substitute it. This is clearly evident in the manner in which this new controversy ended:

The quarrel about who had the right to tax the clergy was a heated one, with both sides wielding theological arguments, and ended in such an unqualified victory for the French monarchy, that it succeeded in forcing the papacy to move its See from Rome to the town of Avignon, on the banks of the Rhone, in 1305. The papacy, although independent in religious affairs, had to acquiesce in political ones, such as the issue of Military Orders. After the Holy Land was lost, the Teutonic Order migrated to the Baltic area, as seen; the Knights Hospitallers continued to be instrumental in defending the sea routes, holding to the islands of Cyprus, Rhodes, and Malta. The Templars, however, did not find a task becoming of their might, so they retreated to France, becoming a nuisance and a danger to that monarchy. In due course, the King asked the Pope to dissolve the Order, which he did by means of charging them with heresies and obtaining false confessions by torture, through 1314. The Swiss achieved their autonomy in 1315. Aragon not only kept Sicily, but acquired Sardinia in 1325.

From 1323 to 1338, the Avignon Papacy lost another theological-legal quarrel, this time with the Empire, leading to the Pope being excluded from interfering in imperial elections. This controversy was interesting because two great intellectual figures were involved: One of them, Marsiglio of Padua, proposed the Church be barred from managing "temporal" affairs. The other, William Ockham, head of the English Franciscans, proposed liberty of cathedra and investigation, without the bishops' authoritarian meddling.

In 1337, the kings of France and England engaged in a dynastic war that would last a total of 116 years -periods of truce included- but in its beginnings saw events that would prove to be a watershed for all Christianity. In 1346, in the Battle of Crecy, an English archers' regiment, men trained to develop the upper-body muscles needed to shoot arrows with the large Welsh bows, massacred the French knights that charged them, as the arrows could pierce their armor. This marked the first time in 10 centuries that a battle was decided by other means than cavalry.

Two years later, the entire population of both countries, as well as that of all Western Christianity, was decimated by the Black Death, a bubonic plague which killed an estimated 25% of the population from 1348 to 1352.

In 1356, the English, again with their archers, delivered an even more resounding defeat to the French, taking the king and many nobles prisoner. To add insult to injury, a peasant rebellion began, and the bourgeois of Paris kicked out the royal officers. So, in 1360 a humbled France asked England for a truce, ceding the Duchy of Guyenne, around Bordeaux, without vassalage.

So it transpired that Western Christianity, after increasing its population to 63 million in 1348, lowered it to 51 million by 1360, to 100 years earlier levels.

6.8.- The Late Middle Ages from 1360 to 1453

This almost 100 year period brought a realization to many in Western Christianity that, in the geographical sense, there were other lands to the east and south of Islam peopled by men of the Mongol, (Indian), and Black races.

For one thing, in the early 9th century, Westerners had entered into contact with a scion of the Eastern Roman Empire called Russia, born in the great northeastern wood or "taiga". A little later, however, several events conspired to leave it in total isolation: the Schism, the occupation of the Ukrainian prairie by Asiatic nomads on horseback, and the terrible Mongol conquest, which destroyed several Russian principalities and subjected the rest to tributary status. On top of that, both the Teutonic Knights of Latvia and the Swedes of Finland tried to conquer the remaining Russian principalities, but failed in the mid-12th century.

In another, Westerners realized that the Mongols had conquered a great part of Islam -in the shape of Central Asia, Iran, and Mesopotamia- so some pondered allying with them, but before they could act on this possibility the Moslem Turks drove the Mongols from Syria (and Egypt) in 1260, and a few years later succeeded in converting the Mongols in Mesopotamia, Iran, Russia, and Central Asia to Islam.

From the year 1300 on, the Ottoman Turks completed the occupation of Anatolia, got a foothold in Europe via the Gallipoli peninsula in the Dardanelles Straits in 1356, took Adrianople in 1361 and made it its capital city, and in 1389 they defeated the

Serbs and Bulgars in Kosovo, conquering the entire Balkan Peninsula. A "Crusade" was organized with the aim of keeping the Turks at bay, but was defeated in Nicopolis in 1396. Fortunately for Christians, the Central Asiatic conqueror Tamerlane defeated the Ottoman Sultan in Anatolia in 1402, and that delayed the taking of Constantinople until 1453.

Thirdly, on the other end of Christianity the Portuguese seized Ceuta, on the African shore of the Strait of Gibraltar, in 1415, thus denying the Moslem fleets a safe passage to the Atlantic Ocean. That done, they proceeded to explore the Ocean, discovering the island of Madeira in 1418 and the Azores in 1431. They then probed Africa's Saharan desert coast until they reached the Senegal river in 1444, arriving for the first time in lands with a black population. Then they reached the Cape in the far west of the African Continent and, off the coast, discovered the Cape Verde Islands in 1455.

Meanwhile, Danes and Norwegians had colonized Iceland and Greenland, and from there had reached the Labrador Peninsula and Newfoundland Island in North America, not knowing it was a new Continent. An ill-fated combination of a cooling climate and attacks from Indians and Eskimos resulted in the loss, by 1450, of all colonies claimed, except Iceland.

In Western Christianity itself, the more advanced, wealthier regions were the northern and central parts of Italy and, trailing them, the Low Countries in northwest Germany, after a seafaring trade between both regions opened up from the year 1340 on. In Italy, the feudal system quickly eroded, modifying many vassalage relationships into ones of exchanging goods and services and, in the political aspect, extending citizenship to many.

The political unit that prevailed in northern Italy, or what we can call the "Provincial State", had acquired, by this time, post-feudal characteristics: 1) A salaried peasantry whose members had the option of becoming "villains". 2) A class of soldiers and priests dependent on the government, with avenues for becoming teachers or artisans. 3) The petty lords had the choice of remaining in their lands as simple rural owners or going into business, as sea merchants, or government officials. 4) The great lord became, as a rule, the head of the "provincial state", the "prince" of Machiavelli, obliged to rule with the consent of the majority of the population, who always numbered in the tens, and sometimes hundreds, of thousands. There was no slavery, but a restrictive principle was always present, reason why in most cases two types of political parties formed, one "patrician" and the other "plebeian" or popular, which functioned informally with a system of "constituencies". Even if their conflicts sometimes deteriorated into street fights, this was the exception, rather than the rule, and gradually a prevalence of the law was achieved, capable of regulating economic life and fostering individual efforts. All this ushered northern and central Italy into a "Renaissance" of arts and science.

The main socio-political events of this period were the following:

1.- In 1378 two popes were elected, one in Avignon and one in Rome, triggering The Western Schism. Its end would come with the XVI Ecumenical Council of Constance, in Swabia, where the delegates voted "by nations" -Germany, Italy, France, Great Britain, and Spain. It was even suggested that the council keep functioning as a kind of Western European parliament. This proposal would be very useful sometime later, for the following reasons: In Bohemia, part of the Empire, Jan Hus, a Czech follower of Englishman John Wycliffe, had been preaching a reform to the Church with such enormous success that he was summoned to the Council with a safe-conduct, but was nevertheless condemned and burned. This set off a rebellion of the Czech people, who in 1420 organized as an army and, led by Jan Ziska, drove back all imperial and papal armies sent against them. So in the year 1431, the XVIII Ecumenical Council had to be convened in Basel. There, an agreement was reached with the Czech moderate party and a coalition of imperial, papal, and Czech moderates' troops defeated the extremists in 1434. Sadly, the reformist and parliamentarian air in the Council could not prevail, so the Papacy threw itself into the Renaissance and each "nation" was left to its own devices. This clearly attainable possibility of unity and reform was totally wasted, and Europe had to wait until the Protestant upheaval to implement Reforms on both sides.

2.- The dynastic war waged from 1360 between France and England saw intermittent periods of relative peace, until 1410 when the French dynasty split in two, because the branch that had the Duchies of Burgundy and Flanders broke with the Royal House and allied itself with the English. The King of England took advantage of this and, in 1415, led an archer-based army and, for the third time, massacred the French knights. This victory allowed the English, with the aid of the "Burgundians", to take all of northern France, including Paris, in addition to the southwest they already had. Hence, the French King, who was insane, was left only with the area south of the Loire. Since no other option loomed, in 1420 the Queen signed a treaty with the English agreeing that, at her incapacitated husband's death, she would recognize the English King as King of France, since her own son, she confessed, was illegitimate.

The death of the French King took place in 1422, but the victorious English King had himself died two months before, so a nine month old infant was hailed as King of both countries. The English Regents did not actively pursue the war, and for this reason the Dauphin of France was able to loll for another six years south of the Loire River. Then, in 1428, one of the most unexpected events in history unfolded: A peasant girl who had traveled on horseback presented herself to the Dauphin and told him that she had been sent to him by God to save France. Bishops and military chiefs examined her and the Dauphin decided to send her to the besieged city of Orleans with a military relief expedition. Success came swiftly and as word spread about her, the motivated French routed the English, and shortly after defeated them in a field battle. Then Jeanne of Arc, for it was she, urged a military expedition to be organized to liberate the city of Reims: It was a triumphal march, and the Dauphin was anointed and crowned King, as Clovis, Pepin, and Charlemagne had been before him. Jeanne's triumph was short-lived, as she was captured by Burgundian troops and sold out to the English, who arranged for some French bishops to have her condemned and burned at the stake.

Nevertheless, the momentum was in place, and the Duke of Burgundy and Flanders, who was in the process of annexing present-day Netherlands, Belgium, and Luxembourg, made peace with the new King of France in 1435, in exchange for recognition as an independent sovereign. The French could soon retake Paris and a substantial part of the northern lands -except Normandy- signing a truce with the English in 1438.

That same year, France can arguably be said to have been the first country in Western Christianity to achieve fiscal independence from the papacy, by means of a solemn decree by the King, ordering the French clergy to hand over all tithes and "first fruits" money to his agents only. With part of that money he financed the manufacture of the first efficient artillery, mounting cannons on limbers pulled by teams of horses, so they could be transported and deployed in field battles. With this new weapon, France defeated the English, recovering Normandy in 1450 and Guyenne in 1453, thus ending the long war.

We've seen how in the Iberian Peninsula, Portugal, in the west, took to the oceans, while in the center, the Kingdom of Castile-Leon still retained a feudal structure. In the east, the commercially active Kingdom of Aragon wrested from the House of Anjou the southern third of Italy in 1443, forming the so-called Kingdom of Naples, which also encompassed Sicily and Sardinia.

Venice, Milan, and Florence -the "powers" of northern and central Italy- made peace in 1453, after waging a long war against each other. For the next 70 years, the Renaissance would soar on this political foundation. The same year, in Germany, Gutenberg invented the printing press with lead movable type.

6.9.- The Renaissance from 1453 to 1516

We will endeavor to visualize the new Era that dawned in the West in the mid-15th century by looking at three "drivers" of novel and intense behavior, noticeable mainly in individuals of the middle class and the lesser nobility, whose members lived their lives with new verve.

Geographically, this dynamism was first noticeable in the three leading "Provincial States" we mentioned, Venice, Milan, and Florence, who were at peace amongst themselves and then suffered no intervention from extraneous powers. Venice already comprised all northeastern Italy and had an active seafaring trade with Egypt and Syria, and even with the Ottomans, when she was not at war with them. Milan was Europe's major manufacturing center, mainly of weapons and protective armor, hence its great involvement in trans-Alpine politics. Florence, although having a lesser commercial and industrial profile, fashioned itself into Europe's banker. The Papal States, which included Latium, Umbria, the Marches, and lower Emilia, had considerable power, since it still received a large share of the taxes of all Western Christianity, and had also preserved a share of its moral authority. Besides, it transformed itself into a great patron of the arts, and continued to be the largest pilgrimage destination. However, this residual power blinded the Church hierarchs and became an obstacle to the performance of its duties of sanctity and service, and prevented it from reforming itself. That made it inevitable for the reform to be forced on it from the outside.

We can call the main driver "Humanism". At its core it was simply an enhanced self-confidence that educated and enterprising men would acquire. This new sense could impel a person to try to excel at some activity, be it the arts, literature, history, or science, or to stand out in navigation or in commerce. These new men continued considering themselves fragile creatures of God but, nonetheless, could better appreciate the marvel of Man and the things he or she could do. They wanted, over and above all else, the moral perfection of Man.

They had various ways and means at their disposal, such as rediscovering ancient wisdom in medieval translations or in manuscripts of Byzantine intellectuals who had fled to Italy -for those who had learned the Greek language- and, as we said, the new printed books. All this unfolding in a relatively prosperous country whose political and religious leaders were willing to pay magnificently for exceptional results.

In the rest of Western Christianity, breakthroughs in the arts and sciences were still uncommon in that 40-year period (1453-1493), as many countries there were busy dismantling part of their feudal structure and forming the new "nation-states" of France, Spain, and England. Not so Germany or Italy itself, where the Empire and the Papacy were major obstacles.

The Burgundian Low Countries sought independent state status under Charles the Bold in a long war with France -from 1467 to 1477- but when he died in battle, the only outcome was that magnificent land being passed through a heiress to the Habsburgs of Austria, since his only daughter, Mary, married Maximilian, son of the Emperor, who negotiated peace with France in 1483.

With that, France reaffirmed its sovereignty and established its northeastern border with the Empire, on the strength of which we can say that it became the first "nation-state", as it succeeded in politically unifying virtually all the French-speaking Western Europeans, and had already attained, as we saw, its fiscal independence from the papacy.

England, meanwhile, once its armies had been definitely routed out from France, suffered the "Wars of the Roses" civil war for more than 30 years, from 1455 on, between two branches of the Franco-Norman Dynasty. When almost all the French-speaking aristocrats had perished in the fight, a distant English-speaking relative, Henry Tudor, inherited the crown in 1485, so the gulf between royalty and commoners substantially narrowed.

In Spain, two of the three large Christian kingdoms -Castile and Aragon, albeit not Portugal- became united by a royal marriage in 1479. They then jointly embarked on, in 1481, the systematic conquest and annexation of the only Moorish kingdom remaining in the Peninsula: Granada. Its capital was recaptured January 2nd, 1492. We can very well say that Spain was born on that date, and its king and queen were bestowed the title of "Catholic Monarchs".

Germany and Italy, hindered by the Imperial and Papal institutions, kept their medieval political configuration, which is why they will form what we may call "provincial states", to differentiate them from the "nation-states".

In the northern and eastern periphery there were other "small kingdoms", like Scotland, Denmark, Sweden, Poland, and Hungary.

The international stage undergoes a sea change from 1494 on, with what we call "the modern European wars". Two factors made them unique: First, their purpose and aims had nothing to do with Western Christianity as such, but were, in essence, nationalistic. Second, the decisive weapon of the field battles was not the noble cavalry, but the disciplined infantries, armed not only with lances and sabers but also with hand-held firearms and backed by horse artillery teams of rapid deployment.

The first disciplined infantries were those of the Swiss: With them they staved off Charles the Bold of Burgundy, who wanted to incorporate them into his new state, and after that, aided by France, they defeated and killed Charles outside the walls of Nancy in 1477. No nation-state had that kind of an infantry for some time after that. It wasn't until France launched the modern wars by invading Italy and capturing the kingdom of Naples from Spain in 1494, and again in 1501, that Spain formed its famous "tercios" (a unit with three columns) of disciplined infantry. Entering into battle in 1503, they expelled the French from Italy. Soon after that, the Empire and France also assembled their own modern infantries, deploying them in the Italian Wars up to the Peace of 1515.

Urgently compelled to make peace among Christian powers that no longer obeyed his orders or even took his advice on political matters, the Pope convened the XVIII Ecumenical Council. In it, only mundane matters were discussed, and the organizers had the impudence of prohibiting making any overt reference to corrupt clerics. The last chance for an internal Reform was thus pitifully wasted, on the eve of the Protestant revolt.

By then the Second Driver –Maritime Exploration- had achieved the following feats: The Portuguese crossed the Equator in front of the mouth of the Congo River in 1483 and reached the Cape of Good Hope in 1487. They mapped out their next step carefully, first negotiating their monopoly of the Eastern Route with Castile in the Papal Court. They then reached India in 1498, brought back shiploads of spices in 1500, discovered the coast of Brazil in 1501, chased off Moslem warships from the Indian Ocean, founded Goa in 1510, Malacca in 1511, and reached China in 1517.

The Castilians, using the Canary Islands as a platform to the west, discovered America in 1492, and colonized the Great Antilles, whose native hunter/gatherer population soon died from exposure to diseases. To replace them as workers, they bought African slaves, who were tropical farmers, from the Portuguese. In 1513 they discovered the Isthmus of Panama and began colonizing South America's Caribbean coast ("Tierra Firme").

6.10.- The Religious Reformation from 1517 to 1560

The nine Popes that reigned from 1455 to 1517 during the height of the Italian Renaissance, were much too immersed in politics and in business, living in a way that seemed ostentatious and mundane to many persons beyond the Alps, particularly scandalizing the devout Germans who made pilgrimages to Rome. That was increasingly difficult to accept in the age of printed books. Half of those made before 1500 addressed religious themes, such as Thomas a Kempis' *The Imitation of Christ*, and the spirited, eloquent writings of Erasmus of Rotterdam, which tended to strengthen individual consciences and place the reader in a position to issue critiques. On the other hand, the rediscovery of the philosophy and history of Antiquity and the breakthroughs in arts and science had the effect of giving a wider and deeper perspective of what Man had done and was capable of doing. Investably, that displaced the dogma and the magisterial position of the Church on that score.

In 1517, Dominican monks began a campaign, by papal order, of selling indulgences in Germany "for pious works", suspecting many that the money will end in pompous displays by high-ranking churchmen. When they reached the Electorate of Saxony in October, Augustinian monk Martin Luther, who believed in man's total incapacity for salvation without God's grace, obtainable only through faith, opposed them and expressed his opinions in 95 theses that he nailed to the door of the castle church of Wittenberg, where he was assigned. His clash with the Church began the following year and in 1519 he reached the breaking point regarding the authority for interpreting the Holy Scriptures. In 1520, Luther mounted an in-depth attack with his "Message to the Christian Nobility of the German Nation", accusing the Church of depriving the Christian people of true religion and of changing the meaning of the sacraments. All this brought upon him his excommunication by the Pope. The Bull was burned by his followers.

All that remained to be seen were the political and social effects yielded by the genius and courage of this man, whose own life hung in the balance at the Imperial Diet of Worms, where he was summoned in April, 1521.

By then, the Habsburgs had forged a powerful monarchy: their scion Charles had inherited the crowns of Castile and Aragon, united now as Spain -complete with its vassal Kingdom of Naples- and in 1519 had become Duke of Austria and the Low Countries and elected Holy Roman Emperor, although effective only in Germany.

Before the Diet of Worms, presided by Charles V, Luther calmly and courageously defended his doctrinal position, his life hanging by a thread, but the immediate popular ardor that spread throughout Germany made many high lords ask Charles to honor his safe-conduct. The Elector of Saxony decided to "abduct" Luther and maintain him in hiding during one year.

Many German dukes and aristocrats began to ponder the enormous political advantages to be had if they were to harness the popular ardor to break free from their fiscal and ideological dependency of Rome: they would then have direct control of Church lands, and would also allow them more autonomy in their relations with the Emperor. The Great Master of the Teutonic Knights acted first, secularizing the Order and becoming the monarch of Prussia and Latvia. Gustav Vasa did the same in the Kingdom of Sweden and later the King of Denmark also embraced Lutheranism.

Other dukes, however, like the one of Bavaria, and several archbishoprics continued to abide being "Catholics", or in obeisance of Rome. So did, obviously, the Low Countries and Austria, as well as Bohemia, in 1526, where a brother of Charles was elected king. In the east, the Kingdoms of Poland and Hungary also remained Catholic.

Of the other "great nations", all the Italian "provincial states", Spain and Portugal, and France remained Catholic, but England, under its second Tudor King, broke with Rome in 1532-1534.

Western Europe soon became polarized into two rival groups of states and braced for battle. It could be thought that the Catholic group, due to its size and population, was more powerful by far than the Protestant one, but that was inaccurate, for the following two reasons:

First, France did not align itself with the leading Catholic power, the Habsburg Monarchy, because it was surrounded by it on all sides and fought desperately to avoid being swallowed up by it, even at the cost of losing the Duchy of Milan and its Alliance with Genoa in 1525. After that, the French became allies of the German Protestants -and even of the Ottoman Turks.

Second, the Ottoman Empire had reached the height of its military power by then, having taken Syria and Egypt in 1517, and under Sultan Suleiman conquered Hungary in 1526. In 1529, it marched an enormous army against Vienna, which was beaten back with great difficulty. Several harsh intermittent wars, both by land and sea, ensued, extending the Ottomans their power all the way to Algiers. In 1547, Suleiman agreed to retain only two thirds of Hungary, ceding the third nearer Austria to the Habsburgs.

So after 30 years of wars, the Habsburg Power could not overcome the combined might of France, the German Protestants, and the Ottoman Empire, but neither could the three defeat the Habsburgs. Hence, it became necessary to make peace inside the Empire. A compromise was arrived at the Diet of Augsburg of 1555: that the religion of the local lord would determine the religion of subjects in his domain, in accordance with the famous formula *cuius regio eius religio*. The following year, Charles V abdicated his crowns, leaving, their patrimonial lands of Austria, Bohemia, and a third of Hungary, plus the imperial title and the alliances of Bavaria and the sovereign archbishoprics to his younger brother Ferdinand; and the Crown of Spain with the kingdom of Naples, the Duchy of Milan, and the Low Countries to his son Philip II.

In 1558, Philip II defeated France and ensured its future neutrality, but lost the opportunity to reign in England at the death of Mary, his catholic wife. He left the throne to Anglican Elizabeth, and retired to Spain.

6.11.- Confronting the Historical Events from 687 to 1560 with the Working Hypotheses

What a tremendous change we saw take place in Western Europe in this almost 900 year period! From a wooded area of one million sq. kms., with some 8 million inhabitants, half of them semi-Christianized and the others still pagan, whose informal leader asked the Catholic Church to be their *mater et magistra*, to a Western Europe triple the size and with some 68 million inhabitants, who had printing presses, firearms, and were accustomed to having the political power divided into two parallel domains: "temporal" and "spiritual".

But they were dissatisfied with two medieval institutions, the Empire and the Papacy. Half of them wanted to substitute the Imperial Temporal Power with nation-states or provincial-states and the Papal Spiritual Power with local autonomous Churches and free interpretation of the Bible. The other half wanted to conserve the two medieval structures, and both were resolved to do whatever needed to be done to achieve their purposes.

Did Western Europeans' morality change during that millennium? It would seem so, if we judge it only by the juridical order: At the beginning of the period the first barbarian invasions were just settling in the Carolingian order, but then others would follow, i.e. those of the Vikings, Hungarians, and Saracens. But is that a good criterion for judging morality? I think not, for the end of the period saw more than half a century of intermittent wars fought with comparable ferocity and violence. The only thing that was new was the reason given for fighting, that perhaps sounds better to our modern ears: Defense of Religion or of our Nation, instead of *habitat, lebensraum* or simply survival.

Indeed, if we examine the Christianization of the barbarians, for example in Fletcher's(4) magnificent work, we can see how the process unfolded: They pondered in mature reflections that the kind of life that the missionaries were offering -of which they gave practical examples in the abbeys they built- was better for their relationships with the people of the lands they had invaded, than their tribal ways. This manner of pondering the issue of conversion is transparent in the stories of chroniclers such as Gregory of Tours or the Venerable Bede, since one realizes that the barbarians scarcely understood the theological arguments, but accepted them nonetheless because they knew they were part of the "spiritual package" included in their conversion deal, which frequently also included their submitting to a "temporal" sovereign.

Nor did the religion, in this case Roman Catholic Christianity, change much in people's appreciation during the six centuries between the birth of this civilization and its medieval apogee: It simply kept consolidating its position, combining during the Carolingian period the administrative structure of the Church with that of the Empire, and both later acquiring a feudal structure in two parallel pyramids. A little before and during its pinnacle, Western Christianity had its frontal clash of the Crusades against Islam, emerging from it with a new cultural attitude, if not yet of tolerance, at least of knowing that other peoples held different religious beliefs, and that converting them was no easy task, mainly when they were also monotheists. In the Late Middle Ages a strong desire and purpose for reforming the Church also began to emerge, seeking for it to fulfill its function of sanctity and service and not be sacrificed at the false altar of political power and mundane life. That was impossible to achieve by internal reform, first because they could, ultimately, crush the Husite Rebellion, and second, because 100 years later the Lutheran explosion polarized Europe into two enemy camps, albeit changing and ill-defined.

To recap: in these 900 years, the changes in morality and religion which occurred in the first 600 years were attendant to socio-political development and, for that reason, merely circumstantial. Only during the last 300 years did a growing desire and purpose of "moralizing religion" become noticeable, and since it could not be done peacefully, it was going to be done by force.

VII.- The Modern Age from 1560 to 1830

7.1.- Panorama of the World at the Year 1560

Over the course of 1380, the Russian princedoms, led by Moscow, dared to rise up against the Mongols, and in 1480, once united, liberated themselves from their yoke. Since by then the Byzantine Empire had been destroyed by the Turks, Moscow considered itself head of Orthodox Christianity. In 1503, after many armed conflicts, Moscow settled its border with the Kingdom of Poland-Lithuania, its western neighbor. In 1547 Ivan "the Terrible" ascended the throne, greatly increasing the power of the Tsar over that of the Boyars, and went on to conquer the khanates of Kazan and Astrakhan.

The Ottoman Empire left by Suleiman the Magnificent in 1555 was a sprawling power occupying: The central and lower Basin of the Danube, the Balkan Peninsula, and the Khanate of Crimea, in Europe; Anatolia, the Caucasus, Mesopotamia, Syria, and Arabia, in Asia; and Egypt, Libya, Tunis, and Algeria, in Africa. Although it had powerful armies and fleets, it did not try to further increase its size, and its administration gradually deteriorated.

Towards the east lay Safavid Persia, already established within the borders of present-day Iran. Beyond it was the subcontinent of India, whose northern portion had mainly been ruled since 1192 by Turkish sultans, and the southern part by Hindu rajahs. From the year 1556 on, the entire northern and central part would be unified by the Dynasty of the Great Moguls, whose Empire, the richest in the world, was to last until 1707.

The Indo-China Peninsula was home to several Buddhist kingdoms, still isolated from maritime commerce. The Malay Archipelago was adopting the Muslim religion and being visited by the Portuguese, since it was the world's purveyor of a myriad of spices; during the 17th century, the Dutch would take over that trade. In the Philippine Islands, the Spaniards established a colony in 1565, administering it through Mexico for trade with China.

China was governed by the Ming Dynasty, whose emperors ascended the throne in 1368 and ruled until 1644. In 1557, they assigned the enclave of Macau to the Portuguese and saw the arrival of Christian missionaries in 1610. In contrast, Japan was visited by Iberian Christian traders and missionaries in 1543, but began to close off in 1587 and went down the isolationist path from 1640 on.

In America, the Spaniards conquered the Aztec Empire and the rest of Mesoamerica from 1517 to 1545, and then colonized the Great Chichimec, which would become the mestizo heart of Mexico. In South America, from Tierra Firme and the Isthmus of Panama they conquered the Empire of the Incas and then gradually colonized the remainder of the landmass. Meanwhile, the Portuguese proceeded to colonize Brazil aided with Negroes embarked as slaves from the coasts of Africa.

At the beginning of the XVII Century began the French, English, and Dutch colonization of North America and the Caribbean Islands.

7.2.- Western Europe in 1560 and the Wars of Religion

The most important change afoot for western Europeans -mainly its middle classes and lesser nobilities- was an awakening their consciences to the importance of religion in their lives, as it was so entwined with morality that their beliefs and practices defined the norms of their public and privates lives. Those who embraced Protestantism felt relieved from priestly pressure, since they could now read the Bible themselves, thanks to its translation into German done by Luther himself during his year in hiding; but from then on, the Protestants also felt a greater weight of responsibility for their own conduct. Those who abominated what they called "that licentiousness" and remained loyal to Catholicism also felt compelled to understand and practice it in a better way. In both cases it was a great strain for them that their rulers did not share their same religious stance.

On the grounds of popular feeling, theologians, both Calvinists and of the new Catholic Order of the Jesuits, contended that a ruler who held the wrong beliefs –i.e. different from the people- could be deposed. For their part, political and religious leaders of both sides endeavored to give religion a refined philosophical structure: the Protestants in the theocratic government of the Swiss canton of Geneva, led by Calvin from 1542 until his death in 1564, and the Catholics in the XIX Ecumenical Council of Trent, which worked intermittently from 1545 to 1564, curiously in sync with its bitter rivals.

The Calvinist doctrine of "predestination", that in certain instances can lead to existential apathy, had the opposite effect on the Protestants, instigating each believer into showing through his/her exemplary life of hard work and irreproachable temperance, that he or she was one the "chosen" or "saints" and that, as such, had a right to govern the still unredeemed masses. It was the beginnings of what Max Weber called the "Protestant Ethic", which inspired the "Spirit of Capitalism" once it unfettered itself from its dogmatic rigidity.

The doctrine of the Trent Counter-Reformation, in contrast, put the interpretation of the Holy Scriptures and the Tradition firmly in the hands of the Roman Catholic Church, including original sin, justification and achievement of grace by means of the seven sacraments, the sacrifice of the mass with transubstantiation, the priestly order and hierarchy, the indulgences, and the veneration of images. Together, this combination tended, in the political aspect, toward authoritarianism and, in the intellectual aspect, toward emasculating dogmatism.

This extreme religious polarization, however, did not erase the great advances made by Renaissance Humanism toward the historical perspective of Man and his capability for action, nor diminish the new geographic and cultural frontiers that maritime navigation had opened. All these circumstances caused the socio-political situation to vary from one great nation to another, so it is convenient to review each one separately.

In the Iberian Peninsula a military and seafaring zenith was being reached, but production and administrative activities were being neglected. The lesser nobility and the middle classes had many things to do in the army, in overseas settling, or as clerics or missionaries, by reason of having decided to commit to defending the two obsolete medieval institutions: the Empire and the Papacy. With industry and commerce in shambles, coupled with the authoritarian and dogmatic attitude toward intellectual activities, it also meant the end of betterment for education. We can explain this situation by what Toynbee called "nemesis of creativity"[2], since the Spaniards held fast to their obdurate religious fervor that allowed them to achieve their "Reconquista", at a time when they would have been much better served by systematic knowledge and negotiations.

In Italy, the drive towards humanism and the arts and sciences was gradually overwhelmed by Spanish militarism, most conspicuously in Milan, by reason of the authoritarianism it fostered, and not only in the Kingdom of Naples and the Papal States, but also in Florence and in most other "provincial states". Venice remained an independent state and imposed controls over its Inquisition, but its level was good only relative to the others, since the loss of its possessions in the eastern Mediterranean made it fall into a gradual decadence.

In France, the most precious gift in its people's eyes was national unity, hence Lutheranism -the first Protestant movement- was considered backward and subversive because its military and political actions came under the command of the feudal lords. Nevertheless, the later Calvinist movement was very well received by the middle classes and lesser nobility in the south, which would give rise to terrible wars of religion.

In Germany, we saw that religious peace was achieved in 1555. So, from then on, the conflict between Catholics and Lutherans would be fought more through preaching and education, with the former in charge of the Jesuits who, by the year 1600, had increased the proportion of Catholics from 30% to 40%.

In the Low Countries, whose monarch was Philip II, also King of Spain, part of the population accepted the Calvinist variety of Protestantism, which would launch them squarely into the wars of religion.

In the British Isles, England and Wales affirmed their Anglican religion under the reign of Elizabeth Tudor, though part of the population adopted Calvinism, known as "Puritans" to the others. Scotland adopted the most extreme version of Calvinism, the Presbyterian religion, which did not admit bishops. Ireland remained Roman Catholic under English rule.

The Wars of Religion had three main settings: France, the Low Countries, and the British Islands, and Spain became involved in all three:

In France, 8 civil wars were fought between 1559 and 1598, pitting the Governments of the three weak sons of Henry II and Catherine d'Medici, supported by the northern nobility's Catholic League and backed by Spain, against the lesser nobility and middle classes of the south, called "Huguenots".
In 1576, Jean Bodin published a book calling on both factions to submit to an absolute monarch who was willing to guarantee his subjects freedom of religious practice: Religion would be considered a private affair, like business and family. This idea gradually gained ground on both sides, until the leader of the Huguenots, Henry of Bourbon and Navarre, inherited the crown of France and accepted to abjure his Protestantism (Paris is well worth a mass!), and decreed the Edict of Tolerance in Nantes, in 1598.

In the Low Countries, Catholics and Calvinists clashed in 1564, and Philip II sent in an army of Spanish "tercios", whose commander crushed the unrest with such ferocity that the Calvinists of the south (Belgium) fled to the north (Holland) where, protected by the easy flooding of the fields, they could receive aid from the Huguenots and the English monarchy. In 1581, the war began to stabilize, with the south firmly Catholic and Holland abjuring their monarch and starting to function as an independent state in 1585.

The Presbyterian Scots dethroned their Catholic Queen Mary Stuart, whom they imprisoned and "sold" to her cousin Elizabeth, who kept her in prison until ordering her execution in 1585. This caused Philip II, King of Spain and, by then, also of Portugal, to launch his famous Invincible Armada against England in 1588, with 8,000 sailors and 19,000 soldiers on board. The English fleet, equipped with longer range "culverins" than its rival's cannons, harried it in the Channel. This fact was not in itself decisive, but it caused the inept Spanish commander, selected only for his being of the high nobility, to take a series of bad decisions: Not to invade England with the "tercios" stationed in Flanders, but instead to sail around the British Isles, losing half his men and ships to the storms. This naval confrontation signaled the decline of Spanish power and the ascent of the English.

7.3.- The Science from Renaissance up to 1650

In matters of astronomy, the Renaissance only inherited from Antiquity Ptolemy's theories, containing two important errors: First, considering Earth as the center of all celestial movement; and Second, although Ptolemy knew it was a spherical body, he miscalculated its circumference as one fourth the actual one, notwithstanding that Eratosthenes had calculated it with remarkable accuracy 400 years before him. This second error led Columbus to discover what he thought was the coast of Asia. The Portuguese had also calculated the real dimension of our planet, having crossed the Equator in 1483, which was established and accepted by all when Amerigo Vespucci published his map in 1507 showing South America as a "new world". The first error had yet to be corrected: It was done by Nicolaus Copernicus in Poland in 1530, because it did not seem "natural" to him, and to other mathematicians, the apparent retrograde motion of the planets. When he calculated their orbits presuming the Sun as the center of planetary movements, he found -what seemed to him- perfect circular orbits. Nonetheless, knowing that the Church arrogated the *auctoritas* to decide what was true or false in astronomy, according to their interpretation of Biblical passages, and that by then the theological discussions were very heated, he deferred the publication of his work until his old age, and sent it to the Pope as a mere dual study: One, if the Earth was at the center, then the planets moved around in coil-like trajectories; if the Sun was the center, then all the planets, the Earth included, described what he thought were perfect circles around it. Indeed, there were many other problems to attend to first and, since no one made an issue of this heliocentric theory, things rested this way for a time.

The practice of chemistry made some headway during the 16th century, thanks mainly to the Swiss Paracelsus, by making better chemical ovens and laboratories, but the theory reached this era so mixed up with alchemy and Aristotelian philosophy, that its followers vainly tried to find an explanation for all changes in matter which were also backed up in the Bible. They never did. Nonetheless, they made some progress in the preparation of medicines and in the application and uses of fertilizers in agriculture, and their methods of analyses and experimentation paved the road for future breakthroughs.

Regarding biological knowledge, the Renaissance first based it on the works of the Roman Pliny the Elder, whose errors and description of monsters were amended first by Barbaro in 1493 and then by others. Through the 16th century there began to appear monographic descriptions of the flora and fauna of recently discovered or visited countries, but the true revolution was effected by the colonizers and seafarers, since the former covered much of America with domesticated European animal species, like cattle, horses, donkeys, goats, sheep, and fowl and the latter took back to Europe new vegetal species such as tomato, potato, corn, tobacco, and cocoa from America.

In regard to human anatomy and physiology, and, consequently, the treatment, healing, and surgical operation of diseases, the Renaissance mainly inherited the theory and practice of Galen, but in this area noticeable advances were made, mainly at Padua University. There, Flemish physician Vesalius, who had studied in Paris, drew a systematic series of illustrations of human anatomy which he succeeded in having Titian paint in his workshop at Venice with an advanced technique. The result was the famous *Humani corporis fabrica* book, edited in 1543, which caused a stir in all European universities by patently showing what a marvel the human body is. His Padua chair was later occupied by Fallopius and others who completed his work. Elsewhere, the Spanish physician Servet discovered pulmonary circulation and English medical practitioner Harvey completed the description of the two circulatory loops and explained the role that the heart plays in them (1628).[3]

With all this, we are approaching the birth of what we call "the modern scientific method"[4]. It seems convenient for us here to distinguish three aspects of it, according to what each of three savants, more or less coetaneous, contributed, since only the combination of those three attitudes and works can give us a complete idea of the obstacles that had to be surmounted in order for modern science to make its arrival. In general terms, we will say that Francis Bacon contributed political respectability, Galileo Galilei filled it with physico-mathematical contents and Rene Descartes gave it formal philosophical rigor.

Francis Bacon (1581-1626) was a minister of England's King James I -monarch of the only one of the great western nations completely free of the Catholic Church's control and under no obligation to follow the opinions held by the Lutheran or Calvinist theologians either. These circumstances are the very reason that Bacon's idea of formally separating the intellectual fields of religion and science, each one respecting the other, not only did not scandalize the English, but were very well received by thinkers in other parts of Western Europe. Bacon demarcated the field of science as that based on systematic observations and experiments designed to understand Nature's processes. This eminently reasonable proposal was designed to avoid confrontations between both disciplines: The sciences abstaining from pronouncing on theological aspects or those concerning the norms for human conduct, and religion having confidence in accepting that the scientific method was the appropriate way for knowing and understanding the works of the Creator, and if its leaders felt there was a discrepancy, they should try an allegorical reading of the Bible. Generally, this stance and attitude prevailed, more among Protestant thinkers than Catholics ones, which is why there was much less confrontation in the northern countries between science and religion, at least for a time.

Galileo Galilei (1564-1642) was a university teacher and researcher in Italy, and his greatest feat was comprehending that the laws of celestial mechanics that a careful observation of the skies permitted to be expressed by means of mathematical formulas, were also valid here on Earth. That a body, the same up above as here below, stays at rest until a force is applied to it, and then keeps moving in a straight line and at the same speed. Here below friction thwarts us from seeing it clearly, but we can deduce it mathematically. This world, then, is not as imperfect as we thought, nor are the skies perfect. He demonstrated thus using the first telescopes available, looking at mountains and valleys on the Moon and satellites revolving around Jupiter. In fact, the Earth was part of the skies, since it rotated around the Sun: He adopted Copernicus' heliocentric theory, amending it with what Kepler had found, that the planets' and Earth's orbits around the Sun were slightly elliptical, with the Sun occupying one of the *foci.* This insinuation of science into the whole of the universe not only attacked the monotheist notion that "The sky is up there, the world here immobile, and hell below", but also destroyed the Platonic world of ideas, and introduced notions that seemed to go against common sense, like the inertia of all bodies, the movements of the Earth, and the imperfection of the skies. So, the Church imposed its *auctoritas* and forced Galileo to recant. ("But it moves", he is said to have said.)

Rene Descartes (1596-1650) was a French official, researcher, and philosopher, famous for his *Discourse de la méthode* in which he tries to begin afresh the entire structure of knowledge, with the solid philosophical foundation of *cogito ergo sum* ("I think, therefore I am") as its cornerstone, and then proceed step by step to build all knowledge, succeeding in establishing deductions with the help of mathematics. Even though it is possible to advance only in a limited part of knowledge with this method, the greater value lies in the obligation it presupposes of making available to all the other scientists or philosophers all that one has been able to discover following its strict and accepted rules of proof. The idea is that everyone understands what was done, what conclusions were arrived at, and thereby be in a position to recreate or design new experiments or make new observations, which would eventually confirm, modify, or reject the proposed hypotheses.

So, by the year 1650 the newly born science had succeeded in ousting religion from deciding what was true or not in regards to the description, quantification, and prediction of how matter behaves, be it in the skies or in Earth; this also applied to living matter, but only on a limited scale. But it had done so at the cost of not only abstaining to opine about what was theologically true or "revealed" and which behavior was morally "good" or compulsory, but also by each one personally accepting the dictums of the Church, if he was Catholic, or what was written in the Bible, if Protestant, in these cases.

7.4.- Wars and Political Ideas from 1598 to 1660

Thanks to Henry IV's minister Sully, France began, from 1598 on, to put its administration on a budget in order to assign priority to public works, such as communications infrastructure, and to direct the energies of the people to hunting, fishing, and colonization enterprises in North America. England also made a similar effort and founded Virginia and Massachusetts during the reign of James I.

Spain and Holland continued warring until 1607, when they signed a 12-year truce. Holland took advantage of it to resolve its basic internal structure, such as the relationships between civil and church authorities and between the central government and the provinces. They also began to sail to the East Indies and displace the Portuguese from the spice trade. Spain did not find anything better to do that expel the last Moorish communities from the Peninsula (those of the Valencia orchard and irrigated fields).

Germany and Italy enjoyed peace from 1598 to 1618, but then a very destructive war began in Prague, capital of Bohemia, in the Habsburg patrimonial lands, that would last 30 years. It started as a confrontation between the Emperor, installed in his patrimonial lands and allied with Bavaria, against the Protestant autonomous lords, but in 1621 Spain and its Italian possessions entered the fray on the Catholic side and Holland did the same on the Protestant camp, being joined in 1625 by Denmark. The Catholics prevailed in 1629. Two great nations, France and England, had remained outside the conflict: The latter, as we will see, will never be involved, while France, under the guidance of Richelieu, minister of Louis XIII, was busy resolving its domestic problems with the Huguenots, and did not feel ready yet.

Nevertheless, in 1630 France felt herself sufficiently strong to subsidize and diplomatically back the entry in the war of Lutheran Sweden, whose King Gustavus Adolphus II proved to be a magnificent general, organizer, and provider for his army: He won three battles against the Catholics but died in the last one. His generals were defeated by the combined army of the Spanish "tercios" and the Imperial troops in 1634.

This battle compelled France to enter the fray as a military ally of the Protestants in 1635. The war expanded and was fought in five land fronts and in the seas of the West and East Indies. The war was bitterly and hard fought, and the contributions in men and money that the entire populations had to provide were of such magnitude that the decisive factor turned out to be, in the long run, the quality of the socio-political institutions of the rival groups: The end result favored those countries which had a larger proportion of bourgeoisie and middle classes, like France, Holland, and Sweden, and some "provincial states", such as Brandenburg in Germany and Savoy in Italy. The Habsburg monarchies, the Spanish and the Imperial ones, were, by comparison, moth-eaten and ossified.

The Spanish collapse began in June, 1640, when the people of Catalonia, tired of supporting the transit of armies through their lands, rose against their King and asked France for help, who immediately sent troops there. In December of that same year, Portugal declared its independence from Spain, opening another military front in the Peninsula, while trying to save Brazil from being entirely taken by the Dutch, who had invaded the northeastern part. In May of 1643 came the *coup de grace* when the Spanish "tercios" based in the Low Countries were almost annihilated by the much better artillery, ammunition, and provisions-equipped French army, led by

Condé. The war still raged on for another five years, but when the "kingdom" of Naples rebelled against Spain in 1648, the Emperor sued for peace and negotiations began.

While this terrible war lasted, Dutchman Hugh Groot (Grocius) wrote what can be called the first book in international law: he tried to demonstrate the imperious need to respect formal treaties between nations. He also argued the need for the warring factions to behave justly and charitably towards the civil population, the prisoners, and the wounded. For Grocius, maintaining social order is the essence of law, since Nature impels us to live in society and we have to obey this "law" or instinct, according to Aquinas' legal scheme.

In the peace negotiations which took place in the Province of Westphalia, Grocius' ideas were taken into account, and, in contrast, no church officials were called in to participate, neither Catholic nor Protestant. Religious tolerance was agreed on for the whole of Germany, and political autonomy for all the sovereign lords. France and Spain fought each other for 11 more years, until the latter recaptured Catalonia.

In England, meanwhile, King Charles I Stuart was immersed in a struggle for power with the Parliament regarding authority, which is why he failed to convene it from 1629 on. This meant, however, that he lacked the income to intervene in wars. When he convened it again in 1640 in order to ask them for contributions, the conflict grew into a schism and an armed confrontation between the royal army and the Puritan militias, with the latter emerging victorious in 1645. This was followed by the dictatorship of Oliver Cromwell, their leader, until his death in 1659, and by the monarchical Restoration in 1660.

During this conflict, numerous political works defending the rebels' position were published, as was also a great work favoring absolutism: Thomas Hobbes'. The former works are usually divided into five groups: 1) The lesser nobility, who comprised much of the government and Parliament and sought an agrarian reform; they remind us of the Gracchi brothers. 2) The Calvinist Puritans, who wanted complete religious freedom. 3) The group of extremist sects, such as the Baptists and the Quakers, who wanted church structures to disappear and leave the faithful alone. 4) The "Levelers", mainly militia troops. 5) The "Diggers" or peasants who wanted a right to occupy land.

We have this to say in regard to Hobbes' book: That he made a much more coherent case in favor of absolutism than Jean Bodin's and included much of the maintenance of social order demanded by Grocius. But Hobbes' postulation was based on what he thought had been "the state of nature" in primitive man: "…solitary, poor, nasty, brutal, and short." This made him commit the fundamental error of believing that each individual acts only for strict personal selfishness, without taking into account, as we saw in Chapter II, that in our evolution as hominids we were conditioned to live in society, in such way that our security, identity, and curiosity-related instincts address both the individual and the group. This error caused him to overestimate the importance of the head of state, who he did not think could be subject to control.

Nevertheless, Hobbes' argument greatly strengthened the separation between politics and religion, making the latter a private affair and the former an instrument for tolerance towards all those beliefs and practices that did not contravene or pose a danger to social order.

7.5.- Panorama of the World in 1650 and Arrival to Limited Government from 1660 to 1715

Shortly before the beginning of this period in 1650, the population of the various regions of the world (ordered by geographical criterion) is estimated as follows:

REGION	Millions of Inhabitants
Western Europe	78.5
Russia and Siberia	12
Ottoman Empire (In Europe, Asia, and Africa)	40.5
Sub-Saharan Africa	32
Iran, Central Asia, Tibet and Mongolia	22
India, South East Asia, Pacific and Australia	162
China, Korea, and Japan	221
America	12
TOTAL	580

Some figures in this table may seem almost incredible to us: i.e. America, which today is home to 14% of the world population, accounted for only 2% then. The reason was that its population, which before the Conquest had perhaps numbered 35 million, had catastrophically plummeted to only 12 million, mainly due to epidemics. Also striking might be to learn the huge scope and population of the Ottoman Empire, but it had already entered into decadence, and, when in 1683 it mounted an ill-advised battle in what is known as the Second Siege of Vienna, it was driven back, and after 16 years of war, Austria recovered all of Hungary up to the Carpathian Mountains and the middle section of the Danube River, up in front the fortress of Belgrade.

The figures that should forcefully impact us, though, are those of the following trends: We saw in section 5.11 that the world saw a population growth from 95 million in the year 350 BCE to some 245 million in the year 650 CE, which means a 2.5-fold increase in 1,000 years. Now we are seeing that in the following 1,000 years, up to 1650, the world population increased to only 580 million, meaning a similar 2.37-fold increase in that period. This is mainly attributable to the devastating plagues of the 6th century, the Black Death of the mid-14th century, and the demographic catastrophe in the Americas for 100 years after the Spanish Conquest. The most mind-boggling data, however, is what follows from the year 1650 up to the present time: In the mere 350 years up until the year 2000, a third of the aforementioned time spans, the world population will multiply 10-fold, from 580 million to 6 billion, or 28 times more rapidly than during the 2000 years before 1650.

What was the cause of this unprecedented acceleration? In truth, a series of "revolutions" or radical changes in the efficiency of the collective manner of operating, that we can call the commercial, political, industrial, and information revolutions. All of them saw the light and developed in Western Europe or in its overseas territories, before being adopted, at times only partially and selectively, by other cultures.

In view of the above, for our purpose we will follow the significant events in Western Europe from 1660 to 1715. During those 55 years, the figure of Louis XIV - the "Sun King" of France- shines, but the most pivotal events for the future took place in England.

Briefly, Louis XIV succeeded in settling the northeastern border of France to its present-day boundary, but was unable to incorporate the Spanish Low Countries (Belgium) or the Rhineland, nor subject The Netherlands to his will, so he signed peace with them in 1698.

A great deal of the political and military gains that Louis XIV was able to secure from 1660 to 1685, were possible because those were the years of the reign of Charles II Stuart of England and Scotland. The "Merry Monarch" of the Restoration liked to deal in financial terms, either receiving sizeable payments from Louis for abstaining to intervene "in the Continent", or paying members of Parliament to be left alone to reign at his pleasure. This easy period ended, however, at the death of Charles, because his brother and heir James II had the unsound idea, politically speaking, of converting to Catholicism, which is why he was deposed by the "Glorious Revolution" of 1688 and had to flee to France. The English pondered what to do: Return to the Republic and then again to civil war? They decided on the middle of the road and clever path of preserving the monarchy but limiting it clearly and formally. To do so, they invited a sister of the king, named Mary Stuart, namesake of her famous great-grandmother, but Protestant and married to the *Stadtholder* of The Netherlands, William of Orange. They would be recognized as Queen and King if they accepted the limitations written in the famous Declaration that later was enacted as the Bill of Rights, whose first three articles say, in essence:

1.- The Parliament makes all the laws.

2.- Parliament is composed of two Chambers, one inherited by the Lords,
   and one elected by the Commons (Middle class owners and lesser nobility)

3.- No English subject can de detained or put in prison without due process of law.

William and Mary signed the Declaration in February, 1689, and it is still valid today, reason why it is, by far, the oldest politically valid constitution of the world, the one which ushered in limited government in one of the great western European nations, paving the road to democracy.

The author of the theory that underpinned this great political breakthrough, and who kept defending it and giving it prestige, was John Locke. Even if he knew that in all the intellectual disciplines of humanism -politics among them- it is not possible to attain certainty to the degree it can be done in the physico-mathematical sciences, he thought that if one examined the results of the recommended actions with an open and tolerant mind, and embraced the responsibility of making the modifications that were needed, we could approach some certainty and come nearer to the truth.

By then, in the field of chemistry, Boyle and Mariotte had, separately, reached the conclusion that the volume occupied by gases is inversely proportional to the pressure applied on them, if the temperature remains constant. In physics, Isaac Newton arrived at his famous law of universal gravitation, which says that bodies attract in direct proportion to their masses and inversely proportional to the squares of the distances between them.

Such were the circumstances at the death, at the end of the year 1700, of Spain's last Habsburg King. He had left in his will as heir to his throne a relative of his who was also a grandchild of Louis XIV Bourbon of France. This threw Europe into a war in which England, already united to Scotland in the United Kingdom of Great Britain and Ireland, took part with armies on the Continent in aid of The Netherlands and Brandenburg, until peace was achieved in 1713.

Austria, which was France and Spain's main rival, had recaptured all of Hungary from the Turks, as we saw, and received from Spain the Low Countries (Belgium), the Duchy of Milan, and the Kingdom of Naples, although it was lost again to Spain in 1734. Brandenburg, which had lands both in the northeast and in the Rhine, was given the name of Kingdom of Prussia.

France hardly lost anything and saw its Dynasty extend to Spain, on condition that the new King, Philip V of Bourbon, renounce his right to the crown of France. Spain kept all its colonies in America and had already accepted the independence of Portugal, which had recovered Brazil in its entirety.

In 1714, because Queen Anne, daughter of William and Mary, died without surviving issue, the crown of the United Kingdom passed on to the Elector of Hanover, George I. Louis XVI died in 1715, and his throne was inherited by a minor great-grandchild. A new era was commencing.

7.6.- Commercial Revolution and Enlightenment from 1715 to 1763

One of the ways to deduce how strong, ideologically speaking, were the organized religions in Western Europe in the period we are starting to see, is examining the state of Freemasonry in each nation. It was founded in London between 1716 and 1723. Who conceived it and why? Liberal politicians and thinkers who felt that some aspects of their ideologies were so "advanced" that they were apt to be rejected by any Christian church. For this reason, it seemed convenient to keep them secret and promote them in confidence, preaching in public only those positions which would not be cause for scandal.

We can also ponder the degree to which individual liberty of opinion and beliefs were respected in each nation, by examining how its rulers reacted to the Masonic Order's inroads. In Great Britain, they were considered groups or clubs with esoteric tendencies or practices within political parties, which after a time divided in two branches, the York and Scottish rites. In France, the situation was different, since its early initiates, like Montesquieu and Voltaire, had to hide in anonymity to publish their Persian and English Letters, and even so they were persecuted and had to express their ideas with the utmost care. In the Catholic part of Germany, the situation was akin to that in France, while in the Lutheran part –Prussia- even the King himself, Frederic II, entered the fraternal organization and had it under his control. In Italy, Spain, and Portugal it was banned during the 18th century, so any activity of this type was illegal.

Regarding each society's capacity for trade, we should examine the ability of its members to establish concerns large enough to engage in the construction or purchase of ships, to hire honorable, capable personnel and crews that could navigate, trade, and wage combat if need be, and to have the capital necessary to pay their sustenance during the trip and provide them with merchandise for bartering and sale and money to buy species and other valuable goods. Among the most advanced in those affairs were The Netherlands and Great Britain, since they applied the Calvinist tradition of forming "social virtues", such as honesty, trust, cooperation, and a sense of duty toward the other members of their community. In France, society tended to family enterprises, so in order to carry out great expeditions, their absolutist government's intervention was always needed. (5)

When did the Commercial Revolution begin? Historians fail to agree even on its existence, let alone its dating, but we can say this: Maritime trade began with the discovery of the Route to the East Indies, since Vasco da Gama returned to Lisbon in 1500 with his three ships loaded with spices. However, it is clear that this and all the other voyages of the Portuguese during the 16th century did not suffice to bring about a "revolution" in the commercial activities of the western Europeans.

Around the year 1550, the Spaniards began to substitute the gold sacked from American civilizations, or mined at their traditional sources, with silver from the mines in Potosi and Zacatecas, and other places, which from then on flowed continuously, though at fluctuating levels. This flow of precious metals gave European trade a new monetary liquidity, mainly to the suppliers of military equipment, on which a great portion of the money was spent.

Around the year 1600, the Dutch broke the Portuguese monopoly on the spice trade and soon displaced them. Nevertheless, I think we should not mark the start of the Commercial revolution until the two great nations that were in the midst of a boom -France and England- entered in earnest into overseas trade and colonization. Even if during the rest of the 17th century both powers continued their colonization of North America and wrested some Caribbean islands from Spain, where they established sugar cane plantations worked by Negro slaves, and all that generated export trade, they could not establish an important commercial presence in India as long as the greater part of it continued to be the Great Moguls Empire, i.e. until 1707.

It is, then, from 1715 on when both nations embark on a major sustained effort to control Indian and North American trade. In both cases, the United Kingdom emerged victorious thanks to her naval fleet prevailing over the French one in the Seven Years War, which ended in 1763. So, it seems that 1715 is a good date for marking the dawn of the Commercial Revolution, also in view of the fact that Spain and Portugal's colonial empires doubled their populations during the 18th century and developed more efficient administrations. Russia began, during the reign of Peter I the Great, to appear on the European scene, both militarily and commercially. We can say that Manchu Dynasty of China reached its zenith in the 18th century, as borne out by the fact that its trade by sea with the Westerners and by land with the Russians began to be significant. The same cannot be said of Japan and Korea, which remained hermetically sealed off.

In Western Europe, a 25-year peaceful period, from 1715 to 1740, was followed by two wars which involved nearly all the European powers: the War of the Austrian Succession from 1740 to 1748, and the Seven Years' War from 1757 to 1763. The latter's main results were colonial and naval, with Great Britain, as we saw, obtaining both India and Canada, and the English navy becoming ruler of the seas. In Europe, there was just one important territorial and population change: Prussia succeeded in grabbing from Austria the rich province of Silesia, which had been Polish but by then was totally German and Lutheran. This change of events so equalized the power of both states that, from then on, one had to refer to the German "Dualism", in which Catholic Austria was going to compete with Lutheran Prussia for the leadership of the rest of the Germanic states.

In regard to philosophical thought, the Scot David Hume wrote in 1740 a theory of knowledge which borrows from Leibnitz the distinction between two types of truths: 1) The strictly logical ones of mathematics, true out of necessity and whose opposites are impossible or unimaginable, and 2) The "truths of fact", assertions about events that may involve a high degree of probability but can never reach total certainty, which is why they are contingent and their opposites do not imply a logical contradiction. To these two, Hume adds a third type which he calls "values", such as goodness, beauty, justice, liberty, or utility, whose definition or relationships contains factors that cannot be rationally demonstrated, and that he calls "conventions".

Consequently, Hume considered absurd trying to reach systems of religion, ethics, or politics through pure reason. He thought that history demonstrates that instincts and passions have led man to establish his purposes and aims. That is why he believed that politics should base its studies on human nature and on sociological facts, such as subjects' interests, usages, and opinions. This "advanced" thought was well accepted even in British conservative circles, despite the fact that Hume fought superstition and did not believe in the immortality of the human soul.

In 1748, Montesquieu published *The Spirit of the Laws* in support of his argument considering laws to be "necessary relationships deriving from the nature of things". For this reason, laws have to change in accordance with the circumstances in order for them to conserve their applicability. He examines the whole course of history and when he arrives to the Europe of his time he makes an argument for the superiority of the constitutionality, libertarianism, tolerance, and uniformity of British laws in comparison with the absolutism, arbitrary mien, intolerance, and wide variety of the local laws of France. He recommends his country to make a transition toward the division of powers: had it been put into practice, it would have arrived at his famous division of the executive, legislative, and judicial powers.

Economic theory in France was based on a kind of illustrated individualism. To develop it, Helvetius and Quesnay advanced opposing strategies, the former a public system for educating the entire population, and the latter that the state abstain from intervening, leaving the laws of supply and demand to operate freely. Turgot, a future minister, introduced the concept of progress, coming about as a result of the aggregate experience that structured and enriched a civilization. All these ideas were widely disseminated thanks to being systematized and published in the Encyclopedia, edited by Diderot and D'Alembert.

Meanwhile, the British colonies on North America's Atlantic coast had been developing in two different groups:

Most of the colonies in the north were established by disaffected Anglicans, who wanted to begin a new type of community based on their own free work. The first one, Massachusetts, was simultaneously joined by the colony of New Amsterdam, founded by the Dutch. Then, Connecticut and Rhode Island broke off from the first colony and New Hampshire was founded farther north. In 1664, the British took control of the Dutch colony, renaming its main part New York and its southern part New Jersey. Lastly, Pennsylvania was assigned to the Quaker Sect in 1682.

In the south, the royal chartered colonies prevailed, and their economies were mainly based on plantations worked by Negro slave labor. The first of them, Virginia, had been joined by Maryland, founded in 1632 by Catholics, and later, during the Restoration, by the Carolinas. Swedish Delaware was later acquired and lastly, in 1732, Georgia, next door to Spanish Florida, was added.

Even in comparison with their home country, the British (and Dutch, and Swedish) colonies in North America had the societies with the most democratically advanced institutions in the world. This was particularly striking in the northern colonies, because it was still very evident in Great Britain the aristocratic mold from which it was emerging, as its lower classes had no properties and could not vote. In North America, in contrast, there was no aristocracy, but neither was there a landless peasant class, since each immigrant had a right to a homestead which he could own if he settled there and cultivated the land.

Up until the year 1763, the American colonials had been very pleased with their British metropolis, since it had won the French and Indian War, thus gaining Canada and ending all French claims in North America east of the Mississippi river. This feat had opened for them a wide perspective for colonizing the immense wooded area to the west of the Appalachian Mountains, up to the great river, without European interference.

So, in 1763 many Frenchmen were acutely conscious that their socio-political system was very inadequate in comparison with the British one, which had defeated them in the maritime and colonial war with only half of their population. The British, on the contrary, were euphoric; that would lead them to impose authoritarian measures on their colonies, driving them to rebellion.

7.7.- The Beginnings of the Industrial Revolution (1763-1795)

In the year 1763, the world was ready to begin its industrial revolution and it was precisely in Great Britain where it took place, since its navy gave it undisputed control of the seas and its merchant marine had multiplied six-fold (6) in the century since Oliver Cromwell had decreed that all imports had to be brought in on English bottoms. All this generated a huge demand for advance products for export, in order to obtain the money necessary for buying the overseas raw materials and luxury products.

First to react to this demand was the textile industry, which made clothes with Egyptian imported cotton, but was still doing it the artisan way, i.e. using only human toil and ability. The problem was being tackled since 1764 with machines that threaded continuously with several spindles, which were then taken to mechanical looms. A great force was required to move all that, so from 1769 on several factories sprung up near water currents, whose force was used to turn a turbine which would actuate a rotating shaft which was installed inside the factory premises and connected to all spindling machines and looms by means of pulleys and belts (7).

But all of this was still precarious: What was needed was a source of motor energy unfettered by considerations of location or power, as water currents were. Coming to the aid of textile manufacturers, some 30 years later, would be the steam engine. As the first and most useful of the applications of the modern scientific method that developed and matured enough to bear technological fruits, we will take a glimpse at its historical development.

Since the mid-17th century, the pressure and vacuum force that could be obtained by expanding overheated water steam had been studied and calculated, and boilers and cylinder and piston engines had been made, but their efficiency was terribly low due to their having to be stopped in order for the steam to condensate at the end of each piston stroke.

In May of 1765, a student of the University of Glasgow, Scotland, named James Watt devised the solution to this problem, which was to provide the cylinder with valves to expel the steam after having expanded at the end of each stroke and admitting new overheated steam. The expanded steam was sent to a nearby vessel to be condensed into water, which could again be sent to the boiler, vaporized and overheated, as many times as needed.

Twelve years passed since this invention was patented until the first engine made with this design was put into operation for pumping water out from mines, since the manufacturing entrepreneur, Matthew Boulton, to which Watt pitched his design had to first convince the mine owners. Then the construction itself took considerable time, as it required specialized personnel and tools in order for the vertical cylinder - whose piston had to be pushed by steam- to produce a forced movement with such a precision that almost none of the expansive power of the overheated steam was lost. Then, that force had to be transmitted by a swing beam to the twin piston in the neighboring cylinder, where water was to be pumped, which required many precision adjustments. Once all obstacles were surmounted, the first steam engine of the world was installed in the year 1777 in a tin mine in Cornwall, where it operated for 125 years, until 1902 (8).

More time was required to invent the connecting rod and crankshaft mechanism which permitted converting the reciprocating movement of the piston into the rotating movement of the power shaft. With it in place, it became possible from 1795 on to install anywhere within a factory a coal-fired water boiler and its condenser to operate a steam engine and, with it, move the main power shaft. In order to stabilize the rotating movement, an inertia flywheel was added to the shaft (9). This breakthrough came just in time, because in the United States, Eli Whitney invented in 1793 the machine for removing the seeds from the cotton fiber, so that cotton production exploded in the southern states.

The Industrial Revolution began to pick up speed once new components prompted the development of others: The steam engine needed cheap, abundant coal to feed the boiler, and steel for making it; in order for the coal to be plentiful and cheap, it had to be transported by river and canal barges, and the canals needed steel aqueducts and bridges built. To produce steel you need coke, and to make coke you have to blast air currents inside the furnace. Between the years 1776 and 1780, the steam engine would prove to be the most efficient way of doing so. Thanks to it, steel could be produced cheaply, aqueducts and bridges easily constructed, and coal effortlessly transported by barges, thus forming a "virtuous circle".

7.8.- Political and Social Events from 1763 to 1830

When the Seven Years' War ended in 1763, King George III, the first Hanover to be born in Great Britain, had practically become the head of the Executive Power again, since he was capable of naming Prime Ministers who were not the leaders of the majority party in Parliament. One measure that seemed called for by his government was to make the colonies help defray defense expenditures since, to begin with, they already numbered 2 million against 9 million in the metropolis and also, a sizeable portion of the navy and military expenses were spent in their defense. Since the colonies did not agree to chip in, legal documents were taxed in 1765. Again a refusal, another step back in London, and then a tax on imported tea, which sparked a simulated Indian attack in Boston Harbor in late 1773.

The fighting began in 1775 and the following year all 13 colonies reached an agreement and declared their independence. In 1778, they entered an alliance with monarchical France, the Netherlands, and Spain. That would lead to Great Britain's first defeat at sea in a century. With that, France was able to disembark troops in North America which, together with the American rebels, secured a victory in Yorktown with the surrender of 7,000 British soldiers.

In the Treaty of Versailles, signed in 1783, Great Britain recognized the independence of the American Colonies and their property over the huge wooded area between the Appalachian Mountains and the Mississippi River, returned some colonies to France and Spain, and recognized the freedom of the seas. This humiliation also meant the end of the personal reign of George III and a return to Prime Ministers being the leaders of a majority in Parliament.

In the Constitutional Convention of 1787, the newborn United States of America set forth a solid system of government, based both on the principles of living together in society and taking into account human fragilities by providing ways to amend errors through a balance of powers, both between individuals and the state and also between the states and the federal government and among the three powers: executive, legislative, and judicial.

This Constitution was ratified by the states in July 1788, and came into effect April, 1789 -one month before the French Revolution began- with newly elected officials, and George Washington as President.

The French assistance given to the colonists allowed many people to become acquainted with this new type of egalitarian and freedom-loving society, capable of sacrificing for others when needed. This had an accelerating effect in shaping their own democratizing ideas.

Probably the most unpopular institution in France was the aristocracy, which was not involved in commerce and industry, but only had roles in government, army, and the church. Aristocrats' mediocre performance over the previous century, however, had taken a severe toll on their prestige.

In contrast, the middle classes, already including the lesser nobility, had greatly grown in numbers and aspired to manage public affairs in a way that the inefficient royal government could not do without endangering its entire structure. That is why when the severe financial crisis hit, the King was forced to convene the States-General, equivalent to a Parliament, in May, 1789, which brought about his demise.

It is well known how events in France followed on the heels of one another, so we will only comment the following:

1.- The socio-political changes that had to be made were so colossal, that the reform movement developed its own momentum and turned revolutionary, overstepping the midpoint and not stopping until the Terror.

2.- Even with that imperfect level of democratization and the disorder prevailing in the country in September, 1792, the *levée en masse* of the French nation was capable of defeating an all-European coalition in the Battle of Valmy.

The strength of the people in arms kept being corroborated over the next three years, until 1795, when it was clear that France could not be defeated by any coalition. Quite the contrary: it had already incorporated Belgium and the Rhineland, where its democratizing moves were very well received, despite part of the population speaking Flemish or German. In The Netherlands, where the Batavian Republic was created, the advantages were less evident, as it was a more advanced society and was reeling from the blow to its trade delivered by the British blockade.

Great Britain, led in 1795 by the young, notable statesman William Pitt, who had managed to bring about the recovery of his country after its defeat 12 years before, did not recognize a regime considered to be illegitimate.

Prussia, with provinces neighboring France on the Rhine, chose to recognize it at the signing of the Peace of Basel in 1795, as did Spain, its southern neighbor, unlike

Austria, which included Bohemia and Hungary, and had somewhat modernized. Italy was divided, Portugal had Brazil. To the east was Russia, who had annexed Poland, and the Ottoman Empire.

The Napoleonic Wars were fought from 1796 to 1815, in which the great vitality awakened in the French people was harnessed in a great military adventure. Even if the adventure ended in formal failure, it nonetheless shook European society to its foundations. Hence, it is convenient to examine how the different nations reacted, according to their type and level of civilization.

If we look at the political map of Europe at the Peace of Tilsit in 1807, we will notice that the Napoleonic Empire plus its "protected" states comprised the entire core of Western Civilization -except Great Britain. Everything else not included was either on the periphery, like the Iberian Peninsula, southern Italy, and Scandinavia, or of a different civilization, like Russia and the Ottoman Empire.

Within the core, the Napoleonic régime had been well received –to a certain degree- in western Germany and northern and central Italy, as it had put an end to the archaic régimes there, which hampered the development of those peoples, whose societies were already ripe for democracy.

Conversely, the peoples of the "protected" régimes of Prussia and Austria, even if their societies were more backward than the aforementioned ones, felt that the Napoleonic hegemony had to be resisted and were not willing to accept "the novelties" of the French Revolution.

Great Britain, Spain, and Russia registered the most flagrant popular opposition. We saw that the rulers of the first saw a demagogic perversion in Napoleonic militarism, evident for them in his barefaced ambition for himself and his relatives. Spain, in contrast, rejected the French for the opposite reasons, considering them atheists "who in former times were Christians" and from which they were not willing to receive anything under duress. In Russia's case, it was simply a matter of their civilizations being so different, that they felt that submitting meant reneging their cultural essence.

The most surprising reaction was that of the French people themselves, whom "the glory" of Napoleon's triumphs blinded and dazed to such a degree that they were unable to detect the profound demagoguery of the skilled adventurer, which is why the Englishmen seemed egotistic to them, the Germans ungrateful, and the Spaniards afflicted by an inexplicable madness.

Nevertheless, many Napoleonic lessons, like the patriotism that he knew how to inspire, the Civil Code which made every Frenchman equal under the law, were notions that every European nation would adopt in time, but at the high cost of each nation going it alone, thus launching a new phenomenon called "nationalism". We can explain it as the effect of public education and centralized administration allowing nations to develop an awareness of themselves.

The Restoration Period, from 1815 to 1830, is notable for the contrast between the ancient political structure which the rulers that defeated Napoleon tried to impose upon the people, and the deep and irreversible changes that the combined effect of the Industrial, American, and French Revolutions brought about in those same people.

Western Germany, for example, was composed of only half a dozen modern states of an advanced level of democratization, and something similar occurred in northern Italy, only that in the latter, the richest ones remained a political part of conservative Austria. France expelled its "divine rights" kings in 1830 and put a "bourgeois" king on the throne.

Great Britain was fortified by the victory it had achieved and was making great strides in its industrialization, so it also pushed ahead with its democracy, approving laws permitting labor unions, liberalizing the policy toward Catholics, and abolishing the Negro slave trade.

7.9.- Evolution of the Philosophical and Religious Ideas through 1830

Referring to the western politicians and thinkers of circa 1763, Mark Lilla [10] says that all had adapted to the principles of what he calls "The Great Separation" and that "those principles did not necessarily touch on the truth of Christian revelation, or any revelation; they simply dictated that for the purposes of political philosophy and political argument, all appeals to a higher revelation would be considered illegitimate."[11] He continues saying that this puts us "on the opposite shore" with respect to all other past and present civilizations (which have always linked theology and politics) and that our crossing to "the opposite shore" has been very difficult.

Nevertheless, he notices that at the turn of the 19th century, there is a noticeable nostalgia in Europe for its religious past and illusions are harbored for achieving a better religious future. Were they not convinced of the abuses by the clergy that Voltaire, for example, had brought to light? Yes, but they did not consider this as proof that conscience is fiction: Men feel they are moral beings and, since the workings of our conscience are somewhat mysterious, they feel inclined to credit it to a benevolent God. [12]

Looking for the origins of that nostalgia, he turns to Rousseau, whom he describes as "a disappointed modern" who sees all the errors of his time. He also thinks that between he and Kant (whom we will see below) began the rift in the manner of judging ideas concerning the theological-political problem between the Anglo-Saxons on one side and the Germanic Protestants, on the other. [13]

He illustrates Rousseau's theological position with his *The Profession of Faith of a Savoyard Vicar* character, who educates the protagonist of his novel *Emil.* Lilla celebrates its conscience, its charity toward one's neighbor, its virtue, its pious awe, but he also signals its non existent relationship with revelation, since it all emerges from the intrinsic goodness of human nature. (14)

So his *Emil* is not naturally religious but naturally ethic, and Rousseau thereby becomes the first to offer man a religion without revelation and dogma, to which one can arrive following these three steps: 1) Man's faculties are limited; 2) Man desires answers that exceed his capacity to answer; 3) He can have some sort of answers provided he formulates them making reference only to his own moral certitude. (15)

This door to a religion without revelation seemed so dangerous to the political and religious authorities that Rousseau was persecuted.

Lilla considers that Kant's moral doctrine is a philosophically disciplined argument of Rousseau's shrewd vision (16), and that his *Critique of Pure Reason* (1781) is, in turn, a new and profound view of all those things that lie outside the possibility of experience.

But Lilla believes that in his *Practical Reason* (1788), Kant subtly lays out the foundation, perhaps unknowingly, of new theological politics. And that he does it because he believes that following the correct moral course would be too formidable for any person, because of the existence of evil, of "the enemy" which has to be fought. Hence, he posits his two famous postulates that he deems necessary for not falling into despair: 1) That God is the supreme cause of nature and metes out happiness in direct proportion to moral behavior, and 2) That the soul of each individual is immortal. But, why does evil exist? Kant had no idea, but he saw man as torn between two opposite forces: selfish pride and cruel remorse. (17)

We can now try to explain the existence of "evil" according to the latest research and opinions we saw in Chapter II, unavailable in Kant's time. When man arrived at high consciousness he or she realized that he himself or she herself, and others as well, were capable of committing actions that could be detrimental to themselves and to his or her family, friends, or the group as a whole. I think that this is what we call "evil" or "wickedness" in a human sense: our capacity for doing them or abstaining from putting a halt to them, compared to natural catastrophes or blind chance of fate. We can add this to what Kant said so well: If we do evil things it is for "selfish pride", that clouds the reason and gives free rein to passion; and if we abstain from doing them, it is because we were able to discipline our will and lead our passions toward a good purpose, in order not to fall into "cruel remorse".

Coming back again to Kant, and to Rousseau, Lilla thinks that both of them opened a crack through which theology seeped through, and adhered a little to Germans' political ideas: Between the two of them they created a purely moral theology, bereft of "dogmatic crutches", but capable of helping man with his formidable issues of conscience, curiosity, and hope. Rousseau proposed that churches be used only as an adequate place to socialize, but Kant went further, since he assigned the Lutheran churches the duty of working toward attaining happiness for all humanity. So, although respecting the principles of "the Great Separation", they opened up the intellectual possibility of "constructing a bridge" connecting both shores. (18)

Meanwhile, those with a background in romanticism aspired for man to become one again with his world, which implied "reconciling" instead of "alienating" his environment. They tried to achieve this by means of esthetic experience, mystic introspection, the structuring of myths, and "leaps of faith". "We need a new mythology of reason", wrote the young Hegel in 1765, and Lilla thinks that this was what, in the end, came to violate the principles of the Great Separation, by reintroducing "a reconciling with the world" in politics. In his later writings, Hegel declared that "the reconciling" had already been achieved, in its main aspects, by the bourgeois state that was born at his time. (19)

In his *Phenomenology* of 1807, Hegel posits that man's moral drama follows a dynamic sequence of negativity, alienation, and reconciliation that allows it to ascend levels in a spiral motion. He also suggests that history is nothing but the collective development of this drama, which advances by creating a human group with a socio-political structure adequate for a particular situation. When the relationship deteriorates because of changing circumstances, a critical situation arises that has to be corrected, and doing so requires measures to be taken until a new level of adequacy is reached in the spiral of historical development.

Hegel's main error was to think that religion is the founding force of societies, when we saw in Chapter II that modern research and thought ascribe that force to morality, which is, precisely, the social discipline for achieving the survival and development of human groups. That is why morality is as old as the hominid genus, while religion is relatively new, a fact that was not available to Hegel.

Considering Lutheran Protestantism as the most advanced religion, he proposed the good citizens submit to its ethical prescriptions, and that the Church should clearly submit to the state (in his case Prussia, since in 1818 he was called to teach at the University of Berlin, and stayed there until his death in 1831). With this, Hegel was disregarding "the Great Separation" (of politics and theology), arduously gained since philosophy fathered the Modern Scientific Method. Not only that: he was also disregarding what we can call, in the spirit of Lilla, "the Great Separation of Powers" ever since St. Ambrose faced Theodosius in Milan in the far away year of 390.

So, from then on, ventured Hegel, the "great" states will play the lead roles in world history, as he thought that the form and organization of the world of his era could be seen as the unfolding of God's will (similar to the "Manifest Destiny" of the North Americans of that time).

Lilla judges Hegel's proposals with a lapidary comment: That what Hegel had really found was a well designed and very reasonable bourgeois God and a very cheap reconciling with the world. (20)

7.10.- Panorama of the World in 1830 and Confrontation of Historical Events from 1560 to 1830 with the Working Hypotheses

When the Restoration conservative period after the Napoleonic Wars ended in 1830, the Industrial Revolution was emerging from its cradle in Great Britain and passing into Continental Western Europe. It is, again, a convenient time to view the population data of that region in some detail, and also that of the rest of the world, in geographical order:

COUNTRY OR REGION	Millions of Inhabitants
Great Britain	21.5
Scandinavian countries	5.5
France	32
3 Low Countries and Switzerland	9
Prussia and the other German states	26
Austria, including Bohemia and Hungary	28
Italian states	19
Iberian Peninsula	17
WESTERN EUROPE	158
Russian Empire	70
Ottoman Empire and North Africa	54
Sub-Saharan Africa	45
Persia (Iran)	14
India	210
South East Asia, Pacific, Australia	38
China	350
Japan and Korea	41
REST OF THE OLD WORLD	822
Anglo-Saxon America	16
Latin America	24
AMERICA	40
WORLD TOTAL	1020

So the world had just passed the 1 billion-inhabitant mark and had a population 1.76-fold that of 1650 (table in section7.5). We can make the following comparisons:

1.- The population of Western Europe also had doubled (from 78.5 to 158 million) but that of the Russian Empire had multiplied almost six-fold (from 12 to 70 million), since in 1830 it encompassed most of Poland, the Baltic countries, and Siberia, and we are also including Central Asia in this amount.

2.- The Ottoman Empire, Sub-Saharan Africa, and Iran practically saw no population increase (the joint figure went from 94.5 to 113 million).

3.- India, South East Asia, the Pacific, and Australia grew from 142 to 162 million, while China, Korea, and Japan went from 221 to 391 million.

4.- America more than tripled its population (from 12 t0 40 million), and the recently independent Latin portion had 50% more population than the Anglo-Saxon part.

What can we say of the evolutions of morality and religion in the 270-year period between 1560 and 1830?

As always, it is very difficult to appreciate if there really was a significant change in humans' morality, its core being so stable and universal. Nevertheless, we saw it operate in settings and circumstances so varied and different in those 270 years of exploration -first contacts between humans of very different types and levels of culture; conquests; religious and trade wars; piracy; slavery; missionary work; exchange of agricultural products, domesticated animal species, food, drink, smoking, new diseases, and new remedies; new cruelties and new heroisms; instinctive fights, friendships, and loyalties between very different persons- that the only thing that we can say is that Europeans held a view of primitive man between two extremes:

That espoused by Hobbes, the pessimistic opinion that their life was "solitary, poor, nasty, brutal, and short", as we saw in Section 7.4, and Rousseau's opinion, whose optimistic nucleus of the intrinsic goodness of human nature we just saw in Section 7.9, led him to his paradigm of the "noble savage". Which of the two was correct? I think the answer is "partially both and completely neither".

This is to say that the first men in possession high self-consciousness of self were as we are, only in primitive conditions, and we are as they were, only in advanced civilized conditions. Then, human nature does not make any strides? Not after only 10,500 years of settlement nor even after 50,000 years of high consciousness, but we can advance our knowledge of ourselves and, consequently, the goals that we should set for ourselves and the social discipline needed to reach them. I will make a concrete proposal for this in the final Chapter XI.

As far as religion is concerned, it is easy to track its evolution -as we have been finding all through history- because, as have been shown, it is nothing more and nothing less than an extension of the feeling of dire poverty or helplessness in the face of "the world powers" and the certainty of our own deaths, what our ancestors felt when they attained high consciousness. The changes in religion are even easier to follow if we limit ourselves to study Western Europe and its overseas outposts, since it is there where the process that we may call "the moralization of religion" unfolded: It consist simply in minimizing the theological aspect and maximizing the role of religion as arbiter of the human moral conduct. This evolution occurred as follows:

After 40 years of reforms and counter-reforms that still attempted to be broad-scoped, by the year 1560 the two "fields of honor" were sharply drawn, although - fortunately and thanks largely to France- not strictly along religious lines. It was also in France where an alternative to the unending war was first visualized: Absolutism in public life and tolerance in private life. Meanwhile, Spain was perishing to a "seigneur" syndrome and a mind-numbing intolerance; Italy was being crushed under militarism and authoritarianism; and Germany was being irretrievably divided. The firmest steps toward democratization were taken in The Netherlands, Scotland, and England.

In the early 17th century, Galileo brought science from the skies down to Earth and began to demonstrate that *Natura é scritta in lingua mathematica*; Bacon began to formally separate the intellectual fields of religion and science; and Descartes gave the whole structure of knowledge a solid philosophical underpinning. All this made it possible to take religion out of deciding what was true concerning the description, quantification, and prediction of matter, but only in exchange for leaving to it the theological and moral fields.

With Grocius (Groot), an international "secular" law began to gain so much acceptance amongst the rulers of the powers, that no official representatives of any church were invited to the peace talks that culminated in the Treaties of Westphalia in the year 1648. With Hobbes' solid arguments, the notion of casting out all and any theological references from even internal discussions of politics gains acceptance.

Finally, in 1689, the politicians of a great nation arrived to formally instituting a limited form of government, inspired and advocated by Locke, which will lead to democracy. Meanwhile, Boyle and Newton were establishing the foundations for modern chemistry and physics.

What was religion's state during the 17th and 18th centuries? We saw that even in liberal Great Britain and its colonies in North America, the Anglican Church and the various Calvinist sects had so much influence that the politicians with the most advanced ideas had to conceal them in the safe haven of the Masonic Lodges, so as not to rouse the wrath of the men of the cloth. The same can be said for The Netherlands and Switzerland.

During the first 25 years of Louis XIV reign in France, the Catholic monarchy had been constructive and popular, and had kept its political independence in its relationship with the Papacy. But in 1685 "the Sun King" succumbed to his own authoritarianism and abolished the Edict of Tolerance: France paid dearly for this harmful measure, since many high and middle class Huguenots emigrated to Prussia and England, and their native country lost their valuable contributions forever. With this, the backward brand of Catholicism strengthened its position in France, and it was against this tendency that the encyclopedists and philosophers of the Enlightenment fought.

In Frederick II's Prussia the notion -which Hegel would later philosophically plead for- that the state should be the sole protagonist and, consequently, should control both the Lutheran Church and the Masonic Lodge, was common.

Austria had to wait until the reign of Joseph II -from 1780 to 1790- to abolish feudal servitude, establish a new penal code, overhaul the tax revenue system, remove obstacles to trade, set up hospitals, asylums, and orphanages, and have an Edict of Tolerance for Orthodoxy and a strict control over the Catholic clergy. In Italy, these measures were applied in the Austrian Lombardy and similar laws already existed there in other northern states.

Notwithstanding all of this, intolerant Catholicism continued to be the rule in the States of the Church, the Kingdom of Naples, and in the Spanish and Portuguese monarchies, both on the Peninsula and in America. Its most peculiar institution was the Inquisition. But even in those countries there was a muffled fight between "royalists" and "papists" -which recalled the medieval fight of Ghibellines and Güelphs- the former more influenced by the Enlightenment but more authoritarian and centralist, and the latter partial to a kind of theocracy, able and skillfully defended by the Jesuits. The fight culminated with the expulsion of the Jesuits from every Catholic monarchy and these, in turn, pressuring the Papacy, until the Order was dissolved in 1773.

The impact of the French Revolution upon Catholicism was highly significant, so it is convenient to review what happened in some detail:

1.- In France, all the reforms that had been carried out in Austria were legislated and put into practice, but to a greater depth and scope in the educational, judicial, and fiscal aspects, and carrying the clergy's civil control to such extremes that many people never again flocked under the Church's wing. All rights were granted to Protestants and Jews, and belonging to the Freemasons ceased being a crime.

2.- During the Napoleonic era, the occupation of Italy by French troops almost brought about the disappearance of the Papacy, since Rome itself was proclaimed a Republic and Pope Pius VI was sent to forceful exile in France, where he died in the crossing of the Alps in 1799. Regardless, a conclave gathered in Venice under

Austrian protection and elected Pope Pius VII. Later, Napoleon let him return to Rome and signed a Concordat with him in 1801, as he had seen how Catholicism was entrenched in the peasant class, and how much he depended on them militarily and politically.

3.- In Spain and Spanish America, since Godoy became favorite of the King and wielded the royal power as Prime Minister in 1792, the liberal ideals of the Enlightenment and the French Revolution had been gaining a foothold in the avant-garde circles of the ruling class, some of them even belonging to Masonic Lodges. However, when Madrid's population rose against Napoleon's troops in May, 1808 - which soon triggered a huge guerrilla movement in the entire Peninsula, including Portugal, most of the rebels upheld the traditional values in the Governing Juntas they formed, while just a minority maintained their liberalism.

4.- In Spanish America, most of the owners of the agrarian "haciendas" and mines abided by the traditional Juntas and deposed the viceroys who had been installed by Godoy. Nevertheless, the fact that this irregular situation prevailed up until 1810 allowed the liberal groups that had been taking shape to overthrow the local authorities, or to spark popular insurrections, as transpired in Mexico, but always fighting against conservative armies. These were aided by Spanish troops sent to America in 1815, and they succeeded in recapturing power everywhere –almost. The notable exception was the Rio de la Plata Viceroyalty, where the creoles, who had already defeated two large British forces in 1806 and 1807, had taken over local power in May, 1810, and proclaimed Argentina's independence in July, 1816. The following year, they deployed an army led by San Martin, who crossed the Andes into Chile and liberated it. Meanwhile, Bolivar was gaining the loyalty of Venezuela's "llaneros", who made up the core of his army, which liberated Colombia, Venezuela, and Ecuador. In 1820, the liberals in Spain had forced the Cadiz Constitution of 1812 on the King, and that would prove the catalyst for the Mexican conservatives to negotiate its independence with the insurgents, which went into effect in 1821. The Spanish liberalism was crushed by conservative French troops in 1823, which is why the liberating movements of San Martin and Bolivar joined forces to liberate Peru and Bolivia in 1824.

The Restoration period in Western Europe -from 1815 to 1830- banned the Catholic Church from recognizing the Spanish Colonies' independence, as well as that of Brazil from Portugal, and saw Pope Leo XII deploring the situation in the "rebelled" countries "contaminated with heretical ideas".

Nevertheless, by the year 1830 Catholicism was extending in the United States, gaining equality under the law in Great Britain, as well as in The Netherlands and Switzerland.

So we can say that, by the year 1830, the relationships between Western Christianity and the governments of the countries with practicing populations fell under one the following modes or a combination thereof:

1.- In the counties with a majority of Calvinist Protestants, such as Great Britain, the United States, Netherlands, and Switzerland, religion had become a private affair, and it was considered spurious for anyone to appeal to theological instances in political arguments. Both Catholics and Jews were beginning to gain the same civil rights as everyone else.

2.- In France, to which we can add the recently created Belgium and the Kingdom of Sardinia, "the Great Separation" will be respected from 1830 on. Their Catholic majorities were by then highly "eroded" by what was being called "religious indifference". They had granted full civil rights to their Protestant and Jewish citizens.

3.- In Prussia and the other Lutheran states in Germany (those in the Scandinavian Peninsula tended to follow those of group n° 1), the Great Separation began to be distorted by a "self-aggrandizing" of the state that sought to politically command both the Church and the Freemasons, at odds with each other. The rights of the Catholics were recognized, but the Prussian State wanted to exert some control over the Catholic Church in the Rhineland Provinces, reason why it negotiated with Rome the "investiture" of the bishops there.

4.- Austria-Hungary-Bohemia, which back then also encompassed the Vento-Lombard "kingdom" in Italy and, for practical purposes, also protected the Pontifical States, were lagging far behind France and there still was an interaction between Church and State, although, as we saw, very reformed.

5.- In 1830, the kingdoms of Spain, Portugal, and Naples were still in the midst of a conservative reaction which kept them in absolutism with its accompanying Inquisition, but were close to breaking free from those ancient shackles. The same held true of the recently independent Latin America.

VIII.- The Strengthening of the West from 1830 to 1914

8.1.- Political Events in the West from 1830 to 1848 / 1852

Great Britain recognized the right of its workers to organize in trade unions in 1824, emancipated its Catholic population in 1829, extended the right to vote to all the middle classes, established the 12-hr. workday in 1833, and abolished slavery in all of its colonies in 1834, reasons why it remained the leader of world liberalism. It soon had its first strikes and then a famine ravaged Ireland, but its socio-political system already had such an ample evolving capacity that it always took the appropriate measures for solving its problems, which in those two cases were to improve working conditions and decree the free import of cereals. For all these reasons, it was the only western European county left untouched by the 1848 revolutions.

In France, this 18-year period covers the government of the "bourgeois king" Louis Phillip of Orleans, when the country "got acquainted with the arts of peace", began to work its coal mines in modern ways, build its railroad network, and began to industrialize. The population's surplus energy was directed toward the colonization of Algiers. But "the people got bored" so in 1848, they launched a second revolution and established a Second Republic.

The Netherlands, Belgium, Luxembourg, Switzerland, and the Kingdom of Sardinia combined in a peaceful "Lotharingia" in the heart of Western Europe.

Prussia and all the other German states also began their industrialization, creating their Customs Union to embark on the road towards unification. They were unable to advance much further because of the huge presence of Austria-Bohemia-Hungary, which also encompassed the Veneto-Lombard "kingdom" and protected the duchies of Tuscany, Parma, Modena, and the Church States.

Spain, Portugal, and the Kingdom of Naples finally began a slow and difficult liberalization, punctuated with crackdowns and setbacks.

The United States of America, which had acquired the immense wooded area between the Appalachian Mountains and the Mississippi River in 1783, had slowly settled it, establishing eight more states there. In 1803 it purchased the Great Plains from France to crest of the Rocky Mountains, admitting Louisiana as a state, founding the territory of Missouri, and buying Florida from Spain. So when Mexico became independent in 1821, they had a common border. In 1821, the USA had 11 million inhabitants, 3 million of them black slaves. By this time it began building its railroad network, mainly in the northern states, where a substantial immigration began to arrive, while in the south cotton exports were booming. The population thus jumped to 17 million in 1842. During the following 10 years, the U.S. fought the War with Mexico, acquiring territories from Texas to California, and negotiated with Great Britain its possession of the northwestern part, reaching its current coterminous extension and counting 25 million inhabitants in 1852.

During the immediate post-independence period, from 1821/1824 to 1852, Latin American countries mostly had negative reactions, as they realized that they had freed themselves from Spain and Portugal only to enter a world dominated by Great Britain, France, and the United States, whose socio-political superiority seemed tremendously out of reach for their societies' type of structure. In addition, the Latin American countries had no control over the huge ecclesiastical organizations they had inherited, as the Papacy did not allow them to exercise "Royal Patronage". All these problems prompted most of the countries to close themselves off in one way or another. Some countries, like Mexico, were rudely awakened by their neighbor's quest to fulfill its "Manifest Destiny", loosing the vast and scarcely populated territories of its far north to the U.S.

8.2.- Political Events in the West from 1848 / 1852 to 1872

These 24 years mark the most important period of Western Europe's buildup, for the following reasons:

First: In Great Britain and France the proportion of individuals with a right to vote increased from one third to more than half of adult men. This factor enhanced their social strength, forcing other nations to take similar measures, in order to cope with them.

Second: Industrialization reached its culminating point then, when the railroad network was completed in the entire sub-continent, the coal-fired iron and steel factories were busy with the anchor site of the chain of production, and sailing by wind was substituted by ships equipped with steam engines.

Third: The Reunification of Germany and Italy took place, the only remaining great nations not unified until then. If we add Great Britain, France, and Spain to them, we will have the five great variants of the Western European "styles of being".

The major exception to the "great nation-state" in Western Europe was the Austro-Hungarian Empire, which included Bohemia or Czechia and parts of Poland, Rumania, and Serbia, and what are now Slovakia, Slovenia, Croatia, and Bosnia. It had a multinational structure which increasingly became obsolete as nationalism kept rising. Besides, there were also small countries not absorbed into any great nation, such as The Netherlands, Belgium, Luxembourg, and Switzerland, which can be joined by Portugal and Ireland. The Scandinavian countries were "a periphery".

The United States opened its era of continental domination by sending a fleet to try to open Japan to commerce and deals with the West, which it eventually succeeded in doing, as well as engaging in trade with China. But domestically, the territorial expansion sent the slavery issue into an acute crisis, plunging the nation into the bloody and protracted Civil War from 1861 to 1865, from whence it emerged badly hurt, but was able to surmount and later unite on a firmer ground.

Latin America -with its second generation of leaders- emerged from its isolation and threw itself into reforming its socio-political structure, achieving the separation of church and state or at least some control over its workings, and adopted liberal/democratic constitutions. But many countries, those with very class-stratified societies, found that putting those principles into practice was impossible. The gap between political theory and practice thus began to widen.

8.3.- Political Events in the West from 1872 to 1914

In those 42 years, Western Europe underwent practically no political changes. Its salient features were its impact on the rest of the world, by means of what is known as "imperialism" or "colonialism", and also its rushing its industrialization into what is called "the second stage", marked by the burgeoning chemical industry, the internal combustion engine, the use of electricity, and telegraphic communications.

Another novelty, albeit an unfortunate one, was the two military alliances at odds with each other. One underlying reason was that in order to achieve its reunification, Germany had to defeat France in the 1870-1871 War and extracted as a prize the province of Alsace-Lorraine, German-speaking but French in national sentiment as a result of its annexation two centuries earlier. So France wanted a *revanche* and knowing that it could not defeat alone the Second German Reich, which had a population 50% larger, with almost the same standard of living, it had to resort to entering an alliance with the Russian Empire. This enormous country was on the threshold of revolution, as its industrial workers grasped the fact of their appalling social backwardness compared to the West. So Germany, so as to not be surmounted in power, offered its alliance to its neighbor Austria-Hungary, which gladly accepted, since it was menaced, as we saw, mainly by the nationalism of the Orthodox Slavs, backed by Russia.

Great Britain and Italy kept out of those alliances, but they were important factors which the four committed powers had to take into account. The same has to be said of the Ottoman Empire, already in an advanced state of socio-political decay, but still so large and strong that it was still a force to be reckoned with. Spain and Portugal, on the other hand, engrossed in their colonial problems, distanced themselves from European woes.

After its Civil War, the United States had carried out its "Conquest of the West", which included turning the Great Plains and California into agricultural expanses. It also accelerated industrialization upon receiving the largest wave of transatlantic immigration in history, some 30 million in this period alone. After imposing its hegemony in the Caribbean Sea after seizing Cuba and Puerto Rico -and the Philippines in Asia- from Spain, the U.S. proceeded to separate Panama from Colombia and to build the Canal, a huge engineering feat completed in 1914.

By then, Great Britain had four "White Dominions", i.e. colonies in which Europeans outnumbered the natives to such an extent, like Canada, New Zealand or Australia, or had imposed a supremacy system, as in South Africa, that they had been granted the right to have an autonomous government.

For Latin America, this period overall was its first peaceful and constructive period since the insurgency started. Various countries were nearing democracy, like Argentina, Uruguay, Chile, and Costa Rica, or had developed benevolent dictatorships, like Mexico and Brazil (the latter had finally abolished slavery in 1888). However, there were also some negative attitudes.

8.4.- The Rest of the World from 1830 to 1914

Czarist Russia emerged from the Napoleonic Wars as one of the stewards of the Treaty of Vienna of 1815, reason why it was apportioned the largest part of Poland and the Baltic Countries and Finland, which it already had, all with a western culture-imbued population. During those wars many of the Russian officers were familiar with and appreciated that culture, and called for reforms, but their movement was crushed. The same happened to the Poles when they rebelled in 1830. Nevertheless, the Russian Empire's vitality was far from waning, so its rulers directed the expansion campaign toward the Far East and Central Asia, and fought the Ottoman Empire in the Caucasus and the Danube. This fight carried Russia to a confrontation against Great Britain and France, which defeated it in the Crimean War of 1853-1854.

After that humiliation, the Czar was forced to make concessions, immediately liberating the crown's 20 million serfs and in 1860 all the serfs of the nobility, which were the majority. Later, employment problems came, partly remedied by industrialization, but then labor problems emerged in an unstable spiral. As a neighbor of the greatest military power of the world, the Second German Reich, Russia sought an alliance with the Third French Republic, whose liberal democratic system was abhorred by the Russian rulers, but there was no other choice. In 1904-1905 it got involved in a war with Japan in which it was defeated. As a result, a revolution broke out in the big cities and was barely crushed, but seemed like a portent of the future.

Although the Ottoman Empire was not involved in the Napoleonic Wars, when they ended it was left with the problem of the new nationalism of its subjected peoples in the Balkan Peninsula, and Greece earned its independence in 1829. Then the sultans had to compete with their Viceroy of Egypt, who practically became independent. After it was handed a defeat by the Russians in 1878, it had to deal with Rumanian, Serbian, and Bulgarian nationalism, yielding Cyprus and Egypt to Great Britain and Bosnia to Austria-Hungary.

In order to stop this decline, a large group of army officers, backed by the emerging middle class, formed the nationalist "Young Turks" party, who gained power in 1908. But before they could consolidate their regime, Italy grabbed Libya and the Dodecanese Islands, which set off the Balkan Wars of 1912-1913. Their defeat in that war left the Young Turks full of resentment against Great Britain and France and ready to side with Germany and Austria-Hungary.

To the west of the Ottoman Empire, and with a base in its overseas territory of Algeria, France imposed its protectorate on Tunisia and Morocco. To its east, the Persian Empire (or Iran) was able to keep the Russian and British pressures at bay and maintained its independence.

In India, the British government had established control over the East India Company since 1774, acting as the sovereign power in the dealings with Rajahs and Sultans, and imposing modern legislation on its directly administered areas. Bentham had been consulted on this, but Company commercial privileges were upheld through 1833. After that year, however, free commerce was introduced, but Indian sugar and textiles were taxed.

The pressure on Indian rulers to change their administrations for the better and the native soldiers' religious sensitivities triggered the terrible Sepoy Mutiny of 1857 in the Great Ganges Plain. It was barely crushed by the loyalty of the native troops of the Bombay and Madras Presidencies and the rapid deployment of several British armies. That same year, the Company was dissolved and the Government of India came under the direction a minister of the British Cabinet, who immediately took steps to improve communications, health, and education. Later on, a Council of State and a High Justice Court were created, and in 1866 native legislatures were elected in the three Presidencies. In 1885, the Indian Congress Party was founded and 1905 saw the birth of the Muslim League. In 1911, George V was crowned Kaiser-i-Hindi and in 1914 the Empire was prosperous and at peace.

In South East Asia, the Indochina Peninsula was divided between British and French rule, leaving Thailand (Siam) between their territories. The Netherlands ruled all of the Malay Archipelago, except for British Malaya, Borneo and the Philippines. The latter passed from Spain to the United States in 1898.

At the turn of the 19th century, the trade surplus which the Chinese Manchu Dynasty had maintained with the West during the whole of the 18th century began to shrink. One of the causes was the introduction of opium from India by British merchants, which caused drug addiction in many Chinese ports; the other was the Industrial Revolution's new and cheaper products. When the Chinese authorities banned the use of opium and burned the stockpiles of the drug, Great Britain attacked Canton harbor in 1839 with steam ships equipped with large cannons, and forced the Chinese to cede the island of Hong Kong to them and allow the entrance of opium and other merchandise to their ports. This was the first of 80 years' worth of aggressions and humiliations.

During the 1850's, a pseudo-Christian religious movement called Tai-ping burst on the scene, weakening the Imperial Government and allowing France, the Netherlands, Russia, and even Japan to join Britain as China's tormentors over the following decades. Then, in 1894-1895 Japan defeated it in the first Sino-Japanese war, seizing Taiwan and the Korean Protectorate. In 1900, an anti-western rebellion, the Boxer, was crushed by a multinational expedition. In 1911 a liberal revolution in the South caused the fall of the Manchu Dynasty, but the north remained in the hands of a general, who intended to start a new dynasty, but died in 1916, during World War I. China was then divided among several military "warlords".

Japan, as we saw, had maintained its absolute isolation since the turn of the 17th century, but by the early 19th century, it began –despite being at peace– to suffer from an internal crisis. Also, news began filtering in of what was happening in China and, in general, in the outside world. That is why the cordial and unaggressive arrival of Commodore Perry's American Fleet July, 1853, brought about the creation of a political Party favoring the deliberate and controlled opening of the country. It launched a muffled confrontation with the conservative Party grouped around the Shogun, or hereditary administrative and military chief. Members of the former party prevailed: the Shogun was overthrown and his throne suppressed, leaving only the throne of the Tenno or religious Emperor, who moved his residence to Tokyo in 1868, thus beginning the Meiji Era.

This Era showcases one of most outstanding collective human actions in history: Painstakingly, Japan carefully "dismantled" its entire feudal structure and substituted it with one of a western type. This means that Japan passed through Renaissance, the scientific method, the Enlightenment, and the Political and Industrial Revolutions in a short, 44-year lapse. The 200 feudal lords or Daimios "returned" -which is what "Meiji" means- their lordships to the Emperor, receiving monetary compensations which they soon invested in industry or banking ventures. The 4 million warriors and administrators or Samurai relinquished their monopoly of swords and their special clothing and hairstyle, receiving reparation, but accepting social equality with the Chonin or merchants and artisans, who had to pay taxes. Finally, the tenant farmers and salaried peasants had the opportunity to buy their lands through long term arrangements, or becoming industrial workers in the new factories.

A universal public education system was established and it was so efficient that in 30 years the entire population could read and write. In industry, the first preferred products were those required by the West -like silk- in order to obtain money by their export; then the heavy coal and steel industry, in order to build the railroad network and steam ships, and to equip the Army and the Navy. We saw how in 1894-95 Japan defeated its *mater et magistra* China, in 1902 it signed a defensive alliance with Great Britain, in 1904-05 it defeated Czarist Russia, annexed Korea in 1910, renewed its alliance with Britain in 1912, and in 1914 had a solid and respected position.

Sub-Saharan Africa (except South Africa) had began to free itself from the shackles of the slave trade in 1807 when Britain forbade it and persecuted it with a naval squadron in Sierra Leone, though the ban was not totally effective until around 1850. There were several French, British, and Portuguese factories on the coast, but the big interior was organized in small "kingdoms" or in tribes.

In 1879, Africa awoke from this sleepy state in an irreversibly altering way when the King of Belgium, Leopold II, engaged explorers to open the huge Congo River Basin and began to grant exploitation concessions to commercial companies. This whetted the appetite of all the European powers, and in order to prevent a free-for-all, Bismarck convened the Second Congress of Berlin in 1884, in which Belgium, Germany, and Italy benefited besides Great Britain, France, and Portugal. They all sent in explorers and missionaries first, and then officials and military men, who began to superimpose territorial administration over the prevailing tribal organizations.

When the tribal people shockingly learned in 1914 that their white masters were killing each other in Europe, the population of the world may be estimated as follows:

COUNTRY OR REGION	Millions of Inhabitants
Great Britain	44
Scandinavian Countries	11
France	42
Low Countries and Switzerland	16.5
Germany	56
Austria-Hungary	53
Italy	35
Spain and Portugal	22.5
WESTERN EUROPE	280
Russian Empire	158
Ottoman Empire (+Balkans +North Africa)	74
Sub-Saharan Africa	105
Persia (Iran)	16
India	326
South East Asia, Pacific, Australia	82
China	428
Japan and Korea	60
REST OF THE OLD WORLD	1,249
Anglo-Saxon America	105

Latin America	82
AMERICA	187
WORLD TOTAL	1,716

During the 84 years from 1830 to 1914, the world population increased 68%, which means that at such a rate it would have grown 86% in 100 years. Between 1650 and 1830, the population jumped from 580 to 1020 million, which is also 86% per 100 years. So the rate of growth was maintained in the latter period compared to the former, because even if in Western Europe the birth index was beginning to descend it was very high in the new settled lands. Most statesmen liked this performance very much, with one of them, President Mitre of Argentina, saying: "To govern is to populate". Fine and dandy for the times! But then, was Malthus wrong in his 1804 prediction? Careful, as it was precisely during the latter period we are seeing that were opened three of the richest regions of this Planet to agriculture: The North American Great Plains, the Ukrainian Prairie, and the Argentinean Pampas. No other opportunity of its kind loomed in the foreseeable future: None similar arose in the 20th century. This is why we are now feeling the effects of that acceleration in the pace of rising population growth, which was only "warming up" during the 1830-1914 period.

Comparing in some detail the numbers in this table with the one in the Section 7.10, The following is evident:

1.- The group we call "Rest of the Old World", which includes much of what we now call Second and Third Worlds and has a majority of the population, grew at a slightly slower pace (52% from 822 to 1249 million) than the average (68%).

2.- In contrast, Western Europe grew faster (77%, from 158 to 280 million) in that period, because even if its birth index was decreasing its mortality rate dropped even faster. But the prize goes to the Americas (467% from 40 to 187 million) and particularly Anglo-Saxon America – the United States and Canada- which grew 656% (from 16 to 105 million) - aided by the largest migratory wave in history crossing over from Europe.

8.5.- The Evolution of Philosophical Ideas from 1830 to 1914

Our aim in this Section will be to try and determine which were, at the onset of this period, thinkers' position on proper human behavior, how they evolved and how they arrived to the terrible ordeal of World War I. In order to situate ourselves within the issue that concerns us, we should clearly delimit and mark it off, which I will try to do as follows:

Whose positions? Those who influenced public opinion to such an extent, that the politicians of the great western nations had to acknowledge them, implicitly or explicitly. What ethical aspects?: Those addressing what was considered proper behavior for caring the poor, proletarian, or lower classes of their own nation and, in cases of war or colonization, the treatment given to people of other countries of the same or different cultures, or primitive peoples.

What religious aspects? Those regarding who wielded the authority to determine what was ethical or not, and those dealing with the issue of scientific discoveries posing a threat to religion's authority.

It is assumed that we are dealing with countries in which the large majority of the people professed a Christian religion, whether Protestant or Catholic, but was not "established" due to their adopting a liberal capitalist socio-political system or to being in the midst of a democratization and socialization process for the benefit of the lower classes.

Since the religious aspect is going to be very important to our discussion, it's advisable to work with three groups of countries:

The first includes Great Britain and the U.S., which we can call "the Anglo-Saxons" and to whom we can add The Netherlands and Switzerland, and call this group "the Calvinists". The second group includes France, Belgium, and northern Italy and we can call it "the advanced Catholics". The third includes Prussia and the other Lutheran German states: "the Lutherans".

First Conundrum: What to do with the poor, unprotected citizens?

In the Calvinist group, the tendency was to not consider assistance for the poor a government concern to be decided by legislators. Overall, this type of aid was on the restricted side, because the "solid citizens" did not want to foster laziness or vice. On the other hand, there were many private institutions, generally for specialized assistance, maintained by private individuals or groups. This kind of assistance used to be substantial.

In the "advanced Catholic" group the legislators decided what had to be done, but part of this function was carried out by ancient institutions of religious orders which had been nationalized, but continued being operated by religious personnel for as long there were enough "vocations", after which they were substituted by lay employees. Private assistance tended to be channeled as patronage groups for the religious institutions that kept operating as private concerns.

In the "Lutheran" group, the legislators also decided what had to be done for public assistance and there were also private institutions of specialized assistance, but the State tended to have a hand in both.

The severity and urgency of this "assistance to the poor and unprotected" issue grew as industrialization advanced, and labor unions and socialist political parties were formed. 1848 to 1872 saw the rise of Marxist parties, culminating with the Paris Commune in the middle of the Franco-Prussian War, which ended in a terrible assault. 1872 to 1902 was the formative period of the great socialist parties, which succeeded in gaining admittance to the political arena in the three European powers, but failed to do so in the United States; even in Europe they had to renounce its extremism and accept liberal democratic rules. From 1902 to 1914 they began to regularly win a growing share of the popular vote, eventually accounting for one quarter to a third of the total vote.

Why was this problem so significant? If we go back to "the Origins of Morality", we saw in Section 2.3 that some specialists tell us that the "ought to be" social discipline in primitive hominid groups included:

1.- Loss of prestige or condemnation of anyone performing acts harmful to others.
2.- Established standards of reciprocity and equity.
3.- Each person's attitudes and actions must be in keeping with his/her position within the group.
4.- Certain bodily functions, such as sexual acts, bathing or washing, eating and excreting, were regulated under purity or contamination criteria.

We can clearly see that the four components of these rules for living together were affected by industrialization. If we look at the simplest one, no. 4, we can say that developing the following inventions was necessary to prevent workers living in cramped housing near the factories from dying of epidemics:

a) Drinkable running water and drainage system in every site.
b) Cheap lye and soap, which launched the chemical industry.
c) Cheap cotton clothes which could be washed frequently.
d) Cheap, washable pottery fired in slow cooling ovens controlled by recently invented pyrometers.

Regarding component no. 3, no worker had any political rights in 1830, so they had to fight for them and it wasn't until 1916, when they were killing each other in the trenches, that they obtained them in full. Regarding component no. 2, how many hours of work were necessary to earn a salary? A workday started out consisting of 16 hours -or all the time except for sleeping- then 12 hours, and finally 8 hours. Regarding component no. 1, which is what we can call "good behavior", both public and private, it cannot be said it changed much.

If we now address the problem morality-religion in this period and in these groups of nations, who decided what was good or bad, how much prestige did religion preserve and how was it affected by the scientific discoveries?

We saw that monotheistic religions, the Christian one in particular, had reeled from the scientific method discoveries, starting with the non-geocentric model of the universe, the Earth's round form which allowed it to be completely circumnavigated, the imperfection of celestial bodies, and the same applicability of the laws of physics in the sky as in Earth. So, man's home was not the center of the universe and his own body was a biological machine, very similar to that of the animals. Ah, but there was still one fundamental difference: his or her immortal soul, with its morality ensconced in his or her conscience, instilled by the Divinity. The problem was that said Divinity had revealed certain things about the origins of the world which increasingly didn't agree with reality.

Besides the abovementioned discrepancies, from the mid-18th century to the mid-19th century the new science of geology had emerged. It had gradually cleared away any doubt about the extreme old age of the Earth, chronicling unimaginably long periods, first of millions, and then of tens, hundreds, and even thousands of millions of years, complete with "antediluvian" faunas, very different from today's, about which the Bible said nay. Fortunately for religion, it was relatively specialized information and a direct contradiction of the Bible could be averted if the "days" of the Genesis were interpreted with sufficient leeway and criterion.

A very different thing happened with the 1859 publication of Charles Darwin's *The Origin of Species*. This seminal work not only showed that some species descended from others, as the "antediluvian" fossils had hinted, but it also identified and demonstrated the natural selection mechanism as the key to the evolution of species.

This directly contradicted both Adam's naming of each species as well as Noah's having saved one pair of each, and a controversy flared. In the bitter discussions that followed, the critical point of the conflict derived from the origin of the human species: Darwin decided to clear this point in a new work in 1871, putting the primates, particularly the great apes, in our direct biological ancestry.

How did the "great nations" react to this science-religion quarrel? Great Britain itself can be divided into two groups: One with a highly religious motivation, like the Puritans, Methodists, and Presbyterians, simply and clearly marked the fields of each discipline: Religion was in charge of morality, mainly in private life, and science was in charge of knowledge; any public behavior problems arising between those fields should be decided by legislation and before the law. The other group was that of the Anglican Church, who tended to adopt a liberal morality, bordering on secular, whose core included moral universalism, tolerance, political progressiveness, and patriotism (1), reserving religion for ceremonial aspects.

In France, the reaction of the majority was like that of the Anglicans, but since there was a smaller proportion of individuals whose "traditional" religion was not Catholic, a frequent implication of the reaction was simply to gradually abandon the religious aspect and take secular morality more seriously.

For the Germany of this period, Mark Lilla makes his magnificent analysis of the philosophical-religious evolution of ideas, not so much as a cause of World War I, but as a description of the ideology that completely shattered when that tragedy became a reality, simply because explaining that tragedy in the terms of those ideology principles was impossible. In the following, I try to offer an abstract of what Lilla says in Chapter 5 of his *The Well Ordered House*.

By adopting Rousseau's and Kant's suggestions for structuring a morality based only on human experience and not in revelation, the liberal German theologians posited that man was the measure of the Christian theological truth, in which they had an unshakable faith. So, what they ended doing was to invest man's religious feelings and its history -which had taken Germany to be the greatest power of the world and, consequently, the main figure of history, followed by the other "Germanic" powers, such as the British Empire and the United States- with a divine character. So history became "the sacred scene" where the drama of morality unfolded and became reality.

Following this downslide, some German thinkers, like Ernest Troeltsch, gradually came to view Christianity as only the contingent product of an epoch, and that the morality that should underpin it was one which the historical facts had justified. But, he asked himself -as Nietzche had done before- would that underpinning resist? It would not: When August, 1914 came and the tragedy of the prolonged war ensued, the entire theological structure came tumbling down. As the American H. Richard Niebuhr tried to explain later: "A God without wrath brought men without sin into a Kingdom without judgment through ministrations without the cross." (2)

IX.- The Two World Wars

9.1.- The Tragedy of World War I

We need to give as close a look as possible to understand where the tragedy lies. We can advance the answer and say that it lies in that its cost greatly exceeded what any and all statesmen and military leaders thought it would cost and, consequently, what they were prepared to "pay" or "waste", not so much in money as in human lives.

Then the following question has to be: Why so many important persons of every country erred so much? A provisional and partial answer may be that in the 100 previous years, from 1814 to 1914, Western Europe had strengthened so much, as we saw, both in the social aspect, by democratizing, as in weaponry, by industrializing. The fact that all their masculine adult population were citizens made them all disposable to be soldiers, so the size of the armies increased from tens or a maximum of hundreds of thousands of men to millions of men at each side. The weaponry, mainly the machineguns and light artillery, made the defensive operations very efficient. But, no one noticed this? Everyone, that is for sure, but only in theory, not in practice, because during those 100 years there had been no general European war. The American Civil War could have alerted them, as bloody as it was, but since in the following Franco-Prussian War the offensive operations, not much bloody, prevailed, they forgot the American event.

The most tragic misunderstanding, however, was not tactical, but ideological. Here we have to delve into which were the two main "concepts" or general ideas that had developed and been put into practice in human history regarding what reasons there could be to fight a general war. One type of reason is called "For Ultimate Ends" (in the religious sense) and the other type simply "Instrumental".

All wars which have been fought "For Ultimate Ends" have been morally justified by the leading actors as follows: Many people are going to die on both sides, and there will be a high toll and destruction, but once our purpose triumphs, it will be the end of all wars, since there will be peace thereafter. The basic reason in these cases is that those who begin the war believe that they have a morally superior ideology, and that ideology is offered to the defeated peoples who, because of this fact, will come out benefiting at the end. Examples of this type of wars are the founding of the Persian, the Roman, and Alexander the Great's Hellenistic empires, because all of them offered a "superior" civilization. The most typical example of religious motivation was the Expansion of Islam, since the Arabs believed that they were offering all the peoples the only true religion. The Christian reaction of the Crusades brandished the same type of justification. In modern times, Communism can be classified under this heading, if we consider as war its call for world revolution.

That type of reasoning for fighting wars began to decline in the West since Machiavelli realized that wars in Italy were fought purely for gain. Later, there was an intensification of wars of religion, but even those gradually gave ground again to the wars for gain, which reached their culminating point during the 18th century and the Napoleonic Wars. It was mainly from studying those wars that von Clausewitz, founder of the Instrumental Theory, structured his ideological concepts, the basic one being that war, for a great nation state or "power", was simply the achievement of its "sacred" interests by other means when diplomacy had not been able to do so. The state was Hegel's "protagonist of history", studied in its bellicose aspect by Clausewitz, who said that "a power" had a perfect right to obtain its interests by means of war, if that suited it, as there was no moral principle above its interests. War was "an instrument" that it could use at will. (2)

Up to this point, all European statesmen and military leaders were in agreement with Clausewitz, but very few of them read the caveat he expressed to warn against the thoughtless use of armed force: Long experience proved that drawing the sword could be dangerous and costly, reason why it was convenient to do so only when there were reasonable expectations that the gains would greatly exceed the costs. So, war was an instrument, sure enough, but one to be used wisely. It seems that nobody read this last caveat, because no one thought of it until it was too late. (3)

As the events of World War I unfolded and operations bogged down in the trenches, many statesmen began to think of a third theory of the general wars that the great Tolstoy had written about in 1865 in his essential book *1812*. He called it Cataclysmic Theory, and we will review it below.

Examining the outbreak of the war, many historians think that it should never have occurred, for the following reasons: The only power which could conceivably start it was the Second German Reich, because the Franco-Russian alliance was purely defensive. Germany would hardly have started it for its own reasons, for it had all it ambitioned in Europe and starting a war for commercial or colonial matters was inconceivable. So, the only possibility was that Austria-Hungary would feel its own existence so threatened that it would demand Germany's backing. Well, that is exactly what transpired when the heir to the throne was assassinated in Sarajevo on June 28, 1914.

For the eventuality of war, Germany had only one strategic plan, named the Schlieffen Plan in honor of its author. Germany had trained its citizens so well and had such an efficient railroad network that it could have 1,500,000 men in the war front in just one month's time. Its rulers knew that France had equally well-trained citizens and an efficient railroad network, but could command only 1,000,000 men in the time lapse, because its total population was less. In contrast, Russia could dispose of only its professional forces for the initial months of a war, as it took it more than three months to enroll, train, and transport new armies. For this reason, Schlieffen's plan prescribed deploying 1.5 million men to the Western Front, knowing that after defeating France, there would be plenty of time to transport the necessary troops to the Eastern Front. The Plan not only threw the entire force against France, it also stationed the troops in such a fashion that it would be impossible to stop them. They surmised that France would station 800,000 men at their shared border, and leave only 200,000 to cover the Luxembourg and Belgian borders, whose neutrality was upheld by all the powers. So the Schlieffen Plan prescribed also deploying 800,000 men at the shared border, but sending 700,000 men through Luxemburg and Belgium, where they would outnumber the French over three-to-one, which was impossible to stop.

It is clear that this Plan implied a brutal breaking of solemn international commitments, so in putting it into action the German government was risking a declaration of war by Great Britain. However, since the Island only had an army of 150,000 men, Germany decided to take the risk.

In the following pages, I will present a brief summary of events for each calendar year, concentrating on the loss of life of soldiers of all stripes, which means not only deaths in battle but also those in hospitals and in POW camps, but in no case including civilians, which were few in comparison.

YEAR OF 1914
It was the only year which saw a mobile war. Germany declared war on Russia and on France August 1 and 3, and received Great Britain's declaration of war on August 4. Austria-Hungary was also at war against the three "Allies".

The Schlieffen Plan failed for the following four reasons: 1) Belgium defended itself, adding 50,000 men to the Allied forces; 2) Russia attacked Eastern Prussia with its Cossacks, forcing Germany to divert 100,000 men from its "right wing"; 3) Great Britain quickly sent in its small but professional army, with 80,000 troops arriving for the initial attack and another 40,000 during the following month; and 4) France withdrew 200,000 men from its border front with Germany and sent them to the Paris area. From there, they attacked the huge German army's right flank, slowing its advance, until it was completely halted September 9 at the Marne river and pushed back. The Germans then took to the trenches, and the Front was then continued to the north, until it reached Belgium's coast October 31, extending 400 kms (250 miles) down to the Swiss border.

On November 5, the Ottoman Empire entered the war on the Austria-Hungary and Germany side ("The Central Empires") against the three Allies.

Thousands of dead in 1914									
Gr.Brit.	France	Other	West	Russia	Germ.	Aus-Hun	Other	Central	TOTAL
25	300	10	335	310	320	140	0	460	1,105

More than one million dead, nobody had won, and all had lost. Why wasn't peace made then? Ah!, because of the Instrumental Theory! How were the politicians going to face their constituents with losses and no gains? No, the stakes were so high, there was no going back! So preparations were made: For the first time in its history, Great Britain established military service, not entirely compulsory, but practically so due to the social pressure. What about Germany? It still had sound reasons for believing in victory in 1915, for even if the first part of the Schlieffen Plan had failed, it still had the second part, which was to defeat Russia, knowing that France would be unable to resist alone. And that is exactly what they decided to do: it stayed somewhat passive on the Western Front and threw all its might, and that of Austria-Hungary and the Ottomans, against Czarist Russia.

YEAR OF 1915

The Plan of the central Empires failed in 1915 for the following reasons: 1) Great Britain increased its army in the Western Front from 150,000 to 650,000 men, and because of that Germany did not send 500,000 men to the Russian Front; 2) Italy entered the war in May on the Allies side, so it impeded Austria-Hungary to send another 500,000 men against Russia.

Regardless, Russia took a tremendous battering, which caused it to abandon Poland and part of the Baltic Countries, and frayed its social fabric further yet, leading to internal conflicts. Great Britain fell short of taking the Straits so it was unable to defeat the Ottomans nor seize Constantinople, but opened new war fronts in the Sinai Peninsula and in Mesopotamia.

Thousands of dead in 1915:

G.B.	France	Other	West	Russia	Germ.	Aus-Hun	Other	Central	TOTAL
125	200	110	435	1,070	525	580	150	1,255	2,760

Almost 3 million dead and no victory in sight: What to do? Let's try putting ourselves in the role of, for example, the Kaiser: How could he go before the representatives of the German people and say that after the deaths of 845,000 of their own and another 720,000 of their main ally, there was going to be "a white peace"? Wouldn't he fear the representatives would ask him: Why did you start the war, then? No, it was impossible to go before them without victory. So he went to his generals and asked them: Is there still a way to win the war? They asked for time to ponder, and then responded: We were unable to find a maneuver which could break the Western Front, but if we bleed France to the extent that it will not be able to replace its losses, then we could win. A horrific solution, no? Madness! Well, this was precisely the solution which was adopted and became known as a "battle of attrition" since it did not have a strategic objective, other than to kill the maximum number of enemy soldiers at the least cost to its own soldiers. Since it was convenient to get it over as soon as possible, there was no sense in interrupting the battle, which had to rage 24 hours a day, 7 days a week, and for as many months as was necessary.

YEAR OF 1916

The city of Verdun with its many defensive forts was chosen, since it was in the inflection point for the entire Western Front, offering a wider supply route for the Germans and a narrow and difficult one for the French. The battle began on February 21st and raged almost 5 months without stopping until July 15th. Unfortunately for the Germans, the Allies, seeing that France was being bled to death, decided to help her: Czarist Russia, in what was to be its last important act in history, launched the Brusilov Offensive on June 4th, which had no other objective but to make Germany bleed from another wound. The effort took more than three months, until it was compelled to stop on September 20th. Great Britain accounted for 60% of the troops in the third battle of attrition, waged on the banks of the river Somme, in which it, together with France, launched a full-scale offensive on July 1 that violently raged for 4 and a half months, up until November 18th .

So it was that Germany, which began this type of battles, ended bleeding through three wounds.

Thousands of dead in 1916

G.B.	France	Other	West	Russia	Germ.	Aus-Hun	Other	Central	TOTAL
350	500	310	1,160	1,220	830	730	150	1,710	4,090

Although the efficiently executed madness took a toll of more than 4 million lives, it did not put an end to the war! It did, however, shatter the European system of moral values, though it largely escaped notice then. For example, that terrible winter of 1916/1917 was czarism's last, and Austria-Hungary's old Emperor Francis Joseph died as well, and all his subjects had the clear impression that the Empire would not survive him much longer. When the President of France went to Verdun to give medals, his official auto was struck by the soldiers, who also bleated like sheep on the way to the slaughter house.

What course did the German High Command follow? Repeating the madness of the "battles of attrition" was impossible and, on the contrary, it proceeded to spare lives, passing, when possible, to the defensive. But the plan to weaken the enemy extended even to the civil population, since everyone was suffering from shortages, even of food. One of the methods chosen was unrestricted submarine war in the North Atlantic Ocean, directed mainly at the North American ferrying of consumer goods and ammunitions to the Allies.

What did the politicians in the United States think about the war? When it began, all parties adopted a position of neutrality. One of the reasons was that the U.S. hardly had an army to speak of; when Pancho Villa raided Columbus, N.M. and American troops entered Mexico, they were unable to catch him and had to retreat. Nevertheless, the madness of the "battles of attrition" struck them as a sign that their "Old Sod" relatives had gone mad, and they had to go and save them, to ensure that Western Civilization would not to perish, and that, on the contrary, liberal democracy kept expanding.

YEAR OF 1917

The Czarist government was overthrown in the middle of March and substituted by one of the bourgeois majority of the Duma, headed by Kerenski. They were immediately faced with the grave dilemma of Russia continuing in the war or not. Some historians believe that if they had withdrawn from the war, liberal democracy could have taken root in Russia, but then Germany would have won the war. As it happened, they decided to continue the terrible war effort, already in very precarious conditions. From the month of April on, communists Lenin, Trotsky, and Stalin established "soviets" in the army, the navy, and the factories, further weakening the Russian war effort.

The United States entered the war on April 7, but took all that year to enroll, train, and equip its new army. Nevertheless, its decision to enter and the supplies it provided raised French and British morale tremendously.

The French army suffered from a "collective indiscipline" which could barely be controlled and kept hidden from the Germans. For this reason, the British had to carry the brunt of the fighting on the Western Front.

Undoubtedly, the year's most significant event was the Communists' accession to power in Russia on November 7, for they immediately put an end to the war effort, to focus on the revolutionary one. Besides Poland and the Baltic States, they had to surrender Ukraine, Belarus, and Finland to Germany.

Thousands of dead in 1917

G.B.	France	Other	West	Russia	Germ.	Aus-Hun	Other	Central	TOTAL
250	200	310	760	920	375	550	150	1,075	2,755

For the first time, the number of dead is under the 1915 figure, but more as a result of fewer troops, tiredness, and indiscipline than because of a decision by the high commands.

YEAR OF 1918

Two things prevented the Germans from gaining victory: 1) They became engrossed and enamored of their territorial gains in the East and left too many troops there to occupy it, and 2) The new American army gradually arrived, some of its units saw action in March, and by the end of the summer it was able to act as a self-sufficient force, eventually playing a distinguished role in the Allied Grand Offensive.

The events unfolded thus: From March 21 to July 17, the German army launched five offensives on the Western Front: The first and third gained a great deal of territory, and were near successes, but were eventually stopped, and by then all their reserves had been spent.

Starting on July 18, the Allied armies, already under the sole command of French Field Marshal Foch, took the initiative and through September 16th "reduced the salients" formed by the German offensives. Foch convinced the French and British governments to give him the necessary means to end the war that same year, and they did so. The Grand Offensive began in September 26, continued throughout all October and Germany surrendered on November 11.

Thousands of dead in 1918

G.B.	France	Other	<u>West</u>	<u>Russia</u>	Germ.	Aus-Hun	Other	<u>Central</u>	TOTAL
250	400	330	<u>980</u>	<u>10</u>	450	200	150	<u>800</u>	1,790

Thousands of Dead in the First World War

Gr.Brit.	France	Other	<u>West</u>	<u>Russia</u>	Germ.	Aus-Hun	Other	<u>Central</u>	TOTAL
1,000	1,600	1,070	<u>3,670</u>	<u>3,530</u>	2,500	2,200	600	<u>5,300</u>	12,500

Notes: In "Others West": are included Italy 900, USA 120, and Belgium 50.
In "Russia" are included dead of Serbia, Greece, and Rumania (530).
In "Others Central" are included Ottoman Emp. 500 and Bulgaria 100.

9.2.- Socio-Political Events in the 1920's

If we want to gain a realistic idea of the profound changes that took place between the world of the year of 1914 and the one which emerged in the 1920's, we should examine two-fold transformations: Those caused by World War I and those which would have been produced anyway by the momentum of the political, ideological, industrial, and scientific advances that were already in full swing. So the result was a strange mixture, akin to a train partially derailed and partially going at full speed. Keeping with this metaphor, we can say that the derailed portion was that of the deep moral values, mainly those related with the religious certitudes, while the industrial and scientific portion not only kept moving forward, but did so at a faster clip, spurred by the war urgencies.

To illustrate these facts, let's recall several of the most profound changes that occurred then, impacting millions:

The Second German Reich, the Austria-Hungary, Czarist Russian, Ottoman, and Manchu Chinese Empires breathed their last, some of them breaking into pieces and others transforming their societies in very significant aspects and degrees. Even the British Empire in India, though it would endure another quarter of a century, lost in 1919 its will to continue that way.

We also see, for example, that for the Ottoman Empire it wasn't merely a case of losing many territories, but that the Turkish Republic witnessed the disappearance of not only the Sultanate, but also of the Caliphate. As a result, Turkish secular nationalism for the first time left the whole of Islam without a visible head.

A significant portion of its Arab possessions, like Iraq, Syria, Lebanon, and Palestine (opened up to Jewish immigration) became British or French colonies, joining Egypt, Libya, Tunisia, Algeria, and Morocco, which were already colonies. This brought about a tremendous feeling of devaluation to the entire Islamic Civilization.

In the spring of 1919, one of the first meetings for India's independence was brutally crushed by British military personnel, which sparked such a commotion that it projected the political career of Gandhi, who preached a non-violent resistance that had extraordinary success.

That same spring of 1919, China was not invited to the Versailles Peace Conference, though matters that affected it were to be discussed. The excuse was that it was divided among several practically autonomous "warlords". College students staged protests against this decision in the large cities and this movement gave impulse to the founding of the first two modern political Parties: Nationalist and Communist.

Eastern Europe, which in 1914 was part of three empires, by 1919 was the home of ten new small countries making their debuts as such for the first time (or again after many years): Finland, Estonia, Latvia, Lithuania, Poland, Czechoslovakia, Austria, Hungary, Yugoslavia, and Albania. They joined three other existing countries: Rumania, Bulgaria, and Greece. One has to imagine what the citizens of these countries felt being neighbors of giants in the throes of convulsions, like Germany and Russia.

The United States, on the other hand, showed its boundless vitality, though with some dark aspects, like rampant racism against any Negro that "went beyond his place", and an isolationism that restricted European immigration, rudely banned immigration of Asian individuals, and proclaimed a Puritan Calvinist-inspired ban of alcohol for consumption, directed mainly against Catholic and Jews. But its brilliant aspects turned the USA, for the first time, into the world leader in many areas, i.e. mass or serial industrial production which made things like appliances and automobiles affordable for most of its citizens, but also in cultural areas, like commercial radio, movies, and newspapers, complete with "comics", soon imitated the world over.

In the 1910s Mexico underwent Latin America's most significant socio-political revolution, and during the 1920's entered its "constructive stage" and organized the "central" unions of workers and peasants. On the other hand, the new rulers tried to hide their economic conservatism by fostering an anticlerical extremism which triggered the "Cristeros" rebellion, which finally drew the limits of the "official" political party's totalitarian advance.

The ups and downs of the European demand for raw materials and foodstuffs during and after the war sent the economies of Argentina and Brazil out of control, fostering in the former a populist movement that has, since then, plagued its democratic system, that was up to that time, the most advanced in Latin America. In Brazil, part of the army became communist, but was overwhelmed by the rest, then swinging to the conservative side.

In tropical Africa, meanwhile, the 1920's and 1930's would be the "golden age" of European colonialism, as it had entered by then a solid stage of establishing territorial administration, and the tribal system had to adapt to it. The natives still had confidence in their white tutors, from whom they received the rudiments of modern socio-political systems, which translated into public order for very different ethnic groups living together, and also in health and educational systems and in new economic activities.

9.3.- Ideological Changes in the 1920's

In the evolution of their socio-political systems, Western Europe's four large nations show us both the traumas of the war and the inertias of their cultural advances. Both Great Britain and France conserved their liberal democracies, but the inroads made by the socialist vote, which in both cases accounted for 30% of the total, turned the traditional bipartisan arrangement into an unmanageable triad for a while. The relationship between social classes and regions (Ireland became independent) already strained by the casualties of the war, became sour.

If that was the case with the two victorious powers, what would happen in vanquished Germany? Besides the above mentioned problems, it had to exert force to rid itself of various communist regimes, and its "Weimar Republic" had to make costly "war reparations and indemnities" payments which caused "galloping" devaluations of its currency. Nevertheless, the German people made a brave effort to adopt the new liberal ideology, and perhaps would have succeeded if "the Allies", driven blind by their own pain, would have had the magnanimity of condoning those absurd payments.

Italy had aligned itself with the winning side, but became sour when was not invited to participate in the spoils, so in 1922 it put an end to its short and troubled liberal stage by adopting an authoritarianism which conserved capitalism and the social hierarchy, but also established a socialism subjected to the state. The hope was that this mixture, termed "fascism", would close the road to the Communism that was taking root in the Soviet Union and threatened to engulf all of Europe.

What about religious sentiment? It was the most devaluated feeling in all Western Europe, although not in North America, because of the senseless killings of the war (so well expressed by Niebuhr). Scientific breakthroughs also had a hand in the theological depreciation: the theories of relativity and quantum mechanics, which explained how matter behaved from universe to atom, left few mysteries to explain. And then came Mendel's biological laws of inheritance, that were helping to explain the natural selection mechanism of Darwinian evolution. British philosopher Bertrand Russell was best at explaining the devaluing of religious feeling.

It so happened that the people of Western Europe were simply leaving their religious beliefs and practices on the wayside, in some cases conserving the formal and ceremonial aspects and in others looking for secular substitutes for them.

In Germany, Lilla points to several theological works, mainly by Karl Barth, in which the "domesticated Christianities" were attacked because, according to Barth, they had led the world toward the tragedy of the war, as the purely benevolent Rousseau, the moralizing Kant, and the history unfolding of Hegel had done. Barth preached that they had to return to the strict theology of St. Paul, St. Augustine, Luther, Calvin and, recently, Kirkegaard. But Lilla points out that, if these theologies "of Redemption" can lead to a pious withdrawal from the world, they can also lead to a passionate course of action in following a new Messiah, and that if a divine one does not appear, then a profane idol can take its place. (3)

At the other side of the world, in Japan, another tragedy was brewing. We saw how this island nation had hermetically closed itself off after the initial arrival of westerners (Portuguese and Spaniards) in the 16th century and had remained so until the mid-19th century, when the British began to open up its *mater et magistra* China by cannon fire. Then, stimulated by the peaceful visit of Commodore Perry in 1853 and once an internal conflict had been settled, it enjoyed its glorious Meiji Era between 1868 and 1912, during which they ascended to the rank of great power. During WWI, they had been an ally of Great Britain, even if their participation was limited to taking two German cities in China and the Caroline Islands in the Pacific. When China was divided among several "warlords" in 1916, Japan made a series of demands which it tried to secure in 1919, but the United States, already a Pacific power due to its presence in the Philippine and Hawaiian Islands, openly opposed Japan's abusive actions, proposing the "Free China" policy in all the international forums, causing Japan to lose face and sowed hate in the Japanese. Both feelings intensified when the United States pressured Great Britain —indebted to it- not to renew its Alliance with Japan in 1922, and magnified when the Japanese were not excluded from the categorization of "Asiatic" in U.S. immigration law.

For all these reasons, Japan, in his thirst for vengeance against the Anglo-Saxon powers, began to imitate Italy in its authoritarianism, albeit of a military bent, which initiated a gradual departure from liberalism.

This leaves Soviet Communism as the only ideological change we have yet to address. This system professed to be based on the doctrine preached by Karl Marx and F. Engels in the second half of the 19th century, which includes a philosophy of a supposedly dialectical behavior of matter, and also of history, politics, and economy. Nevertheless, after Marx death in 1883 his most important followers in Germany, France, and Great Britain founded socialist parties who abandoned the most extremist aspects of these theories, such as the inevitable destruction of the capitalist system, and gradually accepted the political rules of liberal democracy. For these reasons, they had captured between 10% and 20% of the vote before WWI and in the 1920's they had won over roughly one third of the voters.

For all this, the Soviet brand of socialism, which we will call "communism" to distinguish it from the other, was forged in very different circumstances to those of Western Europe, where it was born. In the first place, experience with liberal democracy in Czarist Russia was practically nil and the little there was lost its chance when the Kerenski Government decided in March, 1917 to continue the war effort. That almost certainly saved the Allies, but prevented the middle class democrats of Russia from being able to resist the "soviets" which Lenin, Trotsky, and Stalin organized in the army, navy, factories, and transports.

The war against the neighboring countries that wished to secede from Russia and the ensuing civil war -when the "reds" expelled the "whites" but could not recover Poland, the Baltic countries and Finland, despite gaining roughly two thirds of Ukraine and Belarus, the Caucasus, and Central Asia- were so terrible that, coupled with the upheaval of the first agrarian parceling, caused famine conditions in many areas. The situation became so dire that Lenin decreed in 1922 his "New Economic Policy", permitting the "kulak" or small agricultural owner. This was the last thing he did, as he fell ill and died in 1924. Trotsky wanted World Revolution, but Stalin prevailed in the power struggle with his "Communism in one country first" policy. He consolidated his position in 1927, and Trotsky had to flee to exile.

The road now clear, Stalin was able to implement his two terrible but very efficient five-year plans from 1928 to 1938, when the Soviet Union built new railroads, industrial cities, mining facilities, hydro- and thermoelectric plants, steel and cement plants, and chemical industries, disassembling in the process the "kulak" class and establishing collective mechanized "kolkhozes". The population lived and worked like automatons while the despot killed anyone who opposed him in the least. In spite of all that suffering the Soviet Union rose to become an industrial and military power. Would all this hold up under critical conditions? That remained to be seen. Meanwhile, all religions, whether Christian, Moslem, Jewish, or Buddhist, were banned, and a militant atheism was embedded in the general public education system which was implemented.

So, to summarize: By late 1929 there was a "Broken World" in some of its most profound moral values –namely religious- and it was embarking on two new, terrible socio-political experiments which shared a totalitarian bent and differed sharply from the liberal democracy that continued to prevail in some countries. These capitalist economies saw a wild expansion that decade that led to the Stock Market Crash, whose fallout would be the most devastating economic depression in history during the next decade.

9.4.- The isolationist and Aggressive 1930's

The most representative country of this decade is Germany: The economic depression hit particularly hard there, causing a spiral of bankruptcies of industries that left so many unemployed, that by 1932 they totaled 6 million. The middle class, which was the majority, was desolate due to the loss of their savings, and, consequently, their social status, and by the fear of communism, compounding the guilt they felt for the war. They then realized that there was a political group, though somewhat thug-like, that offered an end to all those terrible problems. In desperation, 42% voted in November for the "National-Socialists" or "Nazis", who soon obtained the few allies they needed. On January 30th, 1933, President Hindenburg appointed party leader Adolf Hitler as Chancellor of Germany. Never one to miss a trick, he soon schemed with his thugs to set the Reichstag ablaze, blaming the communists for it, so he could pressure for and be granted the special powers he wanted and could begin to put into practice the policies he had promised:

1.- He roundly refused to pay a penny more for war reparations and indemnities. His bold action was received with acquiescence by both Great Britain and France, when they had stubbornly refused the Weimar Republic. That measure immediately cured many of the German economy's ills, and the capitalists then proved ready to invest their money.

2.- Then there was the problem of the labor unrest stirred up by the communists. Hitler solved that by sending in his well-armed ruffians against them, so very soon labor peace was achieved by means of beatings, imprisonment, or assassination. From then on, the Nazis were left as the sole arbiters between labor and capital.

But, what were the industries going to manufacture if trade activity had shrunk to a minimum? Well, modern war equipment, such as warships, airplanes, and tanks, paid for with government credit, which would later find how to back it.

3.- That wasn't all: Hitler could also erase the guilty feeling for the war, by telling the German people that they were right in having fought and that they would surely have won, had it not been for "the back-stabbing" perpetrated by the "Jewish traitors". With that, he channeled the hate and frustration of the people against the only minority that -at just 1% of the population- was not large enough to hurt but was sufficiently notorious to make his lies plausible.

These actions of the Nazis charted the course for the world, since the German people, seeing its aspirations fulfilled -although in an authoritarian and, worse yet, totalitarian way- backed this criminal regime in an increasingly fanatical manner, while it pushed the world toward the only policy in which modern weapons could yield profit: war of aggression.

So, in order to put the weaponry to work, in 1936 Hitler ordered the militarization of the Rhine's left bank, breaching the Versailles Treaty. Both France and Britain held a stance of appeasement. The world began to take notice that the only thing that seemed to work was thug-like bravado: Mussolini decided to imitate Hitler and sent 30,000 troops to help Franco in the Spanish Civil War against the Republican Government that France and Britain were supposed to back and aid, but that only the Soviet Union tepidly did.

On the other side of the world, Japan, which had occupied northeastern China since 1931, establishing the puppet state of Manchu-Kuo, attacked China proper in 1937, seizing all the coastal and middle areas, where its soldiers committed atrocities. It was unable, however, to take the interior western third, where two armies were posted to fend off further Japanese advances: Nationalists in the south and Communists in the north.

In March, 1938 Hitler annexed his native German-speaking Austria, with Mussolini's "permission", and started to rant about "the Sudetenland", a neighboring strip of German-speaking people in Czechoslovakia, a French ally, in turn a British ally. Both of these powers ended up appeasing Hitler in Munich in September, who then occupied the Sudetenland, "protected" the Czechs, and detached Slovakia. As soon as Franco won the Spanish Civil War in April 1939, Hitler started ranting about Danzig and the Polish "Korridor", and France and Great Britain realized, too late, that they had negotiated with a thug and that the world was irretrievably sliding into war.

Fortunately, at the same time that the Germans were voting for Hitler in 1932, the Americans did the same for democrat Franklin D. Roosevelt, who installed measures, called "the New Deal", for moving the economy out of the Depression by investing government money in large public works such as irrigation and rural electrification; abolished Prohibition and persecuted the gangsters it had nurtured. Towards Latin America, the USA became "a Good Neighbor". The U.S.' emergence from Great Depression was slower than that of Germany, but it did not lead toward an abyss of hate and aggression.

What about Christianity? The Catholic Church negotiated the existence of the Vatican City State with Mussolini and backed Franco absolutely, although it also issued a slight scolding against some irreligious aspects of Fascism and Nazism. But in general, its position was uncompromised and accommodating. The Lutheran Churches did not oppose the persecution of Jews and tended to march to the beat of the Nazis. In France and Great Britain, their main Churches were so weakened that they practically played no role. Only in the United States did the Churches retain some of their moral authority. In Mexico, Church and Government found a new *modus vivendi.*

Stalin, seeing a new German colossus emerge near its borders, first sought to offer the Allies his help in guaranteeing the integrity of Poland, but the Fascist-like regime there roundly rebuffed the Soviet Union's offer. The Allies accepted that state of matters, although they were left with no practical way to fulfill their commitment. Stalin believed that Hitler's attack on Poland was just a ruse and that he would then proceed against the Soviets, as he had signaled in his famous book *Mein Kampf* and in hundreds of other speeches. So an incredible thing happened: The two despots signed a non-aggression pact in late August 1939 and with that, all the elements were in place for the start of World War II.

9.5.- The Second World War

On September 1st, 1939, Hitler ordered his army to occupy the Free German-speaking city of Danzig and attack Poland, which they did with their famous Blitzkrieg, in which first massive air strikes gunned and bombed the enemy military formations, followed by an assault by massive tank formations backed by a fully motorized and mechanized army. The fight was over in 27 days.

France had protected his army with the Maginot Line, a modernized version of the old trenches, at its border with Germany, since The Netherlands, Belgium, and Luxemburg had confirmed their neutrality, so during the 1939/1940 winter nothing happened on the Western Front. In Eastern Europe, the Soviet Union, in cahoots with Hitler, had occupied the areas populated by White Russians and Ukrainians in Eastern Poland. In October, it occupied the three Baltic Countries and in December it attacked Finland, which rejected its demands. An incredible thing happened: this small country punished the invading Soviet troops trying to penetrate their long and deep frozen common border -extending from Lake Ladoga up to the Arctic Ocean- so severely that the USSR was forced to halt its offensive. In February 1940, it concentrated its troops and artillery at the Karelian Isthmus, thus forcing Finland to request an armistice. Stalin accepted, taking only small territories as a token of their heroism, and took note that his purges had demoralized the Red Army, leaving it in bad shape. From then on he resolved to reform and reinforce it.

In April, 1940, Hitler surprisingly took Denmark and Norway, and on May 10th launched his second blitzkrieg against The Netherlands, Belgium and Luxemburg! Great Britain and France tried to protect them, but the Germans cut the Allied armies in half. Winston Churchill, the new British Prime Minister, ordered the evacuation, aided by France, of the British army. Then the whole German army turned against France and only three weeks in June were enough to defeat her. In the armistice, Germany occupied two thirds of France, including the entire Atlantic coast, leaving only one third of its territory "free", where the Petain "neutral" government of France established its capital in the spa town of Vichy, keeping the Mediterranean coast, critical to managing its colonial empire. Italy took advantage of the fall of France to enter the war on Germany's side, which immediately deployed it against the British in Ethiopia, which it soon lost, and in Libya, which shared a border with British Egypt.

Hitler had no plans for invading Great Britain, and Churchill ordered the Lord Chancellor in July to not even acknowledge any German proposals. So, in August, Goering improvised an aerial attack against the British aerial installations: They not only withstood, but bombed some German cities in retaliation. That angered Hitler, who ordered massive attacks against London and other major cities. Then, Churchill ordered the Royal Air Force to focus on destroying the Luftwaffe's fighter planes, regardless of the damages caused by the bombers. By October, the British had destroyed so many fighters, losing themselves fewer than the new ones being produced, that the Germans had to resort to night bombing in November and finally halted all air strikes in December. The British had won the Aerial Battle of England.

During the 1940/1941 winter, Hitler ordered its army to prepare to invade the Soviet Union with 2.4 million German soldiers, plus the armies of Finland, Hungary, and Rumania. During the spring, Germany invaded Yugoslavia and Greece: that delayed the main attack against the USSR, which only began June 22nd, 1941. Stalin was shocked, even demoralized, for he could not believe that there was someone more evil than himself. It wasn't until his aides informed him that Soviet soldiers were fighting well, despite the surprise and advanced mechanization of the enemy, that Stalin recovered.

During July and August, three groups of Nazi armies, north, center, and south, advanced unchecked. But in September the northern one was stopped outside Leningrad (St. Petersburg), the southern one took Kiev in October, and the central one threw itself against Moscow in November, but was stopped December 5th only 30 kms. from the Kremlin, under brutal freezing conditions.

Two days later, Japan attacked the American naval base of Pearl Harbor in the Hawaiian Islands. As a result, the U.S. declared war on Japan and Hitler declared war on the USA, in the hope that Japan would also declare war on the USSR. That did not happen, and it only facilitated the American strategy.

The United States was not prepared for war, and figured it had to build 14 new aircraft carriers and many other ships to engage in naval battle with Japan, a roughly two-year endeavor. They were unable, therefore, to reinforce their troops in the Philippines, which was lost, as well as all of South East Asia, in early 1942. In a war council with the British, the Americans concluded that trucks and other military vehicles and communication equipment could best be put to use immediately by sending them to the Soviet Union, their new and not very well liked ally, but that was killing many more Germans than the British or Americans could. What route to use?

The safest one was via the Indian Ocean, the Persian Gulf, Iranian railroad, and again by ship through the Caspian Sea and the Volga River and up to the very heart of Russia. Another possible route was via the Arctic Ocean up to Murmansk harbor, but that was dangerous, as the Germans controlled Norway.

Two American carriers had been saved from the Japanese attack, and with the aid of a deciphering feat, the USA could entice the Japanese navy to attack the island of Midway, to the NW of Hawaii, and in the aero-naval battle that followed they could sink the four Japanese carriers in the fleet: So, from then on they did not have to fear attacks in its Pacific coast, and could contain the Japanese general advance in the Solomon Islands and in New Guinea, with the help of Australia and New Zealand.

In 1942, Hitler concentrated his attack on the Soviet Union in the southern part, his main goal being to cut off the Volga supply route at Stalingrad, with the capturing of the oil fields at the Caucasus added as an afterthought. Over the summer, the Germans reached the middle Don River at Voronezh but were unable to cross it; they breached the lower Don at Rostov and part of the army swiftly marched to the oil fields. In September, the main German army crossed the Don where it is nearest to the Volga, reaching the outskirts of Stalingrad and surrounding it up against its banks. The heroic battle, which lasted two months, then began. Meanwhile, the Soviets amassed troops in front of the middle Don River.

The Soviet counterattack began on November 20th crossing to the west the middle Don, marching southeast and then crossing again the Don, thus surrounding near Stalingrad 300,000 German and Rumanian soldiers. Hitler forbade the surrounded troops to try to break the ring, but ordered the Caucasus troops to immediately return and try to break the Soviet ring around Stalingrad, but by the end of December they had failed to do so. In January, 1943, it remained for the Soviets only to go closing the ring: the German commander surrendered on the 30th, the 10th anniversary of the Nazis reaching the power, surviving by then only 90,000 Germans. This was the psychological turning point of the whole war, though not yet from the military point of view.

Meanwhile, the British had driven the Italian-Germans from close to the Nile River, through the vast Libyan dessert, and up to southern Tunisia. In the meantime, the Americans had disembarked in French Morocco and Algeria and had succeeded in having the French side -with their colonial troops- with the Allies. Together, they engaged the Germans in combat at Tunisia's western border, made contact with the British, and defeated the Italian-Germans in May, 1943. On July 10, the Allies disembarked in Sicily, and did the same in August in southern Italy, which surrendered in September. The Germans, however, formed a strong defensive line between Naples and Rome.

During the summer of 1943 the militarily decisive battles of the world war were fought: 1) In the North Atlantic Ocean, the anti-submarine war was won. From then on, huge convoys could ferry troops and supplies from the U.S. to Great Britain. 2) In the skies over Germany, the air war was won by the American Air Force and the RAF against the Luftwaffe, and from then on the Allies were able to massively bomb industrial, marine, and railroad facilities. German cities were consequently being destroyed, and Hitler was forced to divert many warplanes from the Russian Front to protect them. 3) The Battle of Kursk was fought July 5-August 5, and remains the largest in terms of men and equipment involved to date. When it was over, the cities of Orel and Belgorod were freed, and the Soviet people knew that the tide of war had decisively turned in their favor, although much fighting and sacrifices had yet to be made.

Roosevelt -whose Marines were jumping from island to island in the Pacific and was aiding China through Burma (Myanmar)- proposed a meeting in person to Churchill and Stalin, which took place in late November, 1943, in Teheran, the Iranian capital. The Soviets had recovered Kiev on November 7, and had discovered a mass grave of 50,000 Jewish civilians assassinated by the Germans. That proof of unconceivable cruelty helped allies as different as the Anglo-Saxons and the Soviets to reach accords: 1) First, they agreed that neither would negotiate a separate peace with Germany, until its unconditional surrender; 2) Second, American and British troops would disembark in northern France in order to open up a "Second Front".

The year 1944 saw the huge and already well equipped Soviet army advance slowly but surely from the Dnieper to the Vistula rivers, almost 1,000 kms. (600 miles), annihilating much of the German army in the process.

It also saw the Allies disembark 150,000 men June 6 in Normandy, a figure multiplied ten-fold in a one-and-a-half month period. Then, in August and mid September it liberated almost all of France, Luxembourg, Belgium, and half of The Netherlands.

In the Pacific theater, the two largest naval battles in history were fought, one near the Marianas Islands in June, and the other in November near the Philippines, liberated in early 1945. These defeats placed the Japanese "war machine" in a stranglehold, as it could not ship oil and other raw materials from South East Asia, but the military leaders did not budge.

In February, 1945, the "Big Three" met again, this time in Soviet Crimea. By then the situation was very different: There was no doubt that both Germany and Japan were beaten, and so the most pressing thing now was to decide how to "parcel out" Europe. All knew that a very important factor would be the territorial advances the armies could actually make, but were wary of everything depending on that, as it would only benefit the Nazis by producing friction and rivalries among them. So they carefully examined each country's likely situation and tried to forecast its final status: Finland had already made peace with the Soviets, and the Allies agreed on its loss of territory and payments to the USSR in exchange for remaining free. They also accepted the *de facto* annexation of the Baltic Countries into the USSR, though not *de jure*. Poland was the thorniest case: The Allies accepted the territorial changes, with the Soviets being ceded large areas populated by White Russians and Ukrainians, but Poland gaining from Germany the rich Silesia and Pomerania, as well as portions of East Prussia and Brandenburg; what they insisted on tirelessly was that it should conserve its liberal capitalism. The effort proved futile, so they resigned themselves to it becoming communist. They had to accept the same fate for Czechoslovakia, Hungary, Yugoslavia, Romania, Bulgaria, and Albania, but reclaimed Greece for the West. Germany and Austria were also complicated issues and were solved by occupation zones. It was understood that Italy, the Scandinavian and the Low Countries, and France would be "western", Spain would remain isolated and Turkey would not be touched.

The final offensives against Germany were carried out: an Allied one in late March and a Soviet one in mid April, roughly as planned. In early May, all resistance ceased, unconditional surrender was signed, and all members of the last German government were incarcerated. For a time, there were no German authorities, not even for directing traffic.

The "Big Three" met for the third and last time in Potsdam, in the outskirts of occupied Berlin, but instead of Roosevelt, who had passed away in April, new President Truman attended. He told Churchill that the United States had just tested the atomic bomb and asked him if he thought Stalin should also be informed. Churchill said he thought so, and watched while Truman told the news to Stalin through translators: he was not surprised! Later it was known that his spies had told him already. Stalin offered to declare war on Japan.

By then, the Americans had taken the small island of Iwo Jima, which interfered with the bombing of the main islands, and its 20,000-man garrison defended it almost to the last man. Incendiary bombs caused "firestorms" in every large Japanese city, where most of the houses were made of wood. Although millions of civilians died during the first half of 1945, military leaders still gave no signal of surrendering. In April, May, and most of June, the U.S. attacked Okinawa, the largest of the Ryukyu Islands and defended by 100,000 soldiers. What was left of the Japanese Air Force attacked the American fleet with suicide pilots, the famous Kamikazes, and the battle did not end until there were only some 9,000 soldiers left, isolated in small groups, wounded, hungry, thirsty, and almost crazed. In July, when the Conference of Potsdam took place, Japan was not only enduring air strikes, but the American and the British fleets were also cannonading its harbors and coastal areas, sinking ships and destroying facilities. But still the military did not surrender.

When reading of the after effects of the atomic bombs being dropped, almost no one mentions the over a million Japanese civilians who perished from February to July 1945, nor the inhumanity of the military leaders, even toward their own soldiers, by continuing to fight a war which was clearly lost, so it is convenient to ponder its psychological impact: After the atomic bombing of Hiroshima early in the morning of August 6, the military high command in Tokyo lost contact with the city's military headquarters and tried to reestablish it via other authorities and even businesses, to no avail. Since they were unaware of the arrival of an American bombardment squadron, they did not know what to think and immediately flied out a high official to find out what had transpired. Since the Hiroshima airport was in its outskirts, some of its personnel had survived: the one who came out to receive the official had half of his face so badly burned that it was falling off. The official reported that and the disappearance of the city to the high command in Tokyo.

Even after learning of the event, the military leaders were loath to surrender, but on August 9 a second atomic bomb fell on Nagasaki and, in addition, the Soviet Union, which had declared war the night before, began an unstoppable advance in Manchuria against the main Japanese army. That proved too much, and *Premier* Suzuki asked Emperor Hirohito to please order the high command to surrender. He summoned them at 11 PM and said: "The moment has come to bear the unbearable: I drink my own tears and give you permission to accept the proclamation of the Allies". Even then, the military leaders deliberated for three days the possibility of a coup d'état, but when they became convinced that Hirohito would not back them, the leaders of the Navy high command performed a collective *hara-kiri* in front of the Imperial Palace, while some leaders of the Army accepted the imperial order and contacted their troops, ordering them to surrender upon receiving the notice. This was given by way of a radio address by the Emperor himself to the nation on August 15. The army in Manchuria surrendered to the Soviets on August 19, and the formal surrender was signed on board the battleship Missouri, anchored at Tokyo Bay, on September 2, 1945.

9.6.- New Basis for Public Morality and Postwar Adjustments from 1945 to 1953

The bellicose 31-year period had come to an end: It had not only shaken religious values -and not only Christian ones but also those of all other religions- to the core, but this time had also shaken public morality itself, perhaps to an extent not seen since the times of the hunters and gatherers. Why do we say that?

Let us remember that since the era of primitive man, morality has always been the social discipline that better ensures the survival and development of a human group. Let us also remember that primitive morality was very concentric, exceptionally strong at the family level and within the clan or horde, less so at the tribal level, and woefully weak outside of it. We saw also how this concentricity underwent modification in pace with the improvement and expansion of cultural level, in the sense of broadening the type of relationships covered, although frequently at the price of decreasing their intensity. In this fashion, morality initially covered all the people of the same civilization, preventing them for exterminating all their enemies and merely reducing them to slaves, then changing that to feudal vassalage, then slavery again but only of black pagans, then not even that, and, finally, the "natives" had to be civilized.

But the world wars upset and muddled all the progress made: What could have justified the horrible crime of having sent 12.5 million soldiers to their deaths, who represented between a fourth and a third of all men of military age in Europe? And the horrors of the first war pale in comparison to those of the second war: The most brutal occurred in the Nazi attack on the USSR, letting one million prisoners of war die of hunger during the first year and the horrible treatment of civilians that would add to a total of 24 million Soviet casualties. And we have not yet mentioned Germany's "industrial" assassination of six million Jews, the Japanese atrocities in China, the "conventional" bombing by the Allies of German and Japanese cities, and the atomic bombs. All these actions can only be called by a name which Hitler used in his speeches to the high officers of his army: "total war". Fortunately, since 1945 the world has not seen a total war again, as we will see shortly.

Did humanity learn any moral lesson from these violent upheavals? I think two great principles were learnt, by heart and universally. Although far from new, insofar as the core of their content, they had never been expressed in the way their modern applicability afforded: I call them the "there are no" and the "there are" principles, and they appear mainly in the founding charter of the United Nations and in many other charters, constitutions, treaties, etc. But I think that their importance lies not in their formal wording but in their essence, which has been etched in the hearts of all people and that no politician would dare to contradict. In this "popular" form, the two principles say thus:

"There are no races, peoples or nations *inherently* superior to others, but rather any superiorities are *circumstantial*, which is why these do not bestow any one the right to dominate or oppress any other."

"There are moral principles above and beyond the *interests* of any power or superpower, though which precisely they are is open to debate."

So, it is under these two ancient principles, newly expressed or remarked, that the modern international order is based: They have permitted entities as different as the Western World and the Soviet Union and China to live together on this Earth, and prevented the Cold War from getting any hotter.

The first of these principles goes "against the grain" of what our ancestors thought in the primitive era, but it gradually developed since the agricultural era, and after rising through the various levels of civilization has been adopted by monotheist religions as the principle of the brotherhood of man. Even if at times it has lapsed terribly, after the two world wars I think it has finally become firmly implanted.

The second of these two principles goes against what we have called "the Instrumental theory of general wars", described, more than invented, by Machiavelli and practiced by various "illustrated despots" like Frederic of Prussia and Catherine the Great of Russia, taken to perfection by Napoleon, theoretically analyzed by Clausewitz, and adopted by politicians of every power, until the world wars showed us how easily the cost in lives can take it to the realm of the absurd.

The main problems in the practical application of these two fundamental principles of public morality are the following: First, what can be done of the circumstantial differences that do exist between peoples and nations? And second: precisely which moral principles should govern international relations?

In order to see how these principles have performed in recent history, let's review the eight years between 1945 and 1953 when Stalin was still alive and Truman was president of the U.S. They agreed to establish the borders between the "two worlds" and mutually respect the "spheres of influence" of the two great socio-political blocs locked in a muted conflict, which if led to a "little" war was always limited in various ways, and was far from a "total war". We will divide the "compromises" in four areas: I) Europe; II) The USSR's southern flank; III) India and South East Asia; and IV) China, Korea, and Japan.

I) In order to abide by the Yalta and Potsdam agreements, the Allies retreated from several swaths of territory in Thuringia and Czechoslovakia conquered by their troops, in exchange for which the Soviets ceded the western portion of Berlin, which became something of an "island" within the Soviet Occupation Zone, but was linked with West Germany by canals, railroads, and roads.

Europe became divided by a 1,450 km. (900 mile) long "Steel Curtain" extending from the Baltic Sea coast near the city of Lübeck to the Adriatic Sea coast near the city of Trieste. This militarized border separated the occupation zones in Germany and Austria and established the borders of Czechoslovakia and Yugoslavia. It generally lay in wooded country, was 200 meters (655 feet) wide, was a minefield bounded by barbed wire, and guarded from wooden watchtowers by machine gun-toting lookouts aided by searchlights.

Two notable events in those eight years merit being mentioned: First, the U.S. approved and implemented the Marshall Plan, which maintained American taxpayers' steep level of war taxes, but helped all the countries of Western Europe, allies and former enemies alike, rebuild their economic infrastructure. Second, Stalin saw that the West's speedy recovery was very obvious at Berlin, which is why in mid 1948 he ordered all communications to cease, hoping that this "shop window" of the West, which showed communism in a poor light compared to capitalism, would disappear. Truman, however, organized an "Air Bridge" to West Berlin and a trade counter-blockade, which made Stalin forgo his plan by mid 1949.

II) The USSR's Southern Flank and its European "satellites" had borders with only three countries: Greece, Turkey, and Iran, so Stalin put various strategies of subversion and military threats in practice in order to subjugate them. The U.S. responded with the Truman Doctrine, which officially aided any country who asked for help when threatened by Communism, both strengthening it against subversion and negotiating military alliances against military threats. The U.S. made the mistake of opposing the nationalization of Iranian oil, which would eventually cause the fall of the Shah.

Another problem which came to complicate the relationship of the West with the Arab countries, which were in the process of becoming independent, was the creation in 1948 of the new State of Israel, "born" amid civil, local, and foreign wars, which 500,000 Israelis were able to eke out against more then 50 million Arabs and triggered a Palestinian emigration which is still a problem.

III) Since early in the decade of the years 1930's the Labor Governments of Great Britain had offered independence to India, but they could not ever have an agreement between Hindus and Moslems. For this reason in 1947, after having made intense consultations, decreed The Independence of India Act saying how to do it, its main dispositions being: 1) There were going to be two main countries, one named India with Hindu majority and the other Pakistan with a Moslem majority. 2) There were going to be elections and plebiscites in all 20 Provinces of "direct administration": Those in which more than 75% of the voters selected one of the two countries will integrate complete in it; those which between 50% and 75% voted for one or the other will be split and each part will integrate with a different country. 3) The more than 500 princely states will integrate with the country that its sovereign decreed. 4) The countries with a Buddhist majority, like Burma, Nepal, Bhutan, and Sri Lanka will constitute separate countries.

Elections and plebiscites were held: 17 Provinces voted for complete integration in India, just one (Sind) complete for Pakistan and two provinces (Punjab and Bengal) were divided, one part for each country. In the 500 princely states there were few problems since vicinity and the majority religion decided the issue, but in the two largest ones, Hyderabad and Kashmir, problems arose and had to be settled by armed conflict. But the most terrible thing was the immense migrations of millions of peasants which became religious minorities and were attacked by their neighbors, reason why they fled in the midst of massacres and famines and both armies started to fight one another. In his last intervention Gandhi could accomplish that the two armies ceased to fight each other and assured the great migrations continued in some order. But even with this the victims were counted in the millions.

In South East Asia there were two Communist rebellions one in Vietnam which will later provoke a full fledged war, and one in Malaysia, which will be ended and will cause the formation of the new country of Singapore.

IV) China had kept the Japanese invasion at bay in its interior western third from 1937 to 1945, with the Nationalists governing in the south and the Communists in the north. As soon as the war was over, the United States tried to mediate between the two factions, but it was too partial to the former, so the truce ended in 1947. In the ensuing war, the Communists, aided by the Soviets in Manchuria, decisively defeated, in 1948, the Nationalists, who were forced to flee from the mainland and take refuge on the Island of Taiwan, under the protection of the U.S. Seventh Fleet. The USSR returned Manchuria to the Chinese and the latter proclaimed its People's Republic in October 1949, and began establishing the communist system in the whole country.

The Soviets, who in August, 1945 had defeated the main Japanese army in Manchuria, also crossed the northern border into Korea. They agreed with the U.S. to stop mid-country, marked by the 38th parallel north. Specially disembarked U.S. troops occupied the southern part of the Peninsula. Both powers fostered regimes like their own in their corresponding areas of occupation and both pulled out in 1948, leaving Korea divided into two rival countries.

Having invaded the southern portion of Sakhalin Island and the Kurile Islands, the Russians were on the brink of disembarking on Hokkaido, Japan's second-largest island, but were stopped by a forcible refusal by the Americans, so all metropolitan Japan was occupied only by American troops.

Stalin, who had wagered and lost in other three areas, as we saw, thought the fourth time was the charm, so he left the North Korean communist army well supplied with jets and tanks, and in the spring of 1950 pressed them to attack South Korea, which had almost no army despite having roughly twice the population.

The invasion of South Korea took place late in June and initially seemed a success, since the communists took Seoul, the capital, and continued advancing.

Even if it was taken by complete surprise, the U.S. nevertheless reacted well: First it made sure that the UN condemned the invasion and asked member countries to deploy troops. Several of them complied. Second, it sent occupation troops from Japan to the southern end of the Peninsula and secured the defensive perimeter of Pusan (Busan), which could not be penetrated by the North Korean army.

In September came the surprise American landing at Inchon Beach near Seoul, which forced the Communists to immediately retreat in disarray toward the North, being chased into their own territory. UN troops, meanwhile, advanced toward the North Korean border with China.

Stalin then realized that instead of winning the South he could end up losing the North, compelling him to ask Mao, the Chinese communist leader, to intervene, not openly declaring war but sending its troops in as "volunteers". Mao obliged and in a cold November 1950 sent half a million Chinese soldiers to throw themselves against the Americans and their Allies, forcing them to retreat, although not in disarray.

At this point, the American Commander, MacArthur, declared that, if necessary, he would use the atomic bomb against China, something that Truman had forbidden him to say, which is why he was ousted by the President. His successor, Taylor, stopped the Chinese advance south of Seoul, recovered the capital, and by July, 1951, the front had stabilized at a line which diagonally crossed the 38th parallel north, the original border.

The war raged on for two more years, but at a lower intensity, until Truman ended his term in January, 1953. Stalin died in March of the same year, so in July their successors negotiated and signed an armistice, which is still in place and operational.

So, what we call "wars" in Palestine, India, China, and Korea were limited in many aspects, and were very far from being "total", so we can say that humankind had learned its lessons.

9.7.- Panorama of the World in 1950

The world's population in 1950 is estimated as follows:

REGION	Millions of Inhabitants
North America	165
Western Europe	350
Australia & New Zealand	14
WESTERN FIRST WORLD	529
URSS and Satellites	197
Asia (Except URSS)	1,405
Africa	234
Latin America	161
THIRD WORLD	1,800
TOTAL WORLD	2,526

Since the year 1914, the population increased 47% -from 1,716 to 2,526 million- but at different rates, according to the Region:

1.- In North America the population had increased six-fold from 1830 to 1914, from 16 to 105 million, but from 1914 to 1950 it increased a mere 57%, from 105 to 165, as a result of its new isolationism.

2.- Western Europe went from 280 to 350 million -only a 25% increase- partly as a result of war casualties, but also due to a declining birth rate.

3.- The USSR and its satellites only grew to 197 million up from 170 million, a meager 16%, clearly because of wars and revolutions.

4.- Asia (except USSR) went from 944 to 1,405, a 49% increase, practically the same global rate.

5.- Africa before and in the initial stage of colonialism, that is from 1830 to 1914, increased from 67 to 135 millions in 84 years, which means 0.84 % per year. During the "golden years" of colonialism -from 1914 to 1950- increased from 135 to 234 millions, in 36 years, which means 1.54% per year, doubling the previous increase rate. This clearly shows the great benefits which the new territorial administration of the colonial powers, peaceful and progressing, brought to the native population.

6.- From 1830 to 1914, Latin America increased its population from 24 to 82 million, or 1.47% per year, and from 1914 to 1950 went from 82 to 161 million , or 1,89% per year, only moderately higher, so we can say that it was just beginning its population explosion.

X.- The Cold War, The Information Revolution, and the Collapse of Communism

10.1.- The Climax of the Ideological War from 1953 to 1968

It can well be said that this 15-year period was the first "normal" one in almost 40 years: the new democracies of the defeated powers -West Germany, Italy, and Japan- were already operational; the First and Second Worlds had staked out their corresponding "spheres of influence", and the whole world was, overall, at peace. So, the main question was which of the two socio-political systems, Capitalism or Communism, was going to work better, i.e. obtain better results. Those most interested in figuring this out were the leaders of the Third World countries of both types: those who had been independent for more than a century in Latin America, and those who were emerging in southern Asia and northern Africa and would soon emerge in tropical Africa.

Take the Soviet Union: we can see that this period was the time when the people, many of whom descended from peasant serfs of the czarist era, gave their communist rulers the most enthusiastic support, for the following reasons:

➢ They felt that for the first time were well fed, clothed, and housed, had medical services, enjoyed elementary, jr. high school, and in some cases even college education, in addition to many sports and organized recreation activities.

➢ Even if they still lacked many individual liberties, that was compensated by the fact that the communist economies were growing at an annual 6% rate, twice the First World's 3% growth. That seemed to imply that they would eventually attain western standards of living, and then, maybe, they would get their liberties.

➢ Besides, their victory over the Nazis in "The Great Patriotic War", as they called WWII filled them with pride. Also, they reveled in having the atomic (1949) and hydrogen (1954) bombs, and having ushered in the Space Age with the "Sputnik" satellite (1957).

The reason why the communist economies were at that time growing more rapidly than the capitalist ones, was due to the fact that a key part of them was then "heavy" industry, like coal mining, steel foundries, cement plants, thermo- and hydroelectric plants, railroads, etc. Those type of companies benefit greatly from central planning, as it minimizes costs and maximizes production, as was the case with the USSR, not only with its own economy, but also coupled with those of its "satellites".

That was, precisely, what resolved the Western Europeans to start their first economic cooperation organization, "The Coal and Steel Community" (it also included cement and electricity), in order to be able to compete with the huge economies of the U.S. and the USSR.

The United States then underwent an almost hysterical anti-communist stage, prompted by its worry over its economy's lower rate of growth. So, they embarked on a leftists "witch hunt" and began involving themselves in the Vietnam War.

Other important events of this period include: The Egyptian nationalization of the Suez Canal and its thwarted recovery; the decolonization of Tropical Africa; the acceptance by the French of De Gaulle's proposal to not keep Algeria by force, causing an exodus of 500,000 settlers or "colons"; and the creation of the European Common Market with Germany, Italy, and the three Low Countries.

The most surprising event was the triumph of communism in Cuba with Fidel Castro, which caused a failed disembarking of democratic Cuban exiles carried out by the American navy and the missile crisis with the USSR in 1962, which was the nearest the world has been to nuclear war. The Arab armies were again vanquished by Israel in 1967, and early the following year the North Vietnamese's Tet offensive convinced the U.S. to put an end to that war.

Up until that moment, it seemed that the ideological war was being won by the communists, at least in the eyes of the so called *intelligentsias* of the Third World, i.e. labor union and peasant leaders, intellectuals, and leftist politicians, because the higher rates of growth of the central planned economies suggested to the backward countries' leaders that it could be a fast track to overcoming their poverty. The only worrying thing was that the authoritarianism and the lack of individual liberties gave no signs of disappearing. Finally, in early 1968 the Czech leader Dubcek began liberalizing the Party, ordering its officials to receive and process citizens' complaints and to give transparency to their tasks. All the *intelligentsias* applauded this, calling it "The Spring of Prague" and hailing it as a "humanized" strain of communism which responded to the people.

The spring and summer of 1968 saw fervent enthusiasm take hold of many youths of the world, particularly those in France and West Germany, in the shape of political liberation, while in the United States the liberation was in sexual behavior. In Mexico, a college students and intellectuals movement also erupted.

Soviet leader Brezhnev damped their enthusiasm when he ordered Soviet and satellite troops to invade Czechoslovakia, depose the government, and put an end to all liberal openness and transparency. Not only did he do so, but also cynically justified the action, stating that the communist countries had the duty to crush any traitors to "the proletarians" trying to escape from the Soviet grip: this was called "the Brezhnev Doctrine".

This was the end of the ascent of communism because, by then, China was getting out of their failed extremist Cultural Revolution.

Besides, another deeper and eventually more important change was taking place: Computers were being used to process and manage all types of mathematical information, as their electronic components were becoming smaller and cheaper. This caused a "revolution" in the economies by automating many processes of heavy industry, dramatically diminishing the numbers of employees needed to perform physical tasks, although it did require more specialized personnel for programming and controlling the processes.

What was happening, meanwhile, with religion and morality? Religion continued its speedy decline in the beliefs and practices of the people of the First World, but the danger of communism slowed and even reanimated the process somewhat, as many people adopted this *non sequitur*: "communism is bad, communism is atheist, ergo atheism is bad and so religion must be good".

On the other hand, science kept uncovering the mysteries of the world, so much so that one of the strangest things about the universe was that its workings were not mysterious at all. Therefore, all its aspects can be studied, at least those concerning energy/matter and life. By that time, astronomers and physicists were arriving at the conclusion that the universe had started in a primeval explosion, ironically called by some detractors "the big-bang theory", a name that stuck. Life also yielded its most intimate mystery with the discovery of DNA's and RNA's helical strands, while the history of human evolution was being completed with the findings of Australopithecine remains in Africa and also of several intermediate hominid species.

Humanistic intellectual disciplines -anthropology, history, politics and law, as well as philosophy and logic, which had bearing on all others- also made great strides at this time, but most of those advances were controversial, tentative, and makeshift, most notably in the case of ethics and teleology, which addresses the purpose of existence. For this reason, in these two last areas religion continued playing a significant role.

In contrast, as far as morality it concerned, there was a kind of convergence between the two great opposing ideological systems, as we saw above: Both claimed to be pursuing happiness for all people, regardless of race, ethnicity, or gender, and also agreed that no national interest should be put above this moral principle. So, their only difference was: which is the better and most expedient means of achieving this?

10.2.- Political Immobility and Socio-economic Change from 1968 to 1982

This was the state of the world in late 1968: The Soviet Union was in a political immobility which would not budge until Brezhnev's death 14 years later, the United States had decided to get "honorably" out of the Vietnam War, electing Nixon to do so, and China was leaving its cultural Revolution behind and entering into a stage of recovery.

But if that was happening in the power elite circle, real history was being made in engineering companies, laboratories, the media, and university classrooms, which began to account for a larger share of the economies of the First World by employing highly specialized personnel, while heavy industry was maintained and even grew employing less and less workers, only 30% of the active population. Agriculture was requiring less than 10%. In these new conditions, the "liberal-capitalist, democratic, and with social consciousness" socio-political system of the First World demonstrated its unassailable superiority over the "central planned" system of the Second World, whose growth rate had impressed everyone so forcefully when heavy industry had required the largest part of the working force.

Besides the stark fact of the First World system's economic superiority, the political leaders of the other two "worlds" and observers and communicators alike were gradually realizing that certain non-planned events that had unfolded evidenced the characteristics of justice, fortitude, and wisdom of the First World system. It was all the more impressive because it was obvious that the events were not, by any means, propaganda.

One of them was the Watergate Scandal, which ended with the near-impeachment of President Nixon, forcing his resignation, and the reelection loss of President Ford for having pardoned Nixon. This case, and other similar ones in France and Great Britain, although not so well publicized, convinced the rest of the world that, in the First World, nobody was above the law.

Another event began very favorably for the Third World, in one of those rare cases in which a good and courageous leader ascends to power, as it did in Egypt with Anwar el-Sadat: He planned and waged the only war partially favorable to the Arabs. It started on the Jewish holiday of Yom Kippur in October 1973, and came very close to victory, as his Egyptian troops crossed the Suez Canal and pushed the main Israeli army back to the middle of the Sinai. All that remained was the *coup de grace* to be delivered by a Syrian 250-tank column attacking Israel from the north. But the heroic Israeli commander of a small garrison went out with just 5 tanks against "the nose" of the Syrian column and, in an act of cowardly irresponsibility, its commander ordered his men to halt and turn back, which left the column in disarray and out of commission for a number of hours, enough for the Israelis to send reinforcements.

So unbelievable was the outcome that when King Faisal of Saudi Arabia asked the Syrian President, al-Assad, what had happened with his attack, Assad told him that "the U.S. had intervened". Faisal believed the lie and threw such a tantrum that he decided to plot an oil embargo against the First World. He succeeded in convincing the Shah of Iran, whose amity with the West had cooled, the neighboring emirs, and even Venezuela. Soon all OECO members began to close the valves of their oil wells.

That 1973-1974 winter, the embargo was a resounding success because it took the First World entirely by surprise, but the reactions weren't long in coming: Some countries, like Japan, which had no supply alternative but was rich enough, simply paid what was required, leaving others without oil, mainly Third World importing countries, such as India, Brazil, and Mexico at that time.

Other First World countries, such as the U.S., Great Britain, and France invested great amounts in oil field exploration, and soon started finding them: In Alaska's Arctic Slope, the Campeche Sound, the North Sea, and Nigeria.

By the summer of 1974, King Faisal had concluded that the beating he had intended to inflict on the First World had fallen harder on the Third, and realized the Syrians had lied to him, so he began negotiating the end of the embargo.

Meanwhile Premier Chou En Lai was negotiating with Kissinger the mutual recognition of Communist China and the United States, which paved the way to put an end to the Vietnam War: The high class fled, and the rest of the population was subjected by the North Vietnamese communists. Not everyone, in fact: There were Catholic or Cao Dai villages which had or bought junks and set off in them in the vain hope of reaching France or the U.S., as also did many of the Saigon market's Chinese shop owners, who had studied in French schools. Even if many of those endeavors ended in tragedy, the world was surprised to realize that any community with even the slightest veneer of western education would find it unbearable to live under a communist authoritarian ideology.

In the Indian Sub-continent, the U.S. put its humanitarian feelings above its diplomatic interests. The country known as Pakistan, which had gained its independence from the British in 1947, as we've seen, had operated up to 1970 as a country divided into two by 1,600 kms. (1,000 miles) of Indian territory: The NW part, which has kept the name, was located in the Indus river basin, and then (1970) had a population of 40 million; the NE was part of Bengal, smaller but densely populated, with 60 million.

In the 1970 elections, a major victory by a Bengali leader named Mujibur Rhaman entitled him to be the next head of government, an inconceivable and unacceptable thing for Westerners. So they baited Rhaman to go to the capital, where upon his arrival he was arrested and put on trial for "high treason". Foreseeable, the Bengali people rose in protest, but the government ordered its 250,000 soldiers there, all Punjabis or Sindis, to crush the unrest. The crackdown became such a rampage of bloodshed that it caused 6 million Hindu Bengalis to flee to India!

Up to then, the regional problems of its Muslim neighbor had been a source of amusement to India, but the arrival of 6 million refugees wiped the smile off its face. Its chancellor was dispatched to Washington, after which Kissinger tried to convince the U.S.' ally Pakistan to take the refugees back. It rudely refused to receive "those idol worshippers". Kissinger then told the chancellor: If you plan and execute a "fast and clean" war against Pakistan, the U.S. will look the other way, just for a while. The chancellor understood and accepted.

The Indo-Pakistani war was fought from mid December 1971 to mid January 1972. The western border front was purely defensive for India, so it deployed its elite troops and mechanized units to the East, where they pierced the territory like knives, defeating and taking prisoner 250,000 West Pakistani soldiers.

That was followed by the liberation of Mujibur Rhaman, a prisoner exchange, and the three-sided 1974 treaty creating a new country: Bangladesh.

In China, both Chou and Mao died in 1976, bringing Deng Xiao Ping to power. It would take him five years to consolidate his position. In Western Europe, Great Britain, Ireland, and Denmark entered the Common Market in 1973, and by 1976 Spain and Portugal were preparing to do so.

In Poland, two events took place in 1978 which were instrumental in shattering the Communist system's self-esteem: Independent labor unions were organized in the Silesian coal mines and in the Gdansk shipyards in March and April, respectively. Their leader was Lech Walesa, and the Polish government accepted to negotiate with him! In September, surprisingly, a Polish cardinal was elected Pope, John Paul II, and immediately the polish people began clamoring for him to be officially invited to pay them a visit.

Whether the Poles were truly very Catholic or not, what's certain is that the Pope's summer, 1979 visit was an apotheosis, covered by all Western media, giving it worldwide resonance. Besides, that visit so lifted the status of the labor union leaders, that in August 1980 Walesa was able to organize a confederation of all the country's independent unions, called "Solidarity", which immediately became an important political actor for more than a year. That was too much for Brezhnev. He sacked the Polish Premier and installed a military commander in his place, who ordered the dissolution of all independent labor unions and imprisoning the leaders in December 1981. Less than a year later, in November 1982, Brezhnev died, and that marked the beginning of what can be called "the end of Soviet Communism".

10.3.- The Collapse of the Communist System from 1982 to 1991

Yuri Andropov took Brezhnev's place as supreme leader of the USSR. He was a true believer in communism, so he was convinced that it was working badly because many high officers had become old, inept, or corrupt. In the short time he was at the helm embarked on an almost clean sweep of personnel in high positions, with very good effect, as everything began to run better, which didn't go unnoticed by the people. When he died in February 1984, the leader of the new officers tried to accede to his post to pursue the reforms, but he lacked a "good man" within the Politburo and failed. In his place was elected an "old school" communist who did nothing, and the people felt a reversion to the old routines. Fortunately, the old communist died in March 1985, and then Andrei Gromyko proposed Mikhail Gorbachev as supreme leader and he was elected.

Meanwhile, Ronald Reagan was sworn in as President of the United States in 1981, and won a second term in 1985. His government had almost completed the planning and approval of a new weapons system so technologically sophisticated that the press dubbed it "Star Wars". The military chiefs were closely observing two "little wars" in progress, the Iraq-Iran war, and the Soviet intervention in Afghanistan.

Gorbachev gradually took all the reins of his command, "retired" his "good man" Gromyko and installed the Georgian Shevardnadze in Foreign Relations, who began to negotiate with the Reagan administration nothing less than an end to the Cold War. What had always prevented an agreement to defuse a dangerous situation in which both superpowers could mutually annihilate each other -and incidentally take all of humanity with them- by merely pressing a button, was that mutual inspections had never been agreed to. Now Gorbachev faced his high military commanders, who accepted the deal, convinced that it would be very difficult, not to mention expensive, for the USSR to match "Star Wars", at least without sacrificing goods for the civilian population. So the disarmament of automatic firing systems -based on rigorous mutual inspections- was agreed. In the aftermath, international relations immediately relaxed, notwithstanding the two "little wars".

Once the external problem had been solved, Gorbachev focused on the domestic socio-economic problem by adopting his two famous policies: *Perestroika* and *Glasnost*. The former consisted of reforming the economy and worked on two levels: The direct, small or family level, which was a return to "private initiative" without great changes in ownership laws. Put simply, anyone in an urban area could open his/her carpentry, mechanics, plumbing, electrical, or tailoring shop, the only limitation being that you could not employ anyone but family members, though the definition was flexible. In the rural areas, the kolkhozes were simply parceled out among the members, who would share certain equipment and services, but each one could sow and reap what he/she wanted and sell the product in the nearest market.

Making an aside, we must say that Deng Xiao Ping had begun a much larger "experiment" in China in 1981, since he had ordered the land to be rented for periods of up to 25 years to small virtual owners, because the rental contract could be renewed in the same family. With this, the rural economy grew so much that by 1987, just six years later, it had lifted all the light industries, which created millions of new business to supply peasant needs. Later on, heavy industry was also to rapidly increase its production.

In the USSR, things advanced more slowly in the economic aspect, because at the indirect, large, or managerial level, the *Perestroika* only pretended to imitate the free market, which meant that the performance of the managers of medium and large state enterprises was assessed according to the economic results of their decisions on what to produce for market demand.

Nevertheless, the USSR outdid China in another basic aspect, and that was in establishing the *Glasnost* policy of transparency in the handling of public affairs and civil servants' accountability in carrying out their official functions, just as Dubcek had done in the Spring of Prague. This means that the Soviets were advancing toward liberalism, and China was not, as it has not done to this day.

The implementation of these policies in the years 1986, 1987, and 1988 brought about a profound change not only in production mechanisms, but also in the conviction of the Soviet people that the freedom to decide how, where, and in what to work was much better than the communist system, even more so if we add that the civil servants were now more responsible in how they handled the many public concerns. The common people had only to recall the unending lines they had to stand in, that they had to do what authoritarian officials told them to, and that nothing worked properly in the housing projects, to the point that it seemed they were back in the stone age.

For all these reasons, the stage was set for the collapse of communism, because not even the political leaders, nor the high military officers or the common people believed it to be a system convenient to them. The only thing missing was a good, brave man to make a series of difficult choices. That precisely is what Mikhail Gorbachev set out to do. (1)

The collapse of communism has its start in February 1989, with a decision that was overdue, but nobody had dared to take: The withdrawal of Soviet troops from Afghanistan. Gorbachev also reestablished relations with communist China. In March he ordered free elections of representatives to the Supreme Soviet, but still only within the Communist Party.

All these events caused commotion in its satellite countries; Poland asked for freedom of political activities for Solidarity. It was granted in April, and in August the Poles elected the first non-communist government in the Second World. Also, Vietnam and Cuba were given notice that their subsidies were over.

In July, the USSR tolerated the first labor strike in its history and negotiated with the Donets basin and Urals coal miners. It also took no action against protesters asking for independence in the Baltic countries.

In September, Hungary demanded the same liberties than Poland was granted, and was told: Go ahead. It immediately elected a non-communist government, whose first action was to dismantle its stretch of the "Iron Curtain" on its border with Austria. When the East Germans learned of this, thousands of youths headed there carrying all their possessions and crossed into Austria, who sent them into West Germany, bound by its own laws to receive them. Hoenecker demanded that Gorbachev stop the mass exodus, who answered in an October 25 public radio broadcast that the Brezhnev Doctrine was dead and that each country could do as it pleased. Hoenecker resigned and his successor ordered all surveillance withdrawn from the Berlin Wall. On November 9, youths on both sides who realized that they could do it safely dismantled it informally, and this event came to represent the collapse of communism.

Seeing the overall collapse, Czechoslovakia's intellectual opposition leaders elected writer Vaclav as leader in a café on Prague's main plaza. Upon learning that the puppet government members had simply fled, they crossed the plaza, came out on the Palace balcony, and informed the gathering crowd of the change of regime, in what is known as "The Velvet Revolution".

By then, the world's most nervous leader was the new President of the U.S., George Bush (senior), who feared that the USSR might have thought that what was unfolding had been orchestrated by the U.S., so he asked Gorbachev to meet. He agreed, they met in Malta and ratified their amity and confidence. Gorbachev took advantage of his trip and visited the Pope, a Slav like him, and announced freedom of religion in the USSR.

Up until then, not a drop of blood had been shed by the collapse of communism, but in Romania the despot Ceausescu had failed to grasp the inevitability of the process: When the chief of police of the city of Timisoara informed him that there was a protest march, he ordered his troops to shoot at the protesters. This caused widespread anger, and the miners union organized a national protest march toward Bucharest. Ceausescu then fled, was arrested at the border, returned to the capital, tried by a military court, and executed, together with his wife, by firing squad in front of TV cameras that transmitted the scene worldwide. With that, the military could be back in the protesters' good graces, who were then arriving.

By January 1990, fissures had appeared in the USSR itself, with Lithuania and Georgia demanding their independence and Armenia and Azerbaijan fighting between themselves over territory. In February there were new elections in the USSR already without communist monopoly. That same month, Soviet troops withdrew from Hungary and Bulgaria, and the latter elected a non-communist government. In March, the USSR's 15 Republics elected their own officials, with Russia electing the non-communist Boris Yeltsin. From then on, all tax collecting would be performed by the Republics and none by the USSR itself.

The only problem pending solution in all Eastern Europe was East Germany: If it joined West Germany in a single state, then it would be part of NATO, and that could be seen as treason. Gorbachev and Kohl met and agreed that if Germany and the three western Allies recognized by formal treaty the indefinite ban on Germany to manufacture, possess, transport, or use weapons of mass destruction, and also recognized its present borders with Poland as final, then the USSR would have no objection to all of Germany being part of NATO. So it was done: the United States, Great Britain and France, and of course Germany and the USSR, approved and signed the treaty. On October 3, 1990 the unification of Germany was a reality.

A dark cloud was casting a shadow over world affairs since August of that year, when Iraq invaded the rich emirate of Kuwait, and had to be driven out by a military expedition in January and February, 1991. Taking advantage of this situation, a group of *apparatchiks* or high officials who wanted their old authoritarianism and privileges back, schemed in March to depose Gorbachev, but Yeltsin came to his aid with an impressive popular demonstration by Muscovites. From then on, the *apparatchiks* focused on convincing the military to take action, and in August, with Gorbachev on vacation, they succeeded in having the military stage a coup d'état. But again, Yeltsin and hundreds of thousands of Muscovite protesters saved the situation. The army decided to arrest the *apparatchiks* and returned the reins of the USSR to Gorbachev, who returned to Moscow. From then, however, the real power lay in the hands of Yeltsin, as President of the Russian Republic.

In September 1991, Yeltsin demanded that Gorbachev dissolve the huge Soviet Communist Party, which had some 18 million members -9 million of them commissars and one million full-time Party officials- which was something like the USSR's nervous system. Gorbachev was not fully prepared for doing it, but in view of the circumstances, accepted. The party was dissolved in one fell swoop with astonishing ease, and not a single demonstration or rally against this important measure took place.

The only pending matter then was how to dissolve the USSR itself. Some voices, like that of the writer Solzhenitsyn, wanted to conserve "the Slavic nucleus": Russia, Ukraine, and Belarus. President Kravchuk of Ukraine, however, called for a plebiscite for independence on December 1 and 85% voted "yes". In view of that, Yeltsin and Kravchuk met with President Shushkevich of Belarus and formed the Commonwealth of Independent States as a kind of deliberating chamber for coordinating the division of the army, navy, treasury, and many other common Soviet institutions among the new and free Republics. It also set a date when the USSR would cease to be subject to national and international obligations, which would pass on to the three Republics of the Slavic nucleus, the three Baltic countries, Moldavia, the three Caucasian, and the Five Central Asian Republics. It was done in this manner, and on December 25, 1991 Mikhail Gorbachev became a retired citizen.

XI.- The Historical Present and the Projected Future

11.1.- What Basis for the Morality of Globalization?

In some aspects, as Francis Fukuyama so eloquently said (1), there and then is the end of history, at least in the sense that we who make up the colossus called "humanity" should not just wait for events to unfold, but take a more active part in deciding which things have to occur and work hard to make them happen.

In order to take action in general, and in the socio-political aspect in particular, one must know, or at least decide, which is the "correct" way to act: Meaning, what "ought our behavior to be"?

This takes us back to the origins of morality: Let us remember that, from the long-ago time of the first hominids, morality has been the social discipline necessary for the survival and development of the groups in which individuals socialize. However, let us also remember that "this" was based "only" on that and not on the whole of reality. So, nothing guarantees that "this" will be the most convenient way for, let's say, preserving our Earth's ecosystem, now that we are a colossus with as much capacity to destroy as to create and preserve; nor is "this" a guarantee that we have learned that "group" now means, precisely, the whole of humanity.

How can we anchor ourselves in the whole of reality and how do we take measures for the whole of humanity? We can start with some tentative answers: To take the whole of reality into account, we first have to gain knowledge of it and then try to see how to act upon it. To have measures which apply to the whole of humanity, a political mechanism encompassing all of it is needed.

In regard to knowledge of reality, I think that we now know enough about energy, matter, and living things to be able to act in the direction we decide in those aspects. Then, it would only be a matter of reaching a general consensus on the ethical foundation on which to anchor our public morality.

As to the fact that the application of these measures must cover the whole of humanity, the only seemingly possible way of doing so, in my view, is by transforming the UNO into a "global affairs government" that A) is accepted and controlled by all countries and its decisions made through a voting mechanism based on some parameter considered fair for everyone; and B) would be in charge only of those aspects which have or could have worldwide effects.

So we need a consensus on: An ethical basis with global validity and a "government" with a fair decision-making mechanism restricted only to global affairs. Let's try to make headway on the former: How to go about finding that basis? We said that our instinctive morality is based only on the survival and development of human groups, but not necessarily on protecting and preserving the environment. It is also plain to see that humanity's ecological impact could be increasing at such a rate that the planetary ecosystem ceases to be sustainable (as we will see in some detail below). Given these realities, I think that the best way to find and agree on an ethical basis could be as follows:

Project possible future scenarios which humanity could arrive to at given time frames, and select the most desirable at the end of each. The social disciplines considered vital to having a better chance to arrive to each selected scenario, would be the basis of our public morality. This procedure for setting the adequate morality compass would be based on the following philosophical principle: The knowledge that we humans are depositories and trustees of the highest organizational level of matter known to man -the kind of intelligence that allowed us to attain high consciousness- makes us feel that that we ought to behoove our behavior by assuming the responsibility of protecting and developing that inherited gift.

One of the most important intellectual disciplines -although far from being the only one- which can guide us to determine these projected scenarios is bioethics, from which the following normative social practices could derive.

I think the most paramount of all social disciplines would be birth control, since the sheer size and power of humanity are critical factors for all future ecological impacts. This should be the main "commandment" for all individuals, communities, peoples, nations, and religions.

The second most important "commandment" should be some form of austerity to counterbalance the unbridled "consumerism" which the market economy tends to unleash. But I am convinced that capitalism, for all its crises and inequities, must continue to be the favored form of productive activity, as it is -of all the economic systems we know- the one which best develops and channels man's creative abilities and nurtures his liberties and his virtues of perseverance and prudence.

Since both "commandments" -birth control and austerity- cannot be said to be instinctive, they must be rooted in a high quality education, in order to turn them into deep-seated customs and mores.

Building on this bioethical foundation, we will try to figure out in the following section the delegated authority basis suitable for a "global affairs government" to function effectively.

11.2.- Basis and Functions for a "Global Affairs Government"

With the purpose of anchoring ourselves in the reality of our political world and conclude the series of demographic tables we have seen, the one for 2008 follows below. It is accompanied by the Purchasing Power Parity (PPP), which is based on the Gross Domestic Product, but adjusted to real costs. It is shown in two columns: total and *per capita*. I have also included a column showing the population growth rate between 1950 and 2008.

REGION	Data for the Year 2008			
	Million Inhab.	% Incr. Popul. f. 1950	PPP *per capita*	PPP Th. Mill. Dollars
West. Europe +Greece +Israel	495	37.5	32,022	13,703
N. America + Austr.+NZ+ (High Inc.)	372	106.6	45,686	15,048
Japan + 4 Asian "Tigers"	210	66.6	32,994	6,434
FIRST WORLD	1,077	61.7	39,931	35,185
Ex-USSR+Orthodox+Turkey+Iran	472	98.3	11,858	5,502
China + 2 Comm. neighbors	1,340	136.7	5,877	7,875
SECOND WORLD	1,812	125.4	7,381	13,377
Latin America	564	250.3	10,987	6,202
South East Asia & Pacific	579	216.4	4,533	2,637
Indian Sub-Continent	1,571	237.8	3,646	4,158
Arab Countries	276	324.6	8,975	2,474
South Africa+Ind. Oc. Isl.	59	181.0	9,993	589
THIRD WORLD	3,049	240.7	5,267	16,060
Tropical Africa, or FOURTH WORLD	678	360.2	1,554	1,151
WORLD TOTAL	6,679	164.4	10,536	70,368

The data in this tabulation tells us the following:

A) That in the 58 years from 1950 to 2008 the population of the First World grew by only 62%, or an annual rate of 0.8%; that of the Second World more than doubled (1.41% per year); that of the Third more than tripled (2.1% per year); and that of the Fourth almost quadrupled at a sustained rate of 2.66% per year. It is clear that the population growth rate occurred in strictly inverse proportion to the living standards of each Region of the World, as we can see by comparing the second column with the *per capita* one.

B) That the First World -with only 16% of the population- produces 50% of the world's wealth, as adjusted by parity costs (and also produces more than half of its CO_2 emissions).

C) That the Second and Third Worlds are home to almost three quarters (73%) of the world population, so according to the combined growth rates of their population and their standards of living, will increase their share of contaminating effects.

Below is the table showing population percentages, GDP, and "contribution" to the emission of carbon dioxide gases of the regions and the "worlds":

REGION:	Data for the Year 2008		
	% of Population	% of PPP	% of (2) CO_2 Emission
Western Europe (+Greece+Israel	7.41	22.51	25.0
North America + Austr.+NZ+ (H.I.)	5.57	24.15	33.7
Japan + 4 Asian "Tigers"	3.15	9.87	5.7
FIRST WORLD	16.13	54.78	64.4
Ex-URSS+Orthodox+Turkey+Iran	7.07	7.82	15.8
China + 2 Comm. neighbors	20.06	11.19	7.0
SECOND WORLD	27.13	19.01	22.8
Latin America	8.44	8.83	3.8
South East Asia + Pacific	8.67	3.72	1.2
Indian Sub-Continent	23.53	91.85	4.0
Arab Countries	4.13	3.52	2.3
South Africa	0.88	0.84	0.5
THIRD WORLD	45.65	22.82	11.8
FOURTH WORLD	11.09	1.64	1.0
WORLD`S TOTAL	100.00	100.00	100.0

I I suggest that these two tables can also signal to us the parameter that would be acceptable by all countries for the establishment and control of a government in charge of only those functions or "affairs" classified as "global".

That parameter for the purpose of voting rights in that restricted global government, should be the size of the economy of each country, as measured by accounting principles generally accepted at the global level by all countries. The most acceptable way of shaping this parameter probably would be the PPP that each Region or country produces (its size in terms of dollars shown in the last column of the first table and its percentage of the world total in the middle column of the last table). This parameter could also be affected by some agreed upon indexes of quality of life or of ecological control. What I'm endeavoring to convey is that it seems fair to me that each country has an authority and responsibility in proportion to its capacity for acting on the world stage, and that a practical way to determine it is by measuring its economic production, adjusted by a parity to real costs. Another way to ponder the fairness of assigning no more than these proportions of voting power to the richest nations is by taking into account that they inflict more damage to certain aspects of the ecosystem than their not adjusted Gross Domestic Product.

Which functions or "affairs" should be classified as "Global"? In the following pages I present a tentative list of the four main areas or type of activities which tend to be of a global character. Some are presently managed by the United Nations Organization, though not with the desirable levels of efficiency and authority.

I) Control of weapons of mass destruction and use of military forces in international police actions.

II) Conservation of the ecosystem and control of fossil fuels.

III) Control of multinational global trade treaties and regulation of the capital flows and worker migration.

IV) Satellite communications and space exploration.

First, the dissuasive and coercive use of armed forces must come under control. One aspect would be the control of weapons of mass destruction, whether nuclear, chemical or biological. A de facto control is, in fact, already in place, as their possession is limited to the victors of WWII: the United States, Great Britain, France, Russia, and China. They have "allowed" the entry of India, Pakistan, and Israel to the nuclear "club", but are opposed to the entry of North Korea and Iran. We also mentioned the mutual inspections agreement that put an end to the Cold War. This control also means licensing and assisting in the peaceful use of atomic energy in nations that formally renounce their right to possess these kinds of weapons and sign the Non-Proliferation Treaty, as Japan, Germany, Italy, Brazil, Mexico, and others have done.

What should be appended to this arrangement is that the control of nuclear weapons should aim to eliminate, through rigorous mutual inspections, all weapons that could be deployed only on Earth. Only those that could be used for planetary defense, i.e. for the destruction of meteorites on dangerous paths or other uses in space, should be kept on reserve. As for chemical and biological weapons, the main function would be the vigilance and the police actions necessaries to keep them out of the hands of criminal or extremist groups.

Another aspect of this function of the World Government would be the coercive use –and control– of conventional armed forces, like those which on one hand took part in the violent breakup of the former Yugoslavia and on the other failed to intervene in the Rwandan genocide, the present anti-terrorist interventions in Afghanistan and Iraq, and the actions which have not taken place to forestall genocides in Sudan and other parts of Africa. So any actions by rogue regimes or of a criminal nature exceeding the "host" country's capacity to combat it and classified as such by the GAG's voting mechanism would warrant compulsory action. Among humans, order without policing is unconceivable, hence it stands to reason that it would be better to integrate it and have it operate legally, than to leave any country to fend for itself as it deems fit.

Second, we must protect, preserve, and control the Earth's ecosystem and control the production, transportation, and massive use of energy sources, mainly fossil fuels. There is a myriad of ways to damage the environment, but I will use, with minor changes, Jared Diamond's classification (3) in three groups: I) Destruction of the Natural Ecosystem; B) Energy sources, water, and photosynthesis; and C) Emissions of toxic gases and liquids.

In Group A he includes four means of damaging the environment, and I add a fifth, which he originally classifies in Group C: A1) Deforestation; A2) Marine resources; A3) Extinction of species; A4) Erosion of agricultural soils; and A5) Introduction of non-native species.

A1 and A4: Deforestation and erosion of agricultural soils are very similar in their harmful effects of impoverishing the planet's flora and fauna. They are, however, subject to strong pressures, deforestation in particular, mainly in the tropical rain forests because of the huge demand for wood from the rich countries for construction and paper production. But also because the native population is razing them to use the soil, inefficiently, for agricultural purposes, with Brazil being the most notorious case. In Mexico it the erosion of agricultural soils is specially severe, mainly in the central and southern parts of the country, because of the rugged terrain and the ancient custom of tilling those lands without terracing (in the last 500 years, an estimated 5 meters or 16' of soil has been eroded from the Mixteca Sierra (4)). But even in the best lands on the planet, like the Great Plains, the soil used for agriculture is being eroded by wind and water at a faster pace than nature can build it up. A tentative proposal would be to substitute the newspapers by electronic information to customers.

A2: This includes overfishing, that is depleting stocks of certain species, as is the case of some whales, sardines and sea turtles; the use of trawlers hauling vast nets for scooping up tuna and that in the process also kill the dolphins that pray on them; and the destruction of coral reefs, sometimes by their use of dynamite. Today, an estimated 2 billion people eat seafood, but since nobody oversees the open seas, the pillaging of fish proceeds unabated and this source of food is in danger of entering a decline. Proposal: Strict global control of marine fisheries.

Here we can add one component of C2, mentioning that the disposal of toxic wastewater and runoff from the cities into rivers and coastal seawaters, are the reason why many seas near the continents which are not "washed" by marine currents, are seeing their fish, crustaceans, and mollusks disappear and becoming waters in which only ancient medusas thrive, as is largely the case in the Yellow Sea. Proposal: That each nation preserves its coastal seas following global obligatory standards.

A3 and A5: By causing the extinction of large terrestrial animal species by excessive hunting and deliberately or accidentally introducing non-native animal or vegetal species in areas where natural enemies are non existent, we are abusing nature's biota and rapidly destroying the immense diversity that evolved during millions of years of life, and which has maintained the Earth's surface in optimum condition. But since man appeared in sizeable numbers a few thousand years ago, we have put an ever-increasing stress on the environment, first with agriculture and then, starting two centuries ago, with the industrial revolution and the population explosion.

In Group B, Jared Diamond places problems humanity has caused in order to have access to its most basic resources: B1: Energy sources; B2: Fresh water; and B3: Solar energy for the photosynthesis process used by plants to start the planet's food pyramid, by converting nutrients and minerals dissolved in water into living plant tissue.

B3: This is the longest-term issue, so we will only say that it is the comparison that scientists make between the capacity this Planet had, say, 10,500 years ago, before the advent of agriculture, for "manufacturing" vegetal tissue with solar energy in woodlands, rain forests, and prairies –not to mention marine plankton– and its current capacity, with half the forests and jungles cleared, many prairies turned into agricultural or uncultivated lands, and great amounts of land losing ground to urban sprawl, highways, and roads. Most people aren't even aware of this problem and would be surprised to learn that we have already lost half of that capacity: It is yet to be a pressing problem, but it could quickly become one if the population and its consumption keep increasing at an uncontrolled rate and green areas and marine plankton keep shrinking catastrophically through destruction and pollution.

B2: Fresh water is a much better known problem, as it affects billions of people. In many places on Earth, it is used to the last drop in crop irrigation, industrial applications, navigation, and human and animal consumption. It is a problem of far-reaching proportions: its most dramatic manifestations are underground water drying up or a lower water table, farmlands becoming salty, and desertification.

B1: Energy sources are the thorniest, trickiest, and most acute of global issues, owing to its having two approaches or sides: One is that they are absolutely necessary for maintaining and driving our civilization's technological activities, such as industry, transportation, and electricity generation. So the demand for energy sources is huge in the First World and rapidly increasing in the Second and Third ones. But the availability of the highest in demand, fossil fuels –coal and oil– is limited and decreasing, hence the great urgency to find new forms of usable sources of energy: The most abundant is nuclear power, but its main flaw, unsolved as yet, is how to cheaply and safely dispose of its radioactive wastes.

C1: The other aspect of the issue are the carbon dioxide (CO_2) emissions of the two main fossil fuels –coal and oil– which meet 90% of the world's energy demands. Those emissions are so huge and have been rising so steeply over the last two centuries, that they have significantly increased the amount of CO_2 in the atmosphere, trapping more solar heat: the so-called "greenhouse effect" that causes global climate warming. It stands to reason that a "government of global affairs" would have to be in charge of regulating the production, transportation, and massive use of fossil fuels. Being solid, coal is rarely carried far away, so it is mainly used in the same regions where it is mined, but is very important as it still satisfies around 40% of the world's energy demands.   Oil, in contrast, being liquid, is easy to transport, mainly by pipelines and ocean tankers, and there lies its strategic importance. One seemingly possible way of regulating these fossil fuels would be to levy a tax on them, making their use more expensive and earmarking the revenue to developing other types of non-polluting energy sources. Another way of preventing the CO_2 massively produced by large plants' fossil fuel combustion from reaching the atmosphere would be to pump it down very deep shafts reaching saline strata , with which salts the carbon dioxide would chemically react, producing solid carbonates, which can stay buried for a long time. This method is only possible, of course, where those kinds of mineral seams are present.

C2: Toxic liquids, which we mentioned in connection to problem A2, mainly a product of the mining and chemical industries and pesticide production for agriculture, is one area in which intervention by a "government for global affairs" is very sorely needed. It also has an impact on problem B2 –fresh water– by contaminating its sources, and in addition instigates corruption, mainly between big corporations and non-democratic rulers in the Third World.

Third: Another area which a "government for global affairs" could oversee would be the control and regulation of global trade –currently carried out by the UN through the World Trade Organization (WTO), along with the regulation and control of capital flows, both for investment or large-scale loans, and the permanent and temporary migration of workers.

Four charges are commonly leveled against the WTO, in Peter Singer's view (5):

1.- That it puts economic considerations ahead of concerns for the environment, animal welfare, and even human rights;

2.- That it erodes national sovereignty;

3.- That it is undemocratic; and

4.- That it increases inequality between rich and poor.

After a well documented analyses, Singer concludes:

That the first charge has merit, but is very difficult to rectify, as it is easy for big business to have many non-democratic Third World rulers neglect the protection of their country's environment. In addition, very few people are concerned about oceans and atmosphere conservation. This explains the great urgency for the arrival of a real government to protect the Earth's environment. The only aspect of the charges that the WTO is responding to is that of human rights: It is asking the UN for the World Labor Organization to intervene in deciding cases where one country is rejecting the products of countries that exploit or abuse their workers.

In regard to the second charge, he says that the WTO is rigorously correct in answering that all countries are free to enter, forgoing certain aspects of their sovereignty, or to leave the organization. But he points out that it is very difficult for any country to stay out of global trade. This, then, is a perfect example for our proposal: That all countries be subject to the same rules, with a say in legislation and enforcement in accordance with the PPP percentage of the block of nations deciding to vote together. This would also provide the solution to the third charge, of being undemocratic, because PPP-mandated voting is the most democratic decision-making approach that would have a chance of being accepted as binding by all countries, rich and poor, superpowers or not.

After a detailed analysis of the fourth charge –that global trade makes the rich richer and the poor poorer– Singer concludes that there is not enough data to either verify or refute it. He thinks, though, that a responsible, caring, and equitable management will tend to foster, if not equality, at least that the poorest people have access to the most essential goods and services, such as food, shelter, medicine, and education.

What should be regulated regarding capital flows? In the first place, their legal provenance and that there be no way to "hide" them in places that have "secrecy" as their middle name. In second place, the rules of the game, according to the living standards of the origin and destiny countries: interest rates and the conditions for withdrawal.

What should be regulated regarding migrant workers? This is a very difficult issue, because at present all countries conceive their sovereignty as exercised only by its nationals, hence their thinking they have a right to legislate on immigration however they deem most convenient. On the contrary, since the collapse of the Communist system, practically no country regulates emigration, leaving their nationals free to go wherever they wish or can.

It would be difficult to convince the rich countries that the acceptance of a certain number of immigrants should be seen as a counterpart to the investment of their capitals overseas. Equally difficult would be to convince the poor countries to control their emigration and, in particular, examine its causes, such as demographic growth, and try to remedy them. If ever there was a country with this problem it is Mexico, as it is the only poor country with a long land border with a First World power.

FOURTH As far as global management of satellite communications and space exploration is concerned, I think this would be the area of less conflict, as several arrangements and cooperative actions have already been made in this area, which may serve as models for further agreements in more contentious aspects. The only pending aspect would be that of formalizing its international global characteristics.

11.3.- A Practical View of the Proposal and Conclusion

The proposal is to strive to forge a world in which all human beings agree to repay their gift of high consciousness by assuming the responsibility of protecting and developing it. In order to do so, I think the world they forge must possess the following two characteristics:

1st) Have a secular public morality based on those norms of social discipline which better assure the survival of humanity and foster its development in harmony with the environment, in accordance with the best projections of desirable future conditions that can be made. The two main "commandments" of this new morality would seem to be birth control and consumer austerity, at least for the time that it takes to stabilize the global state of affairs.

2nd) Have its national governments legally bound to relinquish part of their sovereignty to a "global affairs government", to be controlled by the votes of nations or geo-cultural blocks of nations, and maintained with funding, both in proportion to the nations' capacity to generate wealth, adjusted to real costs.

What will be the relationship of this new morality and international law order with both the nation-states and the existing religions?

If we try to visualize these relationships through the eyes of our most outstanding politicians, we would realize that the highest aspiration of the best of them would be not only to head their country's national government, not even that of the only remaining "superpower", but to be in charge of global affairs. Consequently, he or she would have to be highly prudent regarding his/her nationalism, in the policies for using fossil fuels, and be very concerned with environmental conservation.

It is obvious that responsible behavior by politicians on those stated terms would be possible only if the great majority of the population of every country were genuinely convinced of the unavoidable need to adopt those general policies, which would so greatly affect their own personal lives. Such would be the case with the two "commandments", particularly birth control for Third and Fourth World denizens, and consumer austerity for those in the First and Second Worlds.

Here is where religions could be of greater help, should they decide to limit themselves to the private lives of their faithful, as Christianity does, mainly its Protestant branch in the First World. The Catholic Church would have to radically modify its own stance against birth control methods or face the loss of prestige which would follow if it persists in its present doctrinal position.

But that would be relatively easy compared to the immense transformation that Islam will have to carry out in order to accept what Lilla calls "the Great Divide" between politics and religion, which has cost Christianity a fight which has already lasted five centuries. Even if Islam has the example of the Turkish Republic, it also has many countries where the religious conflicts have worsened, like Afghanistan, Pakistan, and Sudan, or that consider themselves "heads of the faith", like Saudi Arabia and Iran.

Although these things may seem very difficult to achieve, they are not impossible: It is worth bearing in mind what Chris Brazier said referring to the unexpected, utter collapse of the Communist system, which seemingly was going to last centuries: "(the collapse occurred)…as soon as the public consent and the servile obeisance to their government ceased, and the system melted as fast as snow under the spring sun, notwithstanding the tanks and the secret police." (6)

Conclusion

So we can opt to do nothing and let humanity keep being polarized between rich and poor, and continue damaging its planetary ecological system by means of overpopulation and "consumerism", until nature herself makes us see our folly, with the severity she often employs. Or we can throw ourselves into figuring out and trying solutions which could work. We can do that with the resolve born out of our sense of responsibility that our ancestors consolidated and made sacred when they attained high self-consciousness, which we have inherited.

We have become powerful due to our intelligence and sociability, built on a cornerstone of morality which was very concentric at the beginning, but which expanded throughout history by means of great religions and empires. Now we have reached such power and such a population density that it should prevent our behaving in a selfish and hostile manner, and instead adopt a fully responsible moral posture.

The challenge is already upon us: We are our own enemy! So there is no way around it: Let us set the rules for a new moral for globalization and establish the convenient legal order for converting that morality into good laws for living together equitably and in harmony with our Earth environment. This would allow us to keep climbing safely up the never ending stairs of knowledge, forever committed to the well-being of every man.

NOTES

Introduction
1.- This is how Lilla (2007) calls it.
2.- In his book "The Stillborn God".

Chapter I.- The Biological Evolution up to the Human Species

1.1.- The First Life
1.- Knoll, Andrew H. (2003), for events between 4,500 and 600 mya

1.2.- The Formation of Individuals and the Expansion of Life
2.-. For events between 600 and 7 mya I generally follow: Wells, Huxley, and Wells (1958), Fritz Kahn (1957), Carl Zimmer (2001), Richard Dawkins (1996, 1998), and Collin Tudge (1996) which covers also the next incise.

1.3.- The Hominid Evolution
3.- For events between 7,000,000 and 57,000 years ago I generally follow: David Pilbeam (1971), Stringer & McKie (1996), and Gibson & Ingold (1993).
4.- Reichholf (1990), Chapters 13 and 14.

1.4.- The Conditions for the Ascent to High Self-Consciousness
5.- For the description of the Upper Paleolithic, Mesolithic, and hunting techniques, I follow the same authors of Incise 1.3. For the Great Migrations I follow: Cavalli-Sforza (1993) and Steve Olson (2002), and for the Peopling of the Americas: Brian M Fagan.
6.- De Balbin Berhmann, Rodrigo (2006), his article in the dossier "El Arte Rupestre" in the review "La Aventura de la Historia", Madrid, June, 2008.

Chapter II.- The Ascent to High Self-Consciousness

2.1.- The Evolutionary Pressure of Living in Groups
1.- Cartwright (1953), p. 176, plus my additions.
2.- Arsuaga (2001), Chap. 3.
3.- Cartwright (1953), fig, 7.1, p. 196.
4.- Ibid. pgs. 207-209.
5.- Joyce (1996), pg. 90.

2.2.- The Acquisition of Language
6.- Cartwright (1953), fig. 7.3, p. 208.
7.- Ibid. p. 250.
8.- Ibid. p. 206.
9.- Deutscher (2005), Chap. 7: "The Unfolding of Language".
10.- Smith (1985), pgs. 60, 61
11.- Dowling (1998), Chap. 6

12.- Gibson & Ingold (1993), pgs. 259, 260.
13.- Smith (1985), pgs. 143, 144.

2.3.- The Origins of Morality
14.- Joyce (1992), pgs. 90, 104.
15.- Ibid. p.65.
16.- Ibid. p. 110.
17.- Ibid. pgs. 116, 117, 118.

2.4.- The Meaning of High Self-Consciousness
18.- O'Manique (2003), p. 16.
19.- Ibid. pgs. 17, 18.
20.- Ibid. p. 43.
21.- Ibid. p.51.
22.- Frondizi (1977).
23.- O'Manique (2003), Chap. 6.
24.-Ibid. Chap. 7.

2.5.- The Origins of Religion
25.- As general references, I follow: Mircea Eliade (1964), Claude Levy-Strauss (1962), and Marcel Mauss (1993, 1947).
26.- Marquard (2003) cites Hans Blumenberg in p. 114.
27.- In the imagination of myths I follow: Lewis-Williams & Pearce (2005).
28.- I underlined the "dimensions" that Lewis-Williams & Pearce consider to be the basic elements of religion.
29.- James (1902), pgs. 50, 51.
30.- Trías (2000), p. 51.
31.- Lopez Quintas (1997) quotes Miguel Angel Virasoro in pgs. 253-261.
32.- Frondizi (1972)

2.6.- Panorama of Humanity 10,500 Years Ago
33.- Cavalli-Sforza (1993), p. 30.

Chapter III.- The Neolithic Revolution and the First Civilizations

3.1.- The First Human Population and Ecological Impact
1.- Olson (2002), p. 86.
2.- Diamond (1999), in his book Guns, Germs, and Steel.

3.2.- The Social Aspect of the Neolithic Revolution
3.- Childe (1936, 1951).
4.- Hawkes (1976) Chapter 8,000 - 5,000 B.C.
5.- Lewis-Williams & Pearce (2005), pgs. 140, 141.
6.- Dowling (1998), fig. 63, p. 180.

7.- Lewis-Williams & Pearce (2005), fig. 8, p. 48.
8.- Lewis-Williams (2002).

3.3.- The Second Expansion of the Neolithic
9.- Childe (1936, 1951).
10.- Lewis-Williams & Pearce (2005), Chapters 7 and 8.
11.- Tibón (1984).

3.4.- The Ascent to First Generation Civilizations
12.- Childe (1936, 1951).
13.- Schmand-Besserat (1992, 1996) expounding the origin of the cuneiform writing out of clay "tokens" used by farming Neolithic communities for giving each member his contributed amount of wheat or olive oil to the communal silos or barrels or as proof of his working time for the community.
14.- Margueron (1991, 1996), pgs. 347-392.
15.- Edwards (1947, 1979).
16.- Gonzalez Torres (1985).
17.- Armstrong (2006), p.18.

3.5.- World's Overview around the Year 1,550 BCE
18.- Childe (1936, 1951).

Chapter IV.- The Arrival to Second Generation Civilizations

4.1.- The Crisis of the Propitiatory Polytheism during the Bronze Age
1.- National Geographic Magazine, April, 2001.

4.2.- The Birth of Two Axial Peoples
2.- Armstrong (2006, 2007), This is how Karen Armstrong calls to the peoples (Aryans, Chinese, Israelis, and Greeks) who are going to effectuate "the Great Ethic Transformation" during the IX to IV centuries BCE.
3.- Childe (1936, 1951).
4.- Bright (1966, 1970), Second Part: "The Formative Period".

4.3.- Gestation Period in the Dark Age from 1150 to 750 BCE
5.- Finkelstein & Silberman (2001), Chapter 5 "Memories of a Golden Age?
6.- Finkelstein & Silberman (2001), Chapters 6 and 7.
7.- Armstrong (2006, 2007), p. 95

4.4.- The Axial Period between the Years 750 to 500 BCE
8.- Armstrong (2006, 2007), Preface and section regarding each people.
9.- Holland) (2005, 2007), Chapter I and maps.
10.- Toynbee (1946, 1970).

4.5.- The Forge of Monotheism in Israel

11.- Podhoretz (2002), Chapter 6 "Amos: The Lion Roars".
12.- Finkelstein & Silberman (2001), p. 216.
13.- Armstrong (2006, 2007), p. 138.
14.- Podhoretz (2002), Chapter 8 "Micah: Pax Israelitica".
15.- Armstrong (2006, 2007), pgs. 230-233.
16.- Childe (1936, 1951).
17.- Armstrong (2006, 2007), p. 339.

4.6.- The Democratizing of Greece from 776 to 506 BCE

18.- Armstrong (2006, 2007), p. 211.
19.- Armstrong (2006, 2007), p. 205.

4.7.- The Persian Wars

20.- Childe (1936, 1951).
21.- Holland (2005, 2007), pgs. 255, 256.

4.8.- The Golden Age and the Peloponnesian War

22.- Toynbee (1946, 1970), Chapter IV "The Collapse of Civilizations".
23.- Armstrong (2006, 2007), pgs. 316-322 and 351-365.

4.9.- The Greek Philosophy

24.- Armstrong (2006, 2007), pgs. 346-350, 355-360, and 428-450.

Chapter V.- Hellenism and Christianity up to the Barbarian Invasions and the Surging of Islam

5.3.- The Cultural Components of the Hellenistic World

1.- I follow the main ideas of "The Harvest of Hellenism" by F. E. Peters, and of "El Mundo Helenístico" by Pierre Leveque.
2.- Leveque (1992, 2005), pgs. 153, 154.
5.6.- The Upper Roman Empire
3.- Peters (1970, 1996) p. 446.
5.10.- The West Sinks, the East Persists
4.- For all commentaries on the bubonic plague see "Catastrophe" of David Keyes (1999).

Chapter VI.- Infancy and Youth of the Western Civilization

6.1.- The Birth of the Western Civilization
1.- Toynbee (1946, 1970), V. I, pgs. 39, 184.
6.3.- The Feudal Chaos.
2.- In many things I followed Cantor (1963), Chapter VII, incise II.

6.5.- The Crusades and the Birth of the Bourgeoisie

3.- Lopez (1960, 1996), p. 132.

6.11.- Confrontation of Historical Events from 667 to 1560 with the Working Hypothesis

4.- In regard with the Barbarian's Conversion I followed the magnificent book of Fletcher (1997), mainly its chapters IV and V.

Chapter VII.- The Modern Age 1560 - 1830

7.2.- Western Europe in 1560 and the Wars of Religion

1.- Weber (1919, 1994).
2.- Toynbee (1946, 1970), V. I, pgs. 252-292.

7.3.- The Science from the Renaissance up to 1650

3.- Debus (1978, 1985), I took from this book the main ideas of the first four first paragraphs.
4.- Koyré (1973, 1977), In all the rest of this Incise I will follow him, mainly in his conference "Galileo and the Scientific Revolution in the XVII Century".

7.6.- The Commercial Revolution and the Illustration from 1715 to 1763

5.- Fukuyama, Francis (1995), Chapters 4 and 5.

7.7.- The Beginnings of the Industrial Revolution

6.- Derry & Williams (1960, 1977).- V. 2, p. 401.
7.- Ibid., V. 3, p. 414-418.
8.- Ibid., V. 2, p. 464-466.
9.- Ibid., V. 2, p. 467-468.

7.9.- The Evolution of the Philosophical and Religious Ideas up to 1830

10.- Lilla (2007) In this incise I follow Part II of his book.
11.- Ibid. p. 103.
12.- Ibid. p. 110.
13.- Ibid. p. 113.
14.- Ibid. p. 128.
15.- Ibid. p. 118-120.
16.- Ibid. p. 132.
17.- Ibid. p. 140-146.
18.- Ibid. p. 157-162.
19.- Ibid. p. 171.
20.- Ibid. p. 213.

Chapter VIII.- The Strengthening of the West 1830 - 1914

8.5.- The Evolution of Philosophical Ideas from 1830 to 1914

1.- Lilla (2007), p.248: He refers to the liberal German theologians, but it can also be applied to other European liberals.
2.- Ibid., Chapter 5th, p. 217-250.

Chapter IX.- The Two World Wars

9.1.- The Tragedy of the First World War
1.- Clausewitz (1832, 1968), First Book: "On the Nature of Wars".
2.- Ibid. Outline of the Eight Book, Chapter 3, Incise b.
3.- Lilla (2007), Chapter 6 "The Redeeming God".

Chapter X.- The Cold War, The Information Revolution and Globalization

10.3.- The Collapse of the Communist System from 1982 to 1991
1.- Maidanik (1992), In what follows in this incise I used much information contained in this work.

Chapter XI.- The Historical Present and the Projected Future

11.1.- What Basis for a Morality of Globalization?
1.- Fukuyama (1992).

11.2.- Basis and Functions for a "Government of Global Affaires"
2.- Gonzalez Valenzuela (2008), in her contribution for the work "Una Visión Ecológica sobre Ética Ambiental" of Jose Sarukhan, p. 354.
3.- Diamond (2205).
4.- Information given by Jesus Leon Santos, Goldman Prize in Ecology of 2008, in his June 13th, 2009 conference in Monterrey.
5.- Peter Singer (2002), chapter 3.

11.3.- Practical Visualization of the Proposal
6.- Brazier (2006), p. 187.

Bibliography

Classified by the following subject matter or theme: **Number of Works**

1.- Origin and Meaning of the Universe	7
2.- Biological Evolution (for Chapter I)	6
3.- Human Evolution (for Chapters I and II)	10
4.- Anthropology (for Chapters I and II)	4
5.- Cultural Evolution (for Chapter II)	6
6.- Functioning of the Human Mind (for Chapter 2)	4
7.- Prehistory and 1st Generation Civilizations (for Chap. II and III)	11
8.- World History	3
9.- Historical Atlas	5
10.- History of Religions	9
11.- History of Judaism	5
12.- The Arrival to 2nd Generation Civilizations (for Chapter IV)	3
13.- The Hellenism	8
14.- History of Christianity	12
15.- Infancy and Youth of the Western Civilization (for Chap. VI)	11
16.- The Modern Age from 1560 to 1830 (for Chapter VII)	9
17.- The Strengthening of the West from 1830 to 1914 (for Chap. VIII)	5
18.- Philosophy of Religion	15
19.- Philosophical Anthropology	8
20.- Ethics	12
21.- The Military Art	4
22.- History of Countries	6
23.- The Two World Wars (for Chapter IX)	16
24.- The Socio-Political System of the First World	10
25.- Philosophy of History	9
26.- The Cold War, The Information Revolution and Globalization	10
27.- Ecology and Bioethics	3
TOTAL	211

Works cited in "Notes" are preceded by an asterisk *
(Book titles are in English when there is an edition in this language)

1.- Origin and Meaning of the Universe

Davies, Paul, (1983), God and the New Physics, translated into Spanish in Salvat, Barcelona, 1986.

Davies, Paul, (1984), Superforce, trad. into Spanish in Salvat, Barcelona, 1985.

Davies, Paul, (1999), The Fifth Miracle, Simon & Schuster, N.Y., 1999.

Dilfurth, Hoimar von, (1981), *Wir sind nicht nur von dieser Welt*, translated from German into Spanish in Ed. Planeta, Barcelona, 1983.

Monod, Jacques, *Le hasard et la nécessité*, France Loisirs, Paris.

Rodríguez D. Rafael, (1997), *Del Universo al Ser Humano*, McGraw-Hill, Spain.

Russell, Bertrand, (1935), Religion and Science, translated into Spanish in FCE, Mexico, 1951, ed. 1992.

2.- Biological Evolution (for Chapter I)

*Dawkins, Richard, (1996), Climbing Mount Improbable, translated into Spanish in Tusquets Ed., Barcelona, 1998.

*Dawkins, Richard, (1998), Unweaving the Rainbow, translated into Spanish in Tusquets Ed., Barcelona, 2002.

*Kahn, Fritz, 1953?, *Das Buch der Natur*, translated from German into Spanish in Ed. Aguilar, Mexico, 1957.

*Knoll, Andrew H., (2003), Life in a Young Planet, translated into Spanish in Ed. Crítica, Barcelona, 2004.

*Wells, H.G.; Huxley, Julian; Wells, J.P., (1950), The Science of Life, translated into Spanish in Ed. Aguilar, Mexico, 1958.

*Zimmer, Carl, (2001), Evolution, WGBH and Clear Blue Sky Prod., USA.

3.- Human Evolution (for Chapters I and II)

Ardrey, Robert, (1961), African Genesis, Dell, N.Y.

*Arsuaga, José Luis, (2001), The Neanderthal's Necklace, translated from Spanish into English in Fourth Walls Eight Windows, N.Y.

*Cartwright, John, (1953), Evolution and Human Behavior, Aardvark Ed., Mendham, Suffolk, Great Britain, 2000.

*Cavalli-Sforza, Luca and Francesco, (1993), *Chi Siamo?,* translated from Italian into Spanish in Ed., Crítica, Barcelona, 1999.

*Gibson, Kathleen R. and Ingold, Tim, editors, (1993), Tools, Language, and Cognition in Human Evolution, Cambridge Univ. Press.

National Geographic Magazine, series "The Dawn of Humans", 1995-1997.

*Pilbeam, David, (1971), The Ascent of Man, translated into Spanish in Ed. Diana, Mexico, 1981.

*Reichholf, Josef H., (1990), *Das Rätsel der Menswerdung*, translated from German into Spanish in Ed. Crítica, Barcelona, 2001.

*Stringer, Christopher and McKie, R., African Exodus, H. Holt Co., N.Y.

*Tudge, Colin, (1996), The Time Before History, Touchstone, N.Y.

4.- Anthropology (for Chapters I and II)

Durkheim, Emile, (1898), *Les Règles de la Méthode Sociologique*, translated from French into Spanish in Ed. Premiá, Puebla, 1991.

Herkovitz, Melville J., (1948), Man and his Works, translated into Spanish in FCE, Mexico, 1952.

*Levy-Strauss, Claude, (1962), *Le Pensée Sauvage*, translated from French Into Spanish in FCE, 1st Ed., 10th imprint, Mexico, 1998.

*Mauss, Marcel, (1947), *Manuel d'Ethnographie*, translated from French into Spanish in Ed, Istmo, Madrid, 1974.

5.- Cultural Evolution (for Chapter II)

*Deutscher, Guy, (2005), The Unfolding of Language, Holt paperback, N.Y.

De Waal, Frans, (2006), Primates and Philosophers, translated into Spanish in Ed. Paidós Ibérica, Barcelona, 2007.

*Joyce, Richard, (1996), The Evolution of Morality, MIT, Boston, 2007.
Midgley, Mary, (1978), Beast and Man, transl. into Spanish in FCE, Mex., 1989.
*O'Manique, John, (2003), The Origins of Justice, Univ. Of Pennsylvania Press.
*Smith, Curtis G., (1985), Ancestral Voices, Prentice-Hall, New Jersey.

6.- Functioning of the Human Mind (for Chapter 2)
*Dowling, John E., (1998), Creating Mind, Norton, N.Y.
Edelman, Gerald M., (2004), Wider than the Sky, Yale Univ. Press, New Haven
Pinker, Steven, (2002), The Blank Slate, Viking, Penguin Group, N.Y.
Searle, John R., (1984), Minds, Brains and Science, Harvard Univ. Pr., Mass.

7.- Prehistory and 1st Generation Civilizations (for Chap. II and III)
Bottéro, Jean and Others, *Initiation à l'Orient Ancien*, translated from French
        into Spanish in Ed. Grijalbo, Barcelona, 1992.
*Childe, V. Gordon, (1935-1951), Man Makes Himself, Mentor, N.Y., 1955.
*De Balbín Berhmann, Rodrigo, art. *"Signos para entenderse"*, Review *"La
        Aventura de la Historia"*, num. 116, Madrid, 2008.
*Edwards, I.E.S., (1947-1949), The Pyramids of Egypt, Pelican Books, Gr. Br.
*Fagan, Brian M., (1987), The Great Journey, Thames and Hudson, London.
*Hawkes, Jacquetta, (1976), The Atlas of Early Man, St. Martin Press, N.Y.
*Lewis-Williams, J. David, (2002), A Cosmos in Stone, Alta Mira Press, Gr. Br.
*Lewis-William, David and Pearce, David, (2005), Inside the Neolithic Mind,
        Thames and Hudson, London.
*Margueron, Jean-Claude, (1991, 1996), *Les Mesopotamiens* (2 vol.), abridged
        and translated from French into Spanish in Ed. Cátedra, Madrid, 1996.
*Olson, Steve, (2002), Mapping Human History, Mariner Books, N.Y.
*Schmand-Besserat, Denise, (1992, 1996), How Writing Came About, Univ. of
        Texas Press, Austin.

8.- World History
Duché, Jean, (1963), *Histoire du Monde* (5 vol.), translated from French into
        Spanish in Ed. Guadarrama, Madrid, 1964.
Pirenne, Jacques, (1947-1963), *Les Grands Courants de l'Histoire Universelle*
        (8 vol.), translated from French into Spanish in Ed. Éxito, Barcelona, 1961.
Several Authors, *Historia Universal* (36 vol.), Siglo XXI, Mexico, 1972-1984.

9.- Historical Atlas
Barraclough, G., The Times Concise Atlas of World History, 1972.
Darby and Fullard, The New Cambridge Modern History Atlas, 1970.
McEvedy, Colin, The Penguin Atlases of Ancient, Medieval, Modern, Recent,
        and African History (5 vol.), Great Britain, 1979-1983.
Putzger, F.W., *Historischer Weltatlas*, Berlin, 1969.
Vicens Vives, *Atlas de Historia Universal*, Ed. Teide, Barcelona, 1980.

10.- History of Religions

Armstrong, Karen, (1993), A History of God, Ballantine Books, N.Y., 1994.

Armstrong, Karen, (1996), In the Beginning, Ballantine Books, N.Y., 1997.

*Armstrong, Karen, (2006), The Great Transformation, translated into Spanish in Ed. Paidós, Barcelona, 2007.

Cid, C. and Riu, M., (1965), *Historia de las Religiones*, SOPENA, Barcelona.

Couliano, Ioan P., (1991), Out of this World, translated into Spanish in Ed. Paidós, Barcelona, 1993.

*Eliade, Mircea, (1964), *Traité d'Histoire des Religions*, translated from French into Spanish in Ed. Era, Mexico, 4th Ed., 1981.

*González T., Yólotl, (1985), *El Sacrificio Humano entre los Aztecas*, FCE, Mex.

Larraya, J.G., (1968), *Religiones y Creencias*, DANAE, Barcelona.

*Tibón, Gutierre, (1984), *Aventuras de los Aztecas en el Más Allá*, Univ. Mex.

11.- History of Judaism

.*Bright, John, (1966), The History of Israel, translated into Spanish in Desclée de Brouwer, Bilbao, Spain, 1970.

*Finkelstein, Israel, and Silberman, Neil Asher, (2001), The Bible Unearthed, The Free Press, N.Y.

Freud, Sigmund, (1937), *Moses und die monotheistische Religion*, translated from German into Spanish in Ed. Alianza, Madrid, 1986.

*National Geographic Magazine, "Pharaohs of the Sun", April, 2001.

*Podhoretz, Norman, (2002), The Prophets, Freed Press, N.Y.

12.- The Arrival to 2nd Generation Civilizations (for Chapter IV)

*Holland, Tom, (2005), Persian Fire, trans. to Spanish in Planeta, Mex., 2007.

Nack, Emil and Wagner, Wilhelm, (1957), *Hellas*, translated from German into Spanish in Ed. Labor, Barcelona, 1960.

Paretti, Luigi and Others, *El Mundo Antiguo de 1200 a.C. a 500 d.C., serie Historia de la Humanidad*, UNESCO, Buenos Aires, 1965.

13.- The Hellenism

Cummings, L.V., (1939), Alexander the Great, translated into Spanish, in Ed. Pauser, Buenos Aires, 1946.

Gibbon, Edward, (1788), The Decline and Fall of the Roman Empire (abridged), Dell, N.Y., 1963, 12th printing, 1980.

Goldsworthy, Adrian, (2000), The Punic Wars, Wellington House, London.

*Keys, David, (1999), Catastrophe, Ballantine, N.Y.

*Lévèsque, Pierre, (1992), *Le Monde Hellénistique*, translated from French into Spanish in Ed. Paidós, Barcelona, 2005.

Momigliano, Arnaldo, (1975), Alien Wisdom, the Limits of Hellenization, translated into Spanish in FCE, Mexico, 1988.

*Peters, F.E., (1970), The Harvest of Hellenism, Barnes & Noble, 1996.

Wolfram, Herwig, (1990), The Roman Empire and its Germanic Peoples, translated from German into English in Univ. of California Press, 1997.

14.- History of Christianity

Bruckhardt, Jacob, (1852), *Die Zeit Constantins des Grossen*, translated from German into Spanish in FCE, Mexico, 1945, re-print 1982.

Chélini, J., (1991), *Histoire Religieuse de l'Occident Medieval*, Hachette, Paris.

Dawson, Christopher, extracted from: Religion and the Rise of Western Culture (1950); Medieval Essays (1954); Progress and Religion (1960), translated into Spanish in FCE, Mexico, 1997.

*Fletcher, Richard, (1997), The Barbarians Conversion, Henry Holt, 1988, USA.

Freeman, Charles, (2002), The Closing of the Western Mind, Vintage Books, N.Y., 2005.

Guignebert, Ch., (1921), *Le Christianisme Antique*, translated from French into Spanish in FCE, Mexico, 1994.

Jaeger, Werner, (1961), Early Christianity and Greek Paideia, translated into Spanish in FCE, Mexico, 1965, 5th reprint, 1985.

Johnson, Paul, (1976), The History of Christianity, translated into Spanish in Javier Vergara Ed., Buenos Aires, 1989.

Labal, Paul, (1982), *L'Eglise de Rome Face au Catharisme*, translated from French into Spanish in Ed. Crítica Barcelona, 1984.

Mac Mullen, Ramsay, (1928), Christianity and Paganism in the Fourth to Eight Centuries, Yale Univ. Press, 1997.

Montserrat T., José, (1992), *El Desafío Cristiano*, Anaya y Muchnik, Madrid.

Moynahan, Brian, (2002), The Faith, Doubleday, USA.

15.- Infancy and Youth of the Western Civilization (for Chap. (VI)

Arnold, Th. F., (2001), The Renaissance at War, Wellington House, London.

Burckhardt, Jacob, (1867), *La Cultura del Renacimiento en Italia*, translated from German into Spanish in Ed. Porrúa, Mexico, 1984.

*Cantor, Norman F., (1963), Civilization of the Middle Ages, Harper Collins, N.Y.

*Debus, Allen, G., (1978), Man and Nature in the Renaissance, translated into Spanish in FCE, Mexico, 1985.

Huizinga, Johan, (1924), The Waning of the Middle Ages, Penguin, G.B., 1962.

*Lopez, Robert S., (1960), *Naissance de l'Europe*, translated from French into Spanish in Ed. Labor, Barcelona, 1965.

Manchester, Wm. R., (1992), A World Lit only by Fire, Back Bay Books, USA.

Plumb, J.H., (1965), The Italian Renaissance, Harper, N.Y.

Salvat, Manuel, (1967), *La Era de los Descubrimientos,* Ed. Salvat, Spain.

The Fontana History of Europe, G. Holmes, Hierarchy and Revolt 1320-1450, J.R. Hale, Renaissance 1480-1520, G.R. Elton, Reformation 1517-1559.

Tuchman, Barbara, (1978), A Distant Mirror, Ballantine, N.Y.

16.- The Modern Age from 1560 to 1830 (for Chapter VII)

Aston, T. H., (1948), The Industrial Revolution, trans. to Spanish in FCE, Mex.

Chaunu, Pierre, (1964), *L'Amerique et les Ameriques*, Armand Colin, Paris.

*Derry T.K. and Williams, T.I., (1960), A Short History of Technology from the Earliest Times to a.d.1900 (4 vol.),trans. to Spanish in S. XXI, Madrid, 1977.

Friederici, Georg, (1925-1936), *Der Character der Entdeckung und Eroberung Amerikas durch die Europder* (3 vol.), translated from German into Spanish in FCE, Mexico, 1987.

*Koyré, Alexandre, (1973 posthumous), *Etudes de l'Histoire de la Pensée Scientifique,* translated from French into Spanish in Ed. Siglo XXI, Mexico, 1977.

Parry, J.H., (1949), Europe and World Expansion, translated into Spanish in FCE, Mexico, 1975.

Tarle, Evgeni V. (1939), *Napoleon,* translated from Russian (or from a French version?) into Spanish in Biografías Gandesa, Mexico, 1963.

The Fontana History of Europe: J.H. Elliot, Europe Divided 1559-1598; G. Parker, Europe in Crisis 1598-1648; John Stoye, Europe Unfolding 1648-1688; David Ogg, The Ancien Regime 1715-1783.

*Weber, Max, (1919), *Protestantische Ethik,* translated from German into Spanish in CINAR Ed., Mexico, 1984.

17.- The Strengthening of the West from 1830 to 1914 (for Chap. VIII)

Herring, Hubert, (1968), A History of Latin America, from the Beginnings to the Present, translated into Spanish in Ed. Univ. of Buenos Aires, 1972.

Morazé, Charles, (1956), *Les Bourgeois Conquérants,* translated from French into Spanish in Ed. Labor, Barcelona, 1965.

Morison, Samuel Elliot, (1965.1972), The Oxford History of the American People (3 vol.), A Mentor Book, USA.

Morris, James, (1968), Pax Britannica, A Harvest / HBJ Book, USA.

The Fontana History of Europe, Jacques Droz, Restoration and Revolution 1815-1848; J.A.S. Greenville, Remodeled Europe 1848-1878; Norman Stone, Europe Transformed 1878-1919.

18.- Philosophy of Religion

Becker, Ernest, (1972), Escape from Evil, trans. into Spanish in FCE, Mex.

Becker, Ernest, (1973), The Denial of Death, trans. into Spanish in FCE, Mex.

Bloch, Ernst, (1968), *Atheismus im Christentum,* translated from German into Spanish in Ed. Taurus, Madrid, 1983.

Buber, Martin, (1952), *Gottesfinsternis,* translated from German into Spanish in FCE, 1970, 2nd Ed. Mexico, 1993.

Compte-Sponville, André, (2006), *L'Esprit de l'Athéisme,* translated from French into Spanish in Paidós Ed., Barcelona, 2006.

Dubos, Rene, (1983), A God Within, translated into Spanish in Salvat, Barc. 1986.

Fierro, Alfredo, (1979), *Sobre la Religión,* Taurus, Madrid, 1979.

*James, William, (1902), The Varieties of Religious Experience, Penguin Putnam, 1958, USA.

*Lilla, Mark, (2007), The Stillborn God, Alfred. A. Kopf, N.Y.

Onfray, Michel, (2005), Atheist Manifesto, Translated from French into English In Arcade Publishing Co., N.Y., 2008.

Saramago, José, (2001), *El Evangelio según Jesucristo,* Alfaguara, Madrid.

Savater, Fernando, (2007), *La Vida Eterna,* Ed. Ariel, Barcelona.

Sújov, A.D., (1967), *Las Raíces de la Religión,* translated from Russian into Spanish in Ed. Grijalbo, Mexico, 1968.

Trías, Eugenio, (1995), *La Edad del Espíritu,* Random House – Mondadori, Barcelona, 2006.

*Trías, Eugenio, (2000), *¿Por qué Necesitamos Religión?,* Plaza Janés, Madrid.

19.- Philosophical Anthropology

Bohler, Eugen, (1966), *Die Zukunft als Problem des modernen Menschen,* translated from German into Spanish in Alianza Ed., Madrid, 1967.

Buber, Martin, (1942), What is Man?, translated from Hebrew into English in 1948 and into Spanish in FCE, Mexico, 1949, 13th reprint, 1985.

Cassirer, Ernst, (1944), Philosophical Anthropology, translated into Spanish in FCE, 1945, 9th reprint, Mexico, 1979.

Fromm, Erich, (1964), The Heart of Man, translated into Spanish in FCE, 1966, 5th reprint, 1977.

Landmann, Michael, (1957), *Philosophische Anthropologie,* translated from German into Spanish in UTEHA, Mexico, 1965.

*López Quintás, Alfonso, (1977), *Cinco Grandes Tareas de la Filosofía Actual,* Ed. Gredos, Madrid.

*Marquard, Odo, (2000), *Philosophie des Stattdessen,* translated from German into Spanish in Ed. Paidós Ibérica, Barcelona, 2001.

Miró Quesada, Francisco, (1965-1992), *Escritos sobre el Ser Humano Naturaleza e Historia,* Ed. Paidós – UNAM, Mexico, 2003.

20.- Ethics

Dewey, John, (1922), Human nature and conduct, translated into Spanish in FCE, Mexico, 1968.

Escobar Valenzuela, Gustavo, (1968), *Ética,* Mc Graw-Hill, Mexico.

*Frondizi, Risieri, (1958), *¿Qué Son los Valores?,* FCE, Mexico, 1967.

González Valenzuela, Juliana, (1996), *El Ethos: Destino del Hombre,* FCE, Mx.

Habermas, Jürgen, (1984-1987), *Schriften als Moralität und Sittlichkeit,* translated from German into Spanish in Ed. Paidós Ibérica, Barcelona.

López Gil Marta, (1998), *Obsesiones de Fin de Siglo,* Biblos, Buenos Aires.

Oppenheim, Felix E. (1968), Moral Principles in Political Philosophy, translated into Spanish in FCE, Mexico, 1976.

Rawls, John, (1971), A Theory of Justice, translated into Spanish in FCE, 1979, 2nd Ed. 1995, reprinted in Mexico,1997.

Sánchez Vázquez, Adolfo, (1999), *Ética,* Ed. Crítica, Barcelona.

Savater, Fernando, (1998), *El Arte de Vivir,* Ed. Planeta, México.

Selsam, Howard, (1965), Ethics and Progress, translated into Spanish in Ed. Grijalbo, Mexico, 1968.

Todorov, Tzvetan, (1991), *Face a l'Extrême*, translated from French into Spanish in Ed. Siglo XXI, Mexico, 1993.

21.- The Military Art

Clausewitz, Carl von, (1832 posthumous), On War, translated from the German in Routledge & Keegan in 1908, Edited by Pelican Books, 1968, 3rd reprint Great Britain, 1976.

Caillois, Roger, (1963), *Bellone ou la pente de la guerre,* translated from French into Spanish in FCE, Mexico, 1993.

Lidell Hart, B.H., (1974), Strategy, A Signet Book, 1974.

Sun-Tzu (aprox. 350 BCE), The Art of War, translated from Chinese into English by S.B. Griffith, Oxford Univ. Press. N.Y., 1963.

22.- History of Countries

Botton Beja, Flora, (1984), *China, su Historia y Cultura hasta 1800,* El Colegio de México, Mexico.

FitzGerald, C.P., (1966), A Concise History of East Asia, Penguin Books, 1974.

Gowen, H.H., (1939), A History of Japan, translated into Spanish in Ed. Ercilla, Santiago de Chile, 1943.

Mansfield Peter, (1976), The Arabs, Penguin Books, 1990.

Tinker, Hugh, (1966), South East Asia: A Short History, Praeger, N.Y., 1967.

Wallace Robert, (1968), The Origins of Russia, trans. to Spanish in Time-Life.

23.- The Two World Wars (for Chapter IX)

Balfour, M., (1972), The Kaiser and His Times, Penguin, London, 1975.

Brown A.C. and Mac Donald, C.B., (1977), The secret History of the Atomic Bomb, A Delta Book, N.Y.

Churchill, Winston, (1951), The Second World War (6 vol.), Mifflin, Boston.

Esposito, V.J., (1964), A Concise History of World War I, translated into Spanish in Ed. Diana, 1966, 4th reprint, Mexico, 1975.

Elleinstein, Jean, (1975), *Histoire du phénomène stalinien,* translated from French into Spanish in Ed. Laia, Barcelona, 1977.

Hamilton, Allistair, (1971), The Appeal of Fascism, Avon Books, N.Y., 1973.

Hitler, Adolf, (1924), *Mein Kampf,* translated from German into Spanish in Ed. Arroyo, Mexico (no date).

Home Alistair, (1962), The Price of Glory, Penguin Books, 1968.

Jackson, Gabriel, (1965), The Spanish Republic and the Civil War (1936-1939), translated into Spanish in Ed. Grijalbo, Mexico, 1966.

Reader's Digest, The Great Chronicle of World War II 83 vol.), translated into Spanish, Madrid, 1966.

Schirer, W.L., (1959), The Rise and Fall of the Third Reich, Simon & Schuster, N.Y., 1960.

Sontag, R.J., (1971), A Broken World 1919-1939, Harper & Row, N.Y.

Toland John, (1965), The Last 100 Days, Random House N.Y., 1966.

Tuchman, Barbara, (1962), The Guns of August, A Dell Book, 1973.

Tuchman, Barbara, (1966), The Proud Tower, Bantam Books, 1981.

Werth, Alexander, (1965), Russia at War 1941-1945, An Avon Book, N.Y.

24.- The Socio-Political System of the First World

Arendt, Hannah, (1959), *Was ist Politik?,* translated from German into Spanish in Ed. Paidós, Barcelona, 1987.

Bobbio, Norberto, (1977, 1979), *Equaglianza e Libertá,* translated from Italian into Spanish in Ed. Paidós, Barcelona, 1993.

Bobbio, Norberto, (1985), *Stato, governo, societá. Per una teoria generale della politica,* translated from Italian into Spanish in FCE, Mexico, 1989.

Habermas, Jürgen / John Rawls, (1996), Debate on Political Liberalism, translated into Spanish in Ed. Paidós, Barcelona, 1998.

Hayek, F.A., (1988), The Fatal Arrogance, tr. to Spanish in Unión Ed. Madrid.

Laski. Harold, (1936), The Rise of European Liberalism, translated into Spanish in FCE, Mexico, 1939, 11th imprint in 1989.

Mill, John Stuart, (1859), On Liberty, translated into Spanish in Alianza Ed. Madrid, 1970, re-imprinted in Mexico, 1989.

Sartori, Giovanni, (1962), Democratic Theory, translated into Spanish in Ed. Limusa-Wiley, Mexico, 1965.

Various, (2003), The Fight is for Democracy, Harper Collins, N.Y.

Weber, Max, (1922 posthumous), *Wirtschaft und Gesellschaft*, translated from German into Spanish in FCE, 1944, 2nd Ed. 1964, 7th imprint, Mexico, 1984.

25.- Philosophy of History

Brazier, Chris, (2007), World History, tr. into Spanish in Intermon-Oxam, Spain.

Darlington, C.D., (1968), The Evolution of Man and Society, translated into Spanish in Ed. Aguilar, Madrid, 1974.

Dilthey, Wilhelm, (1911), *Theorie der Weltanschauungen,* translated from German into Spanish in Alianza Ed., Mexico, 1990.

Durant, Will & Ariel, (1968), The Lessons of History, Simon & Schuster, N.Y.

Habermas, Jürgen, (1963), *Theorie und Praxis,* translated from German into Spanish in Alianza Ed. Madrid 1988, printed in Mexico in 1993.

Habermas, Jürgen, (1971-1997), *Israel oder Athen,* translated from German into Spanish, in Ed. Trotta, Madrid, 2001.

Spengler, Oswald, (1917), *Der Untergang des Abendlands,* Translated from German into Spanish in Espasa-Calpe, Madrid, 1923, 11th print 1966.

Toynbee, Arnold J., (1946), A Study of History, abridged in 3 volumes, translated into Spanish in Alianza Ed., Madrid, 1970.

Tuchman, Barbara, (1984), The March of Folly, Ballantine Books, N.Y.

26.- The Cold War, The Information Revolution and Globalization

*Fukuyama, Francis, (1992), The End of History and Last Man, Avon, N.Y.

Fukuyama, Francis, (1995), Trust, Free Press Paperback, N.Y., 1996.

Kennan, George F., (1982-1995), At A Century's End, W.W. Norton, N.Y.

*Maidanik, Kiva, (1992), *De la Perestroika al Golpe de Estado,* Ed. Nuestro Tiempo in coordination with Nat. Aut. Univ. of Mexico.

Nye Jr., J.S., (2002), The Paradox of American Power, Oxford Univ. Press, NY

*Singer, Peter, (2002), One World, Yale Nota Bene, 2nd Ed. New Haven, 2004.

Soros, George, (1998), The Crisis of Global Capitalism, translated into Spanish in Plaza-Janés Ed., Mexico, 1999.
Talbot, Strobe, (2008), The Great Experiment, Simon & Schuster, N.Y.
Toffler, Alvin and Heidi, (1995), Creating a New Civilization, translated into Spanish in Plaza-Janés Ed., Mexico.
Zakaria, Fareed, (2008), The Post-American World, W.W. Norton, N.Y.

27.- Ecology and Bioethics

*Diamond, Jared, (1999), Guns, Germs, and Steel, W.W. Norton, N. Y.
Diamond, Jared, (2005), Collapse, Penguin Books, N.Y.
*González Valenzuela, Juliana, coordinator, (2008), *Perspectivas de Bioética,* FCE and Nat. Aut. Univ. of Mexico.

INDEX

N